FRANCIS AIDAN CARDINAL GASQUET, O.S.B.

CARDINAL GASQUET

A MEMOIR

BY

SHANE LESLIE

P. J. KENEDY AND SONS
NEW YORK

Library of Congress Catalog Card Number: 53-11512

PRINTED IN GREAT BRITAIN BY
SPOTTISWOODE, BALLANTYNE AND CO. LTD.
LONDON AND COLCHESTER
FOR P. J. KENEDY AND SONS, NEW YORK
599

THIS BIOGRAPHY IS DEDICATED TO THE
ABBOT AND COMMUNITY OF DOWNSIDE ABBEY,
WHO AFFORDED EVERY FACILITY NEEDED BY
A BIOGRAPHER WITH A GENEROUS KINDNESS
ONLY EQUALLED BY THEIR WISDOM IN
DISCLAIMING RESPONSIBILITY FOR
COMMENT OR CONCLUSIONS

FOREWORD

THIS Biography covers certain periods and the most remarkable seams in a busy and vivid career.

A fragment of antiquated Autobiography occupies one chapter; an account of Edmund Bishop, Gasquet's inspiring literary partner, another.

A full and possibly final chapter deals with the controversy about Anglican Orders in which he took a stirring part in 1896. A good deal of forgotten detail has been brought to light. Diaries, letters and Gasquet's famous but indiscreet interview in America have been used. Another frank document is Gasquet's personal account of his exclusion from the See of Westminster in 1903, which he left for publication after the death of all concerned.

One chapter is devoted to chips and scraps of the correspondences which filled his letter-bag. The most important are more fully represented:

1. The War letters (private and personal) of Pope Benedict XV.
2. The personal letters of Cardinal Merry del Val.
3. The exchange of letters with Father David Fleming.
4. Letters to Edmund Bishop.

An important chapter covers the Cardinal's sturdy fight for the Allied Cause in Rome during the First War: when he stood almost alone in diplomacy against the rest of the *Curia*. The two-volume ratio allotted to English Cardinals has been reduced to one. Anecdotes, trivial but true, take the place of eulogy.

The Pontifical Secret covers unfortunately the significant parts he played in the election of two Popes, his dear friends, Benedict XV and Pius XI, but some historical gossip about the Conclaves electing Pius and Benedict may be accepted.

Visits to the United States, the revision of the Vulgate Bible and the aftermath of the Peace he lived serenely in Rome cover the rest of the book. One chapter estimates Gasquet as a historian, which was far from being the principal or most successful part of his varied vocation.

The thanks of the author are due to the Abbot and Community of Downside, and especially to the late Abbot Ethelbert Horne and Dom Urban Butler, and to the late Dom Philip Langdon of Douai, who all knew the Cardinal so well.

To the Franciscan Prior at Forest Gate for letters. To the late Lord Perth, the late Henry Harris and the late Duncan Gregory for information about the British Mission to the Holy See during the First World War. May they all rest in peace.

Others, who have helped with anecdotes or by criticism, will recognize their handiwork. I must thank Mr. Nigel Abercrombie for introducing me to the treasures in Edmund Bishop's Papers now at Downside.

1946–1952   SHANE LESLIE
   Glaslough
      Co. Monaghan

CONTENTS

I

INTRODUCTION

THE lives of monks are seldom fields for biography; especially when they have closely kept the Benedictine rule. Cardinal Gasquet was essentially a monk and the only life he would have valued to record would have been monastic, the life of *Ora et Labora*, the combined symbolism of the ant and the bee—spiritualized in the Heavenly hive.

His life extended in many directions outside the cloister. Providence, the ecclesiastical eddies, the orders of superiors and his own merits carried him into industrious and illustrious paths, not unnoticed by the world. He was a constant traveller.

From time to time he passed out of seclusion into the world of learning or Roman affairs. He met emergencies, which led him to higher tasks and higher levels until they touched the only eminence he really welcomed, that of the Sacred College of Cardinals. The humble novice became a Prince of the Church—and the black skullcap under his cowl became scarlet as hyssop.

His memoir arranges itself accordingly. Against the austere background of a monk's life certain lively chapters of variety and interest present themselves through document and men's memories.

The biographical facts are simple. Born in London on October 5, 1846, Francis Neil Gasquet lived till April 5, 1929. He was the son of Dr. Raymond Gasquet, a London physician, descended from French Royalist stock. His grandfather was the pilot who steered the English ships into Toulon and out again when the expedition against Bonaparte failed. The family escaped from the Revolution but kept in touch with their rightful king. There survives a letter from Admiral de Grasse about the Order of St. Louis conferred on *Monsieur Gasquet Lieut. de vaisseau à Londres* (Oct. 25, 1814). In the same year the Count de la Chatre, Ambassador of Louis XVIII in London, conferred the Cross of the Royal and Military Order in accordance with the wishes of the king. So much for Gallic blood, a Royalist heart and birth as a British subject.

In the 'fifties Gasquet's early life was associated with Bayswater, where Archdeacon Manning, freshly received into the Church, had settled with the Oblates of St. Charles. At St. Mary of the Angels' the boy Frank served Manning's first Mass in this particular beginning of diocesan life in London. The acolyte did not join Manning's Community, for his schooling at Downside in Somerset drew him to the Benedictine life. In January 1866 he entered Belmont Priory as a postulant. After a year of training he returned to Downside, was professed a monk and finally was ordained priest in 1874. Those years also marked milestones in Manning's career. In 1865 Manning became Archbishop of Westminster and in 1875 Cardinal. Ten years later he exercised a decisive turn on Gasquet's whole life and occupation, who always had the luck to find providential superiors and path-fellows.

Meantime Francis Gasquet had done his best to obliterate himself. He buried himself in an Enclosed Order. He changed his Christian name to Aidan. He ceased to possess goods. His personality became secondary to vows, obediences and devotions. The black robe of the Benedictines and their deathlike cowl seem to denote halfway ground between the living and the dead: dead to the world, but living the varied and busy life of the monastery. The notices of Closura upon monastic doors mark the cemetery of worldly delights, but open the Garden of the Soul. During his strenuous years at Downside Gasquet filled almost every office in the community. Naturally he taught in the school, history for choice, but under obedience he professed mathematics and physical science. This helped him to realize the need for educated lay-masters when he became Prior in 1878. In 1878 Downside was a small place of twelve monks with a school of 60 boys. Thenceforward affairs moved fast at Downside. The school was reformed and rapidly became a great public school.

Gasquet realized the importance of the Catholic schools entering into national life. The patron of reform at Downside was Lord Petre and his lead was both applauded and resisted. In the end there emerged a school without traces of penal or continental days in the past. The national games attained their proper levels and neighbouring schools realized that a sporting rival had arrived in the West. Cricket and Rugby football flourished.

The Priory and above all the great Church began to rise in Gothic amplitude.

A letter illustrates his activity (Nov. 24, 1878): 'I have written to the President for leave to build the Cloister and on that permission coming I shall attack Dr. Bennet, who has shewn no signs of being generous as yet. Madame de Paria and her sister each promised a Chapel. Then I have asked Hansom to tell me what a pillar and half of each arch in the Church would cost. . . . Build it we must somehow or other or I shall go out of my mind. I dream of it all times, particularly *Meditation* times.'

Gasquet was not alone. Life always brought him splendid understudies. There were great Priors and builders at his side like Edmund Ford or inspired Headmasters like Leander Ramsay, both of whom became Abbots. Gasquet knew how to depute and encourage others. He built the transepts for others to complete. Above all he knew how to submerge the old traditions into new circumstance.

Gasquet found himself in an Ancient Order scattered in old-fashioned missions through Victorian England. They represented the famous black monks, who once served the Abbeys of Glastonbury and Westminster and built the great Minsters, since wrecked or appropriated to the State. Gasquet took the lead in bringing back the modern monks from isolated missions and forlorn Priories. His gentle zeal enabled him to stand between the restorers of the real mediaeval life and the old-fashioned monks, who lived like parish priests, as it was said 'served by a housekeeper and a cat,' instead of multiplying communities of Benedictine life. His influence prevailed and the change was really settled after the visitation of the same Cardinal Persico who had courageously visited the Irish Hierarchy in the 'eighties. Persico had seen in a moment that monastic strength was being dissipated into the dioceses while the imagination and knowledge of

England showed that the country had never forgotten the Benedictines in their proper surroundings. Great choral and educational Abbeys, mighty Minsters and modernized schools filled Gasquet's dream. Incidentally it was necessary to break down the prickly prejudice which Protestant historians had taken four centuries to sow.

It was during Priorship that the providential break came in his life. The increasing labours and services, responsibilities and anxieties wore him down in the flower of his age. He suffered a severe illness and was given six months to live. He resigned the office of Prior in 1885. He could have been well satisfied with the fruits of his work. He had changed Downside outside knowledge or expectation. If he had returned to the infirmary and thence to the monks' cemetery, he would have left a brave memory in the annals of his Order.

He consulted Cardinal Manning, who proposed that he should devote himself to historical research in the British Museum. History had been one of his self-taught subjects. If he were willing to take up London residence, the all-powerful Cardinal could arrange the Pope's permission. Manning had lived through a lifetime of controversy and had realized at the Vatican Council that History could be as powerful as Theology in the battles of the Church. Apologetics had been wrung dry in England. The time had come for Catholics to challenge the historical verdicts which were always given against them: above all in condemnation of monastic life. Had the Abbeys and Priories been a social pillar and a religious light to England or merely centres of laziness, ignorance, scandal? It was an open question even among Catholics.

From Rome came no uncertain voice. There had arisen a new Pope, Leo XIII, who was not afraid of History, though at the Council, like Manning, he had watched the great historians of the Church, inspired by Lord Acton, prolong the Opposition against the ultramontane theologians. Leo encouraged Gasquet to enter as a student into the British Museum and search the documents on which the English view of the Reformation was built.

From those twenty years few personal traces remain of Gasquet's activities. He became one of the best-known figures moving amongst the treasures of the Manuscript department where he always sat close to the Superintendent of the Students' Room. Mr. J. A. Herbert writes: 'My Chief and I agreed emphatically in regarding Gasquet as a model student, always cheery, quiet, using MSS. with due care. *O si sic omnes!* we used to say about him.'

From their successors comes a note:

'As to Cardinal Gasquet, we have not much in the way of material here. He presented us in 1891 with a MS. song by George Peele, late 16th century (Add. MS.); in 1899 with some photographs of a Roger Bacon MS., in the Vatican Library (Add. MS.); and in 1920 with the collections of F. J. Baigent relating to Hampshire.'

There was the Record Office as well, where for twenty years Gasquet studied and transcribed the silent witnesses of the Past. He settled down with a companion near the Museum and became a familiar figure under the dome of the Reading Room, which has sheltered and fed so many of the unrewarded rank and file of research. Patiently he sought his quarry. He uncovered records covering the great monastic houses, their troubles, their treasures, their condemnation and specious spoliation. The field was immense and he rapidly harvested a multitude of transcripts and abbreviated notes. He copied and he condensed. His notes were accurate and legible. His summaries were hasty. His handwriting was worthy of the monastic Scriptorium and survives in hundreds of notebooks. Out of his full research his printed books developed naturally.

In 1888 he published his first and most memorable work in two volumes: *Henry VIII and the English Monasteries*. Before the second volume was published the first had reached a second edition. He found himself famous not only in Catholic circles but amongst historians. The reading public were interested and he took the first step towards becoming a national character.

Though he had buried himself first in his monastery and secondly in the British Museum, Destiny seemed determined to drag him into the limelight not once but often during his long, laborious life. Some would speak of his luck, others of Providence, when summarizing his self-sacrificing succession of friends.

His literary career became associated with the genius of Edmund Bishop, a consecrated layman, who possessed that fine liturgical sense which is denied to most ecclesiastics. The faithful *Achates* had come, and not for the last time, into the life of *Pius Aeneas*. Henceforth Bishop's stores of unique learning, immense and unfailing memory and powers of ferreting out forgotten tradition or remote rites were at Gasquet's service. Gasquet, always a man of many different occupations and concerns, fell back on the splendid erudition of an astonishing mind.

Working with Edmund Bishop, he produced *Edward VI and the Book of Common Prayer*, a plummet of deep research into the minds of the Reforming Bishops and the doctrinal intent of John Bull's Prayer Book. It was Bishop who worked the liturgical depths, and Gasquet who arranged the interesting finds such as the Debate of the Lords on the Eucharist, the distant ancestor of the Commons Debate on the revision of the same book under George V, for England still sends her conscience to Parliament. The book was not controversial, but with the approaching conflict over Anglican Orders bore irreproachable testimony to the real intentions of Cranmer. The reader could henceforth feel assured whether the Anglican priest was saying the old Mass or reciting a beautiful translation without the least wish or intent to cause Transubstantiation. Then and now and ever it was the Mass which mattered. Gasquet's book appeared in 1890 and in 1894 came the appeal to Rome by Lord Halifax on Anglican Orders. Were they valid? What indeed did validity mean? It is not too much to say that behind the immensely learned Commission appointed by Leo XIII the effective blow was dealt by the investigations of Gasquet and Bishop: not controversially but by the uncovering of lost, forgotten documents: lost by the Church herself and forgotten by her counsellors.

From Gasquet's notebooks there continued a steady flow of books devoted to the same periods and subjects: the Black Death and Monastic life and the great Abbeys of England and the whole phase preceding the Reformation. Hitherto he had contented himself with facts and the pigeon-holing of the so-called historical facts. When not under the supervision of Edmund Bishop he tended to Theory, the perennial infirmity of historians. Theory may be decked up with facts but is nevertheless born of bias. Bias and pre-judgment have been the characteristics of British historians in a sublime degree. The Catholic School have tended to accumulate facts without expounding controversy or experimenting with Theory: Lingard, Acton and in his first phase Gasquet. They could all be classed as plodders on Liberal, unbiassed lines. No doubt Acton sometimes gave way to his feelings about Persecution, but Lingard was simply a steady transcriber of national records. Gasquet began as a pure transcriber but his immediate success led him to turn on some occasions to Theory. His most remarkable Theories were:

1. The deep and abiding influence of the Black Death on the character of the English Church. Frankly, it excused the resulting low levels of religious life which led to the need of Reformation.

2. The claim that the Wycliffe translation of the Scriptures was not the work of one reforming priest but the 'Old Catholic Bible.' This was a *volte-face*, which, if successful, would have outflanked the whole popular view of the Church and the Bible in the Middle Ages.

When Catholic historians find occasional blots in the Church's record, they can roar like Acton or like Lingard say nothing beyond the fact, or like Gasquet they may sigh apologies, which of course do not explain. Gasquet's historical tendency was Liberal (for want of a better word). In his book on *Henry III and the Church* he dealt frankly with English grievances and Papal exactions. Liberalism in historical inquiry is very different from Liberalism in doctrine, of which he was at one time accused. He was obviously chosen as the proper editor of Lord Acton's Letters to Richard Simpson, most gifted and far-sighted of the Oxford converts. Acton's letters to Mary Gladstone[1] had contained passages which caused 'scandal,' the bugbear of Catholic readers and writers. Gasquet showed courage in editing

---

[1] Daughter of the Prime Minister, Mr. Gladstone.

the Simpson series but could not help transmuting phrases instead of using asterisks. They were not serious or even necessary changes but to the strict modern historian they are very wrong. 'Inverted commas' supply a sanctuary which must not be knowingly tinkered. Gasquet changed whatever would have brought his Liberalism into sacristy disrepute.

Gasquet has been persistently and sometimes accurately questioned in consequence. Criticism of a rude and querulous nature he ignored, but he accepted the comments of a Creighton or a Gairdner: both of whom welcomed his early achievement. A biographer can accept such a sentence as that of Adrian Morey[1]: 'No doubt he was, like many historians, a careless copyist and corrector of proofs, and he did not always trouble to distinguish sufficiently between quotations in full and his own abridgements.' There indeed was the rub that frayed so many of his critics.

But Gasquet was many things besides a historian. He was a schoolmaster, a Prior, a builder, a lecturer, a preacher, an organizer, and an Abbot. Finally, as a Cardinal *in Curia* (that is a Cardinal resident in the Papal Court), and Vatican Librarian and Archivist to the Holy See, he ceased to have the time to write or revise books. All his literary scholarship was given in his last years to supervising the collation of the text of the Vulgate Bible: an immense task which only a great Religious Order could undertake, covering many libraries, thousands of photostats, many nationalities and many Biblical puzzles.

His early works were those of a pioneer. He dug deeply and extensively, showing the lines and possibilities open to an English Catholic school of History. He had not the time to re-edit his own work, which it is surprising that no follower or secretary found time to perform. Nor did he withdraw in the face of criticism. His time was given firstly to the multiple devotions of a monk and secondly to the accumulating affairs of the Church. The making of books came third. He had shown the way for Catholic historians by breaking new ground. He left his varied works to successors to edit or emend. The outbreak of war, and the greater parts he was called upon to play for Church and

---

[1] 'Cardinal Gasquet the Historian,' *Cath. Hist. Rev.*, Oct. 1929.

country, made it impossible for him to return to the desk of scribe and copyist, rearrange facts or re-estimate theories. This may be regrettable, but the originality and breadth of his original achievement remains. He had changed the popular English view concerning the old Religious Orders. If there were plenty of social defects and moral disasters to be traced, the old view that the Monastic system was throughout a national millstone and ghastly scandal, mercifully concealed by Wolsey's suppressions and Tudor confiscations, was proven a myth. In several ways Gasquet made the English Abbey return as an honoured feature of English life.

After the Pope, chiefly at Gasquet's hest, had 'condemned' Anglican Orders in 1896, Gasquet entered into the thought of Rome. In 1900 he was created Abbot President of the English Benedictines and Downside was raised to the rank of an Abbey after immense struggles within the Order. His life's work might now seem completed, but the crown awaited him. He was constantly rumoured for the Red Hat, but that sublime solace of ecclesiastics, even as a consolation prize, constantly flitted past.

Gasquet's personality became so well known in the English Church that his name appeared on the *terna* of candidates selected by the Chapter to succeed Cardinal Vaughan at Westminster— with Mgr. Merry del Val and Bishop Hedley. He came within the proverbial inch of becoming Archbishop. The true story of the Westminster election is part of his Autobiography. The result left him free to undertake tasks compared to which the archdiocese was parochial. He was able to make important tours in the United States. He founded Benedictine studies at Cambridge, an example followed by almost all the Religious Orders in Oxford. His last tour in America was an effort to raise money for his supreme task of revising the text of the Vulgate. The same Pope Pius X who had imposed this grandiose task upon him raised him to the Cardinalate in May 1914. He proceeded to Rome where he assisted in his first Conclave and remained during the First Great War, giving the next Pope, Benedict XV, the benefit of his counsels and his country the immense value of a fighting champion at a focal point of civilization. Through his strong influence

the Foreign Office was made to realize the heaven-sent opportunity of establishing relations with the Holy See. With an
English Legation at his back he fought as hard and powerfully
against pro-German influences as any diplomatist in the field. In
fact he was the spearhead of Allied hopes and controversies at
Rome during those embittered years.

Meantime Pope Benedict XV had placed him in charge of the
Vatican Library and Archives, upon whose order he immediately
set the mark of efficient management, learnt in Bloomsbury. The
death of Pope Benedict allowed him to assist at his second Conclave, out of which his friend and fellow-librarian Cardinal Ratti
emerged as Pope Pius XI. In 1924 he celebrated the Jubilee of his
priesthood and proceeded from Cardinal Deacon to Cardinal
Priest. In 1927 he presented the Pope with the first volume of the
new Vulgate: the Book of Genesis. The Palace of San Calisto,
into which he settled with his secretaries and students, became a
scene in Vulgate history only less famous than the cave of St.
Jerome, but with a British version of the Lion in the doorway.
Here death found him at fourscore years and two. God the
Merciful spared him the Second War and witnessing the destruction of his beloved Monte Cassino.

Over twenty years have passed since his death and the natural
desire has arisen that a monk so characteristic of the English
Benedictines should be commemorated by some manner of
Memoir, a little more extensive and picturesque than the clear
recital of his life in the *Dictionary of National Biography*. Excellent
as it is, and accurate and filial, coming from the pen of Abbot
Cuthbert Butler, the editorial rules reduced it to a meagre limit.

This Memoir is in the nature of a series of Essays touching the
high peaks emerging from a life devoted otherwise to the sunken
tranquillities of Benedictine vocation. Though Gasquet seemed to
bury his talents under the cowl, providential circumstances drew
him on occasions into arenas of controversy, historical research
and high ecclesiastical politics. A character at once so gifted,
simple, dogged and pious in the forthright English manner
enabled him to serve his Community and his country in ways
that neither would wish forgotten: *Pro Patria atque Patre Benedicto!*

The Cardinal's Papers are preserved at Downside and could afford many volumes. We have used only a tithe, including an Autobiography, dictated in old age and unfinished, which is chiefly valuable for glimpses of his early life and of the old Downside. It appears abbreviated to a chapter.

More valuable are:

1. Diaries which record the Commission which sat at Rome to decide the validity of Anglican Orders (1895–96).

2. Diaries describing visits to the United States of America (1904 and 1913).

3. A Diary kept *in Curia* as a Cardinal during the Great War (1914–16).

He left an outspoken Memorandum to explain what happened when he narrowly missed becoming Archbishop of Westminster in 1903, and another recording how he became President of the Anglo-Benedictines.

One chapter contains selections from the varied correspondence he received from all quarters. Two collections have been left in Benedictine custody untouched save for passing historical mention.

1. The troubles, struggles and successes achieved within the Order in Gasquet's time under the great Abbot General of the Order, Hemptinne.

2. The unceasing controversy between Cardinal Bourne and Bishop Amigo of Southwark about their diocesan bounds. These letters rather belong to the lives of the protagonists, or to the history of their distracted dioceses. Gasquet found himself holding the balance in Rome and advising the Pope as well as he could from his knowledge of the two most stubborn of prelates. There can be no doubt in which direction he informed Pope Benedict, who was immensely puzzled and vexed by this stand-up controversy between English Ecclesiastics. Let their biographers eventually see to it, for it does not fall to Gasquet's!

II

PERSONALITY

This Cardinal
. . . was a scholar and a ripe and a good one;
Exceeding wise, fair-spoken and persuading;
Lofty and sour to them that loved him not;
But to those men that sought him sweet as summer.

SHAKESPEARE

CARDINAL GASQUET'S personal character survived the monastic routines even to humour and a charming lightness of speech. Incessant services, prayers and works lowered his physique but brought out his characteristics: an outspoken sense of humour tending to be grim, a practical imagination tending to ambitions. Needless to say he ambitioned for his monastery, for his Order, for his Church, and not for himself. He was restless in passing from one task to another and from book to book, from article to article. Completion in his aims or corrections in his writing he left to others, friends or foes. He allowed the tide of his surprising career to carry him forward. Yet he never pressed himself to the fore and always gave the utmost credit to those who helped him building, reforming or compiling.

He was an uncompromising Englishman, fearless and bluntly outspoken. For ostentation or hypocrisy he had no excuse. His scorn for priests who took airs socially was tremendous. He said he could forgive Mgr. Capel, one of Manning's henchmen, for talking about a *pi-annar* for piano, but not for his snobbery. In spite of a somewhat stern attitude to all that was flimsy and fiddle-daddle in character, he showed courtesy, dignity and ease in conversation with the great or the humble. His common sense did not admit shades or innuendo in conversation. His yea was yea and his nay meant nay. He loved his Order, his Abbey and his country with intense feeling and loyalty. He was John Bull in a Benedictine robe, though his appearance was more ascetic and less jovial than the national figurehead. He looked the Cobbett rather than the Falstaff type of Englishman, but a Cobbett such as Holbein could have gladly painted. He was a builder, and whether he built Abbey or book he built in the same large, uncompromising manner. He was no mystic. Baron von Hügel, when seeking an introducer to his book on St. Catherine of Genoa, wrote to Father Tyrrell: 'Dom Gasquet would not do because he has always made no secret of his fear and dislike of even the moderate Mystics.'

Coupled with a mobile nobility of countenance was a soft pleading voice. He could sing an old English ballad. At the Altar he sang well enough on a note which musicians could not recognize. But what matter *pourvu que le son soit beau!*

He had a turn for old-fashioned anecdote, when he had the time, and he lightened the long serious hours of his brethren with unfailing humour and paternal consideration.

It was a sense of British fun which caused him one Ash Wednesday to drop the ashes into the open mouth of a Downside schoolboy who had mistaken the ceremony!

Everybody who came in touch with him carried away one story at least. He was once kind enough to talk to us about Manning, whose personal influence had fallen upon him, but not to the exclusion of Newman. Catholics used to range themselves angrily with one or other of that memorable twain. To have known Manning in childhood and to have served as his acolyte meant a life's friendship, though perhaps without that full understanding which comes only to a fellow-convert. In later years Gasquet told Manning bluntly that Liddon, the High Church preacher at St. Paul's, must be insincere. 'Do not say that! They used to say the same of me' was the oracular contradiction. Manning took a family interest in the Gasquets. It was Manning who obtained the letter from Leo XIII which transplanted Gasquet for twenty years into the British Museum. When Gasquet's books began to appear, Manning admitted that he had thought very little could be said for the English Monasteries. 'I was wrong': and it was not often Manning said those words.

ANECDOTES

While he was Prior, the great Church at Downside was still a dream unvisioned by the Community. One morning he received a large cheque for the Lady Chapel. After breakfast he felt inspired and rushing out trod out the present noble proportions, leaving pegs where the nave should reach and eventually did.

A monk died during the hot weather and a speedy burial was necessary. At two in the morning Gasquet was awakened by the workmen hammering the coffin. He arose in the kindness of his heart, brought them meat and beer and told them not to lose their night's sleep but to go home in the morning. He had the old monastic sense that the workmen he employed were part of the Community.

In later days the Rose window of the Church was in course of building. Gasquet was anxious to take advantage of the scaffolding to put in the coloured glass. The subject chosen was of the Elders casting down their crowns before the Lamb. Briefly and wittily he put the monetary question to the Council. They hesitated, but he was in a great hurry and he simply asked them to cast their half-crowns down before the same Sacred Emblem.

He could put his spirituality into epigram: 'Any act of ours not supernaturalized is—nil.'

As a Cardinal in Rome his humour flowed into anecdote. A few may represent the sallies that collected about his memory.

Once he came to dine at the Beda College in Rome during the Christmas holidays. The Rector explained the absence of some of the students on vacation: 'Some of our men are very much interested in ski-ing.' 'Yes,' answered the Cardinal, 'I noticed the mistletoe in the main corridor!'

His rebukes took exquisite form. Once travelling north by train, he noticed two schoolboys mimicking his lips as he murmured his Office. When he had closed his book, he entered into conversation with them. They were returning to a famous school. 'Surely not!' he said. 'I knew many men from there, but they would never have forgotten they were gentlemen and mimicked an old gentleman saying his prayers.' An apology followed and conversation became easier.

When d'Annunzio approached the Cardinal for admission among the Benedictines, as a man of letters naturally joining a literary Order, the Cardinal said: 'No, you are not respectable enough. You had better become a Friar. They have had many poets and some crackbrains!' No one laughed more in telling this story than Archbishop Paschal Robinson, himself a Franciscan, who also related to us an amusing account of a famous drive he had shared with Cardinal Gasquet from Rome to Frascati to attend a dinner. The Cardinal had endured a very heavy day in Rome and was in no mood for small talk or even for prayer. In the car was a priest of the Irish College and Archbishop Kelly of Sydney, who was renowned for incredible tactlessness (such as once addressing nuns on birth-control!) as well as for his deep piety.

During the ante-prandial drive Dr. Kelly turned to the exhausted Cardinal as the senior ecclesiastic present and invited His Eminence to avert the dangers of the route by reciting the *Itinerarium*.

The Cardinal set his weary jaw and muttered: 'Never heard of it!'

There was a pause and the Irish-Australian marvelling, though no doubt excusing the deplorable ignorance of an English Catholic, took a simpler line and suggested:

'Will your Eminence lead us in saying the Rosary?'

The reply was the same!

The silence until the car reached Frascati by all accounts was devoted to profound meditation by all present. The Irish priest said that though he had disagreed with Gasquet on many political questions, he forgave him all for *that*!

Before the Conclave which elected Pius XI Gasquet was asked what would happen if an American Pope were elected. He answered: 'He would *guess*—infallibly!'

His relations with Pius XI were always intimate, so much so that he could converse with him familiarly. On one occasion he used the common *cliché* of conversation—'Well, we are none of us infallible.' The Pope started and quietly drew smiling attention to his inadvertence.

This is also recorded of a conversation which he had with Benedict XV, whom he was trying to console after the world's Press had received a Papal utterance more unenthusiastically than usual.

The Cardinal had a way of talking bluntly to the point. It was the English in him. When King George V received him at a Royal Garden Party, the King suggested that Archbishop Mannix should be kept out of politics and given a high place in the Vatican. 'God forbid!' was the Cardinal's comment, which caused some royal laughter.

The most downright reply of the Cardinal occurred in Rome soon after the election of Pope Benedict XV. The German Cardinal Hartmann offered cordiality by saying 'We will not discuss the War.' 'Nor the Peace!' rapped the English Cardinal. This little saying travelled far and wide during the time, and it certainly set the tone for Roman amenities while the conflict lasted. The Cardinal thought it wiser to record it was *ben trovato*. When taking possession of his Titular Church, Santa Maria in Campitelli, in 1914, he said: 'We are fighting for the might of Right not for the right of Might.' He was speaking amid a pro-German Vatican to a neutral Pope who heard him gladly.

It was our privilege to visit Cardinal Gasquet during the *Sede Vacante* which followed the death of Pope Benedict XV. The Cardinal was distressed by the lack of consideration with which the Pope had been allowed to die. As soon as the Papal agony began—doctors in stiff uniforms, Chamberlains in mediaeval dress, Cardinals and prelates crowded not only the ante-camera but the bedroom of the Pope, breathing up all the valuable air. In fact, he was stifled by the atmosphere and, as the Cardinal explained, simply died because he could not clear his throat. The humblest of the faithful would have been happier dying in a ditch. It was the Cardinal's immense human sympathy which struck us on that occasion. The Pope's discomfort in dying left him in tears.

While we were having tea, a Cardinal was announced and we

rose to salute the Archbishop of Milan, Cardinal Ratti. We offered to withdraw but Cardinal Gasquet insisted on our remaining while the British teapot went round and the conventional subjects were discussed. Once more we rose, as we felt that at this critical moment in the history of the Church one Cardinal had not called on another for nothing. Again Cardinal Gasquet insisted on our remaining, though Cardinal Ratti showed signs that he wished more intimate conference. Finally he lost all patience and strode to the door. While he was standing there, his English host said loudly to us: 'You see there a very wicked man! We are going to shut him up for life in the Vatican!' and laughed uproariously at his humorous way of putting it.

Cardinal Ratti's face was a study on that occasion, but he realized very well whom the other Cardinal intended to vote for in the approaching Conclave, without making a promise in private. In fact ten days later he became Pius XI and we know personally that he had Gasquet's vote.

This story is confirmed by a passage in the memoirs of Mary Anderson; a great friend of the Cardinal:

Pope Pius XI was a great friend of his and spent his last night before the Conclave under his roof at San Calisto. On rising to go to bed, Cardinal Gasquet grasped his hand and said: 'This is the last night you will spend outside the Vatican.

When an American lady asked him why Catholics told lies, he smiled and supposed that as the Church was so hard on the cardinal sins, she had to allow a little indulgence to the imagination!

He announced his Cardinalate on a postcard to Father Sargent as 'the most extraordinary event to happen in this extraordinary Pontificate.'

III

AUTOBIOGRAPHY

Men of little showing
For their work continueth
Broad and deep continueth
Great beyond their knowing.

KIPLING

IN his last years the Cardinal began to dictate recollections in
response to publishers' appeals. They were not extended beyond
1904 and rambled over his early life pleasantly and discursively:
but he had lost his touch of phrase and it has been necessary to
restrict the text.

Many of the paragraphs are useful to biography, as they recall
and sometimes describe memories otherwise forgotten.

The Autobiography touches the French origin of his family
and describes the massacre of his great-uncles at Toulon during
the Revolution, and how his grandfather and father settled at
Somers Town whence he was brought later as a child to Bayswater. He describes his youthful friendship with Dr. Manning in
the 'fifties. There are glimpses of the Great Exhibition, of Charles
Dickens, Cardinal Wiseman, Sir Francis Burnand and a Debtor's
Prison.

Reminiscences follow of Downside, as a schoolboy, monk,
Prior, and of the big break in his life leading him to the British
Museum and a literary career. They conclude when he became
Abbot-President of the Benedictines in England. Included were
two important correspondences:

1. With Lord Acton on contributing to the *Cambridge Modern
   History*.
2. With Cardinal Vaughan on staffing Westminster Cathedral
   with a choir of monks in imitation of the mediaeval
   Minsters.

The Autobiography (which follows) then breaks off. He had begun to write his Memoirs too late. His memory had been worn away by his constant industry.

I WAS born in London on October 5, 1846. My father was of French origin, but naturalized an Englishman, my mother was from a Yorkshire family, named Kay. My father's family was Provençal from a strong Royalist family settled at Toulon. My grandfather was a Chevalier of the Order of St. Louis and Vice-Admiral of the Port of Toulon. His naval position brought him into relation with the English when they held the Port in the struggle of this country against the Republicans. He had a little property on the very hill upon which the young Napoleon planted the cannons which commanded the arsenal and rendered the English position in the Port untenable. When it was determined to abandon the city, the English naval authorities offered to convey my family on an English man-of-war to England. The story of the firing of the arsenal and the embarkment of the fugitive Royalist is told by the novelist Besant in *The Holy Rose*. The account is exactly what as a child I heard from my father and uncle. It was December 18, 1792, and the scene is Toulon harbour.

All night long, until within a couple of hours of daybreak, the ships' boats were running to and fro between the fleet and the shore, swiftly yet without haste, as if the work had to be done without delay, yet must be done in order. They were embarking the English and Spanish troops, for the town was to be abandoned.

It was on this night that the people of Toulon discovered that the English and Spanish troops were leaving the town and that they were left to the tender mercies of the Republicans. As for their tender mercies, it was known already what had been done at Lyons, and what at Marseilles. What would they not do at Toulon which had not only pronounced against the Republic, but had even invited the English and Spanish to occupy and hold the town? And now their allies were embarking and they were without defence.

In the afternoon of the next day, December 20, when the English and Spanish ships had departed and were standing out to sea under full sail there was enacted, as my grandfather subsequently learned, the strangest sight that Toulon had ever seen. The scene took place in the Place d'Armes and amongst the many Royalists who were brought up for condemnation were two or three of my uncles.

The Royalists, who had been found in the city, were treated as traitors to the cause of the Republic, and they were no sooner accused than they were forthwith condemned. Amongst those who perished, as I have said above, were two or three of my great-uncles. So that, with the exception of my grandfather and his family who had been carried into England, the whole family perished on this day in the Place d'Armes.

The *émigrés* were landed at Fareham in Portsmouth harbour, and when they had settled down and became somewhat accustomed to life in their changed circumstances and in a strange land, my uncle and father went to Winchester with the intention of studying for a medical career. In those days it was the custom with young men joining that profession to be apprenticed, and so they were soon apprenticed to a well-known doctor of the city, named Lyford, and after having completed their studies they both joined the English Navy as surgeons. From the time of their landing in England my family found a great many Frenchmen everywhere. At Porchester Castle, for instance, there were lodged many hundred prisoners of war and at Winchester through the Christian charity of the English Government 660 priests were sheltered in the old Royal palace. There they used to chant their Office together, and my father was wont to describe how the mighty wave of their prayer could be heard all over the city.

When my grandfather and his family moved on to London, they naturally were attracted to the French colony at Somers Town, for which a well-known French *émigré* priest, the Abbé Carron, had established a centre.

With the advent of Cardinal Wiseman in London a great change became apparent in the religious celebrations in our churches. One of the first things to be introduced in all churches was the *Quarant 'Ore* in Lent, and most people made a point of going daily to visit the church in which it was being celebrated. I remember often going round and seeing everywhere the gathering of people to do honour to the Blessed Sacrament. The Cardinal introduced more solemnity into the ceremonies at which he assisted. He made Mgr. Edmund Stonor his Master of Ceremonies besides acting as chaplain to the convent in Blandford Square. He always accompanied the Cardinal and directed the ceremonies as they were wont to be in Rome. I, as a small boy, frequently went to act as train-bearer with the Cardinal and Mgr. Stonor, sitting down at the bottom of the carriage between the legs of His Eminence and Mgr. Stonor.

I have often tried to determine my first recollection. (I believe that in my case it is a very uninteresting and stupid fact, but let it be set down.) In the days before the modern 'night lights' were invented, in the night nursery it was usual to have a rush light, which (to insure against the chance of fire) was set in a basin of water on the floor, and placed over it was an iron cover pierced by holes. This sent out over the room round circles of light, and I recall, about the age of three (I fancy), lying awake and wondering what these circles of light were and whether they meant anything.

About 1850 I recall being taken by my father to see the great glass house which was being prepared for the Exhibition of the next year. I was struck by the fact that gradually a big elm tree of Hyde Park was being covered in and the branches were then crowded by sparrows, making a great noise. Of the contents of the great Exhibition I remember little. One thing I recall, a very long engine and a pyramid of a gilded substance, which was said to represent the amount of gold found in the California diggings.

The following year I remember the arrival in London of a French cousin (of my father), from Toulon. He had been on the Republican side in the siege of the city and had joined the forces subsequently as surgeon of Napoleon in many of his wars, and (amongst others) he was with him in the ill-fated march upon Moscow. He had come to England in 1851 to try and find any relations who had taken refuge in England. He stayed with us some time to try and persuade my father to return with his family to the old place at Toulon, and in fact, my father thinking of it the following year with my eldest brother went over, but by this time he had become so Anglicized that he gave up any idea of again claiming French nationality. It used to be said that one day when this French cousin was chatting I said to him: 'Why don't you talk English, it is much easier!'

One early recollection of mine at this time was connected with seeing a Debtor's Prison. A lady friend of my mother—a Miss Matthews—was carried off to the Debtor's Prison, and out of charity my mother used from time to time to go and see her. On one of these visits she took me to accompany her, and I thus saw some of the scenes so vividly described by Dickens, and which ultimately led to imprisonment for debt being done away with. The name of Charles Dickens reminds me that once looking down the stairs at home I was shown someone, described as the great novelist, who had been to consult my father as a doctor and was leaving the house when I chanced to see him.

Amongst others I remember to have seen in those early days at home was Mother Connelly, the Foundress of the Institute of the Holy Child. She had great difficulty with her husband (as we may learn from the history) and at one time it was thought probable that she might be compelled, as the result of a case brought before the English Courts, to return to him as his wife, and she was determined in that event to take refuge abroad. To be prepared for this, my mother gave her shelter and we consequently saw her at that time. It was not, however, our first acquaintance with Madame Connelly, as my sisters were among the first pupils in the school she had opened at St. Leonards.

All my early recollections are centred round the old French church at Somers Town. The priests who served it were always honoured and welcomed guests of my parents and we children got to know them well. To one of them, Father George Rolff, I made my first confession, and I recall that when that business was happily over, Father Rolff showed me a conjuring trick, by which he appeared to bore a hole in his nose and pass a piece of string through it. It was to him that about the same time there came for his first confession a boy, one of the Dolans, who had thought it necessary to learn by heart the full examination of conscience in the big *Garden of the Soul*, and this he repeated as his confession! Afterwards, when his mother understood what he had done, she was horrified at this child having accused himself amongst other things of murder. She said, 'But, my dear boy, what on earth did the Father say to you?'—'Oh!' he replied, 'when I had finished he said "There's a good boy: don't do it again."'

Besides my own brothers and sisters there were living with us the two daughters of a convert clergyman, named Glennie. He had given up his living at Salisbury to become a Catholic, and Cardinal Newman in one of his letters says: 'It is sad to think of poor Glennie, he has given up everything and has a sick wife and some children. Someone told me that he had seen him, too poor to keep a servant, sweeping down the stairs himself.' The great desire of Mr. Glennie was to become a priest, and on the early death of his wife this became possible but for the three children dependent on him. At the suggestion of Cardinal Wiseman, my father, who already had six children of his own, offered to admit the two daughters into his home—the boy, Dunstan, who had always been ailing, died. And the two daughters became part of the family and their father, who was thus free to pursue his studies, was naturally a constant visitor. He subsequently became the head of the Catholic Training College at Brook Green and later Canon of the diocese of Southwark. Him we regarded as part of the family and when he came to his end it was my mother who nursed him and closed his eyes at Weybridge.

My father died in 1856 and shortly afterwards we moved away to the new district of Bayswater. At that time speculative builders had run up many houses which remained for years mere shells. To prepare for the expected people, had been erected the shell of a fine Protestant church, which long remained unfinished and which was surrounded by skeleton houses and was always called the Church in the Fields.

In the same way the Catholics had begun the shell of a really fine church which, when I first remember it, was without windows or pavement. The Catholics of the district were then looked after by Dr. MacGee, and for their religious services they had a small school chapel almost adjoining the skeleton church. When in 1854 Dr. Manning returned permanently to London with the intention of devoting his energies to the cure of souls in London, at Wiseman's suggestion he considered taking the mission of St. Mary's of the Angels, Bayswater. I recall a certain Sunday morning when Father Moore told us about the changes then in contemplation and how it was probable that Dr. Manning, one of the most distinguished of the converts, had agreed to take the mission. To have a man of the eminence of Manning as Superior was a future of which no one had dreamed (for Dr. Manning was beginning to be well known in London, and hence the proposal that the eminent convert should take charge of what promised to be a great centre of Catholic activity). To this proposition Manning agreed and on Whitsunday 1857 he and the first members of the Oblate Community took over the district. Manning himself had come a few days before, and as a small boy I had the pleasure of serving his first Mass in the School Chapel, and from that day for many years I was in constant relation with the Oblates and the Father Superior.

For eight years Dr. Manning worked to form the Community and to develop the parish. All that time he lived in a small room, like the rest, which he looked after himself. Reflecting upon the high position he had held in the Established Church, his life in those years was little less than heroic. He had taken a big corner house at 12 Sutherland Place for the Community. This became a place of pilgrimage for souls desiring help, advice and instruction in the Faith. We there constantly saw people well known in the world of letters. Ecclesiastics from Rome came, and I recall an Auditor of the Rota, Mgr. Nardi, and that celebrated Orientalist Ceriani of Milan.

Amongst the small Community at Bayswater in those early days there were Father Herbert, afterwards Cardinal Vaughan, Father Dillon whom we had first known at Somers Town, Father Richards, and an American Oxford convert, Father Herman Charles Denny, who returned to America and became a

Jesuit. Years afterwards I paid him a visit with Cardinal Gibbons when in America. In those days young converts unmarried thought that it was necessary to try to become priests. Amongst those who thus came to the Oblates was one well known later as Sir Francis Burnand, for many years editor of *Punch*. He was an unfailing source of life to us in the Community.

In 1916 he writes from Ramsgate: 'Heartiest congratulations to you on the fiftieth anniversary of your clothing and on everything generally that has gone and is going well with you, and I wish that you may always have with you as now a "virile sense of humour" (as the Right Rev. Bishop of Clifton puts it—Bravo Right Rev!), and a saving sense of the huge amount of genuine fun that can and ought to be got out of life in the Cloister. Don't let this saving sense be ever out of the cloister, and to adopt the Divine Welcome "the world is my cloister," in which I do not suppose I have to remain very long, as I am 80, *tout complet*.'

Yet Bayswater and the choir seem but a short distance off, and our practices with the harmonium in the large room, and our look-out for a visit from the Father Superior who, however, only just looked in and then wisely retired.

Burnand kept us alive with his overflowing humour. I recall one time when he had been reading to us a semi-comical poem he had written, and in the midst of our laughter the door opened and Dr. Manning came in and asked Burnand, 'My dear boy, did you write that?' And on Burnand's reply he said: 'Well, can you never learn to be serious; really if you continue like this you will be more fit for a cobbler than a priest,' to which Burnand instantly replied: 'Well, I should still have the care of soles, Father.'

An endless crowd of people were seeking his advice or instruction. Florence Nightingale, I remember, and Miss Taylor, who also went out to nurse in the Crimea and afterwards became the Foundress of the Poor Servants of the Mother of God.

I remember about 1859 listening to the Abbé Ratisbon giving an account of the miracle which had led to his conversion at S. Andrea delle Frate. He came with his brother in London to establish a convent of Notre Dame de Sion at Bayswater.

Sunday after Sunday Provost Manning attracted crowds by his preaching so that extra seats had always to be brought into the church. Thither came well-known persons, especially converts, to see and consult him: Father Faber and Father Dalgairns and Dr. Ward, who came to live in the parish.

Religious Communities were attracted to the neighbourhood and within a very short space there sprang up the Franciscans, the Poor Clares, the Little Sisters of the Poor, etc.

The district was not always quiet and orderly, and on more than one occasion I remember passing along one road with the Father and seeing him pelted with mud and stones.

DOWNSIDE

In the summer of 1862 my mother took my brother and me abroad and we spent some two months in Belgium, Switzerland and France. After spending a couple of months in Paris on the way back I did not return to the Oblates, but instead I was destined to go to Downside (September 1862). After spending a day or so at Princethorpe where the chaplain, Father Charles Comberbach, was an old friend of my mother, we went to Bath and so on to Stratton-on-the-Fosse where, arriving too late to go up to the college, we had to spend the night at the old village inn, and next day went to the Monastery for the High Mass at which I remember Father Wulstan Richards preached his first sermon.

A severe accident had incapacitated several of the Community. A party was driving back from Shepton Mallet, when the horse took fright on Nettlebridge Hill and bolted downhill. The old phaeton was upset against the wall and all were thrown out. Father Manus McKenna was so injured that he never properly recovered and passed most of the rest of his life in Belgium. We used to hear stories of him when someone would go over to see how Father Manus was getting on. One of the patients accosted a stranger in the village and demanded why he had not taken off his hat to him, saying: 'Don't you know I am the Angel Gabriel?' The stranger replied: 'But only yesterday you told me you were John the Baptist.' Whereupon the patient replied: 'That's right, but it was by another mother.'

The Community in 1862 consisted of some fifteen members and they had more to do than they could get through. The Prior, Father Cuthbert Smith, was of the most kindly disposition, but at times did not hesitate to speak strongly to his overworked Community. To us boys perhaps the best-known members of the Community were Father Clement Clarke, who was just beginning his long term of office as Prefect, and Br. Vincent Dolman who was always ready to join in our games.

The old chapel was much beloved by us though it sometimes astonished people seeing it for the first time. The choir stalls mounted up very high, on the one side to the organ loft, and on the other to the level of the old top dormitory. Here a very frequent visitor used to be seen in the person of the convert Oxford man, the Scholar John Brady Morris, the friend of Newman and the author of many books. Another frequent visitor was old George Count Mazzinghi. He was generally to be found in the organ loft where he, as a musician, was compelled to blow the organ by the boy whose office it was. Poor old George! He was well known to many generations of Old Gregorians and everyone used to play tricks on him. When Cardinal Wiseman paid a visit to Downside, Frank, afterwards Mgr. Weld, composed for him a speech which he was to make when asking the Cardinal to obtain a whole holiday for the school. In this he was made to say that he hoped it would not be the *first* time that the Cardinal would come to St. Gregory's. The father of George Mazzinghi was a well-known Court musician in London. Through his intimacy with the Prince Regent he was able to purchase for Downside the old organ of the Pavilion, Brighton. (He used to tell many stories about the Regent and his friends.)

During my time in the school at Downside, which had come in 1814 to their new home from Sir Edward Smythe's place at Acton Burnell, where he had welcomed them when they were forced by the French Revolution to abandon Douai, we kept the Jubilee of St. Gregory's.

At the great dinner in celebration of the Jubilee there were present several Downside Bishops. The first was Bishop Morris, Titular Bishop of Troy, well known in London, who had been

Bishop of the Mauritius, having in his jurisdiction the great
district of New Zealand and Australia. It was Dr. Morris who
got Dr. Polding sent as first Bishop of Australia. Dr. Polding
asked for Dr. Ullathorne and then for Dr. David of Downside.
Later, Fr. Roger Vaughan succeeded. Thus all the first founders
of the Church of Australia were Downside monks.

In 1864 the then Prior of Belmont, Fr. Roger Vaughan, came
in the Lent to give the boys a retreat. It was much liked by all,
and certainly with me it was the turning point of my life. I had
long talks with Prior Vaughan on the matter of my vocation.
However, there was plenty of time to determine, since my
mother, by the advice of Bishop Ullathorne, decided that before
I took any step, I should be living at home for a year at least. It
was however my last term at Downside and in the summer of
1865 I went home and set to work during the time I had to wait.
In the autumn Prior Vaughan came to see me, and after a long
talk with me he saw my mother and suggested that if he could
arrange it I should go to the Noviciate at Belmont at the beginning
of the year and wait till the following autumn to ask for the habit.

My mother agreed and in the month of January 1866 I found
myself at Belmont.

BELMONT

I came to Belmont as a Postulant in January 1866. The Prior
was, as I have said, Roger Vaughan, and the Subprior, who was
also novice-master, was Father Anselm Gillet. I was only Postulant and was put with the Juniors whose master was Father
Wilfrid Raynal. Our studies were directed by Father Cuthbert,
afterwards Bishop Hedley. I have always looked upon it as a
special providence that I came to know Father Cuthbert so well,
and to his teaching, and to his example as a student, I owe more
than I can say. In literature he was a safe guide as to the books
that should be read and mastered. Sometimes his ideas of books
were not those of Father Raynal, from whom we had to get leave
to read out of study time. I remember once asking to read the
Diversions of Purley. The frontispiece of the volume was a plate
of Mercury without much on, and I was refused permission.

Another time *The Essays of Elia* were condemned, I suppose on account of the name!

I have ever remembered the walks which we used to take under the guidance of Bishop Hedley. They are delightful remembrances, and with him we explored the country churches of Herefordshire, within reach of the Monastery. The conversation of our guide was always interesting, improving, and amusing.

I remained as a Postulant at Belmont till the autumn of 1866, when after spending a couple of weeks at home I returned to receive the habit. I got back on the day before the new Choir and Sanctuary were opened. Archbishop Manning came and preached on the occasion, and remained at Belmont for a few days. There were seven of us: four from Downside, two from Douai, and one from Ampleforth.

Of my special friend at Belmont, Prior Vaughan, I saw practically nothing, except in the hours in which he gave Brother Benedict MacKay and me some lessons in Italian. This stand-off attitude of the Prior was at first a great trial to me; but I soon got to know that he regarded the office of Superior as requiring that there should be no idea of any personal friendship for any of his subjects. 'A Prior,' he used to say, 'is like a Captain on board a ship. He must stick to his quarter-deck, and remain alone.'

Looking back now after more than half a century, I can see how the months from January to September 1866 were a special providence to me, and the delay in following out my vocation, which I regarded at first as a disaster, was in reality a blessing. This is another instance in my life of how I was taught that it was not what I wanted that was to succeed, but what God judged best.

DOWNSIDE AGAIN

In 1867 I returned to Downside and had to take part in the teaching. The Community was very small in numbers, but there was a great spirit of work, and the musical side was much in evidence. We were fortunate at this time to obtain the services of an old student of Einsiedeln, who was an accomplished musician, and could play almost any instrument. By his help we got up two school bands: a brass band, which had existed in some form or other for many years, and a string band, which was much appreciated. In the first I played the cornet and in the second the cello.

In 1874 I was ordained priest by Archbishop Errington, as Bishop Clifford had met with an accident and could not use his arm. I said my first Mass on December 1, 1874. I was almost at the same time named Sub-Prefect under Father Clement Clarke.

In 1877 I became Prefect of Studies and Professor of Theology at Downside. The previous year Bishop Ullathorne came and gave us a familiar retreat in preparation for taking possession of the Monastery. It was throughout a solemn warning not to be content with magnificent buildings, and not to sing *Templum Domini, Templum Domini, Templum Domini est.* The buildings were useless unless they were the symbol of work and interior spirit. This was the Bishop's last talk with us, and I believe that he enjoyed the time as much as we did.

In 1878 I was elected Prior of Downside in the place of Father Bernard Murphy who had been a martyr to ill-health. Two years later, 1880, there was the great celebration of the millenary of St. Benedict at Monte Cassino, and at the request of our President-General I undertook to write a brief sketch of St. Benedict's mission in regard to England. The pamphlet was not long, but it was ready in time and aimed at showing the intimate connection of the Benedictine Order with England. Cardinal Newman wrote a few lines of acknowledgement in which he speaks of it as a 'beautiful composition.'

1880 was a year of considerable activity. In July the *Downside Review* was started on its long career, during which there were published a large number of articles not only in connection with the School, but of general Catholic interest. Father Gilbert Dolan and Edmund Bishop were constant contributors, and I wrote for the *Review* (as the first article) a memoir of Bishop Brown[1] who died in the early part of April. He was one of the first boys at Downside, coming from Acton Burnell in 1814. He was born at Bath as long ago as 1798, and was from the first a determined

[1] Right Rev. Thomas Joseph Brown, O.S.B., Vicar Apostolic of the Welsh District 1840–1850, of Newport and Menevia 1850–1880.

little defender of his religion. I have heard him say, said Bishop Hedley in his funeral sermon, for any matter of his Faith he never blushed or made a compromise, and speaking of those young days he could say: 'I never was beaten.'

The Prior, Dom Peter Kendal, died at Woolton Hill on his way back from purchasing the property. Bishop Brown was one of the party which, under the old Maurist Monk, Dom Leveaux, had been directed to journey by coach to Bath. They spent the night at the Star Inn at Worcester, and I have often heard the Bishop describe the astonished look of the waiters when old Dom Leveaux commenced to sing the *Graces* at dinner, as they had been used at Acton Burnell. On the second day they reached Bath, and the party of boys was left there whilst the Religious pushed on to Downside. Here very little preparation had been made for their coming. Their furniture, which had been despatched from Shrewsbury by canal to Paulton, had not arrived, and there was scarcely a table or chair for use. To add to their miseries, the last days of April became bitterly cold and they had no store of fuel to warm their empty houses. Dom Leveaux, their temporary Superior, was a strict disciplinarian and did not recognize in these circumstances any sufficient reason to depart from the usual routine of monastic duties. The Office was recited under great difficulties, and Bishop Brown used to speak of the great embarrassment they experienced when they were told to study, as no books had arrived and they had no tables to sit at.

With his rhetoric class, it was his practice to read us examples in English composition of chosen passages from the Waverley Novels, such as the descriptions of local scenery and of personal portraits, as well as the occasionally beautiful moral reflections that are met with so often in the novels of Sir Walter Scott. For instance: the picture of Osbaldeston Hall in *The Antiquary*, the portrait of Graham of Claverhouse in *Old Mortality*, and the meditations of Father Eustace during his forest ride in *The Monastery*. When he perceived the lively delight such selections gave his youthful hearers, he invited them to his room in the long summer evenings and read through to them in his own animated manner, several of the choicest of the Waverley Novels, such as *Ivanhoe*,

The Monastery and *The Abbot,* accompanying the reading with critical remarks.

This same year we began to prepare for building the transepts of the proposed church at Downside. We had after considerable thought and discussion determined to undertake the work without any contractor. It was only in this way that we could do it, for the great amount necessary to pay a contractor was impossible. Still there were not a few who looked on me as mad to undertake the work in this way, and several attempts were made to stop me, but I felt that I had the loyal trust and co-operation of my Community and the result proved that I was right. Still, naturally, the building entailed a great amount of anxiety and a great amount of time spent over the details, and I doubt whether it could have been carried out at all but for the loyal and capable assistance of Mr. James, who became practically builder. And so during two years I spent a considerable part of each day with him overseeing his work and even practically assisting him. I recall two or three days especially when we were setting out the centering for the arches of the transept and arranging for the purchase of timber for the roof.

The following year the transepts of the church were finished and we had a solemn opening at which Bishop Ullathorne preached a remarkable sermon. After the dinner he made a characteristic speech in which he described the process by which the modern world was being de-Christianized, and declared that the great hope for the future was the upholding of Benedictine principles which would again save the world. In this same year I prepared an article for the *Dublin Review* on the vexed question of Adrian IV and Ireland.

The year 1885 brought a great change in my life. In the spring, as a natural result of trying to do too much, my health broke and after a trip abroad to Gibraltar and Spain during the Lent time, I returned to Downside only to resign. It seemed at the time that I was at the end of all things and that my life's work was over. Again I found that God in overruling my desires was preparing me for other work, not immediately connected with

Downside. My heart was rather bad and I at first went to my mother in Russell Road, Kensington, to rest and abstain from everything in the way of work, physical or mental, and I remained there with the family till 1890. Whilst I was staying with my mother, one evening it became necessary to go and ask her doctor, a certain Dr. Mennell, to come and see her. Whilst chatting with this new medical friend, he suddenly said: 'You do not look very well,' and on my saying what was the matter, he said: 'I suppose you had dropsy after scarlet fever.' I said this was not the case as I remembered having had scarlet fever, and that there was no case of dropsy after it. He said then, 'I believe that I am right, for you look to be like a typical case of heart after that dropsy.' I said no, sure at the time, but the next morning laughingly told my mother about this affair and how I had denied having had any touch of dropsy, when she said: 'But you had it and we were for a time very anxious about your heart.' This so struck me that I went back to Mennell and told him my case and asked whether he could do anything. He asked me what I was doing, for he thought it would be a great mistake after having led a busy life to get into the way of doing nothing. I suggested going to work at the British Museum and the Public Record Office, and to this he agreed on the sole condition that, if I at any time found myself rather overdone, I would at once give it up for the time. This was the beginning of many years of daily working either at the Museum or Record Office or at both.

No sooner was I settled down in my mother's house than I undertook work in which I had the advantage of the help and advice of Edmund Bishop. This was an Introduction to the new print of the English translation of Montalembert's *Monks of the West*. I took the opportunity of writing down my firm view as to the basis of the Benedictine Order and setting down how it differed from the Constitutions of the more modern Orders: each House to be a complete family and not a regiment of an army under a General. The work took some time and trouble, and shortly after it was printed in English it was translated by the advice of Cardinal Satolli into Italian, and he presented it to Pope Leo XIII.

I had many letters on the subject from various points of view. At this time in London I became acquainted with the great American Prelate, Archbishop Ireland of St. Paul, who was called by the witty Archbishop Ryan of Philadelphia 'The Consecrated Blizzard of the West.' We had discussed together the Benedictine Constitution and he wrote from St. Paul:

> I have just finished the reading of your *Costituzione Monastica*, and I felt that I ought to tell you how much pleasure and instruction I derived from the pages of that little work. I renew also the very valued acquaintance which it was my good lot to form with you in London.
>
> How much you do say! I never before understood the grandeur, the wisdom of St. Benedict and of the Rule which he inculcated. Better far, in my opinion, for Religious Orders and for the Church, if the Benedictine Rule had remained more than it has, the type of the religious life.
>
> One remark you made struck me much—when you speak of the relations of the monasteries with the Episcopate, the result of these relations being that the religious life, so acted out, was an element of activity, of strength in the Church, without assuming to be or appearing to be the Church. No one can be a Catholic without admiring the 'religious life,' and without according to it a large place in the Church's action: but there are Catholics who take objection to the religious life, when, as in the case of the Society of Jesus, it aims consciously or unconsciously to be the whole Church.

On coming to London I went to see Cardinal Manning and he told me that he thought that my settling down in London was most opportune. After Pope Leo XIII's letter on Historical Studies and his throwing open the Papal Archives to students, he had been urged to try to get some people to take up historical work seriously as the best service at the time for the Church. 'We want facts,' he said, 'to correct fancies,' and the Cardinal told me that it was necessary to set down the absolute truth and to try to hide nothing and he repeated what the Pope had said to him, that if the Gospels had been written in our days, the history of the fall of St. Peter and of the treachery of Judas would have probably been left out as not edifying! The Cardinal after my interview wrote to Rome to say that he had found someone to take to historical work and in the course of time I had a letter to say that Pope Leo XIII approved and blessed my work and that I was to consider myself dedicated to it. This came just when it was proposed that I should go and serve the small mission of Acton Burnell as Chaplain to the Smythe family.

[Gasquet must be considered fortunate to have escaped being condemned to a small obscure Mission. Manning's interference was doubtless due to Edmund Bishop who noted in 1889: 'I *did* pull Gasquet out of his coffin.']

Living quietly at home I went every day to the British Museum Library or Record Office, and frequently on my way back home I went in to have a chat with Cardinal Manning in his room. Generally he was glad to talk of early days at Bayswater and to discuss what I had been working at in the Libraries. I told him the state of the Religious Houses on their suppression in the reign of Henry VIII. What I felt was that the story as it was generally told and believed against the moral character of the Monastic Houses was a most powerful argument in the hands of non-Catholics. But was the picture true or libel? This seemed to me the question which wanted examination. The Cardinal held firmly that it was probably true and used to say that Lingard had left a tradition that the less stirred up the better. My contention was that, if the story was as black as supposed, it was well to probe and see. Thus I started and worked steadily in the Record Office and British Museum at every document I could discover. I passed some time at Oxford and went to several Cathedral archives and to libraries abroad and also to Trinity College, Dublin. By the end of 1886 I had gathered together most of the necessary material and spent 1887 digesting and writing the first volume of *Henry VIII and the English Monasteries*, the Preface of which I dated from Downside on October 27, 1887.

On the publication of the first volume in 1888, Cardinal Manning reviewed it in the *Dublin Review* in order, as he said, to put on record that he had changed his view altogether and considered that it had clearly shown that the reputation which had been given to the old monks was the result of calumnies and false interests. The Cardinal forwarded to Pope Leo XIII the volume and I afterwards received a note to come to the Archbishop's house where he gave me a document and the oath on appointment as a Doctor of Divinity. There was some difficulty about the biretta and the only one available was the Cardinal's own. Manning, putting it on my head, said: 'The colour doesn't matter and perhaps some day you will get one like it.'

As my stay in London was now permanent it became necessary to find some place to live, as I could not continue for much longer to live at my mother's house. Looking about I found a place near to the Museum and the Record Office, at 4 Great Ormond Street, and this I was able to take through the long continued generosity of the Duke of Norfolk and Lord Emly. Cardinal Manning did not at all approve of a permanent Benedictine house in London, but for the sake of the work in which he was interested, he refrained from refusing his blessing. Fortunately at this time my friend Edmund Bishop retired from the Education Office and devoted himself to literary work, and proposed to come and live with me. For me nothing could have been more providential, for he was the best guide that anyone could have in historical work, for not only had he studied for years deeply in every branch of Ecclesiastical History and especially in Liturgy, but he had a retentive and accurate memory, so that he was immediately able to point out where to find what was wanted and to say what edition of any special book was best consulted. I cannot say all that he was to me during the years we lived and worked together.

Another friend for many years was the Baron Frederick von Hügel with whom we used to have long walks and talks on Hampstead Heath. Through him I got to know Mrs. Anderson and her famous actress daughter, Mary Anderson, who became a firm friend, and with her and her husband Anthony de Navarro I have passed many restful and happy days in their house at Broadway in Worcestershire. The von Hügels introduced me to the Caves of Ditcham Park, Petersfield, and after a short time I agreed to act as their Chaplain and used to go down to their country house every Friday evening, returning home to London on the Monday morning. As I became perfectly at home at Ditcham I was able to do a good deal of work in the country quiet on Saturdays and Sundays.

At this time the President of our Congregation, Abbot O'Neil, was appointed by Rome as Bishop of the Mauritius. This entailed an election of a successor as President, and in the General Chapter I was elected. My first thing to do was to preach at Warrington at a feast at St. Alban's Church and I obtained from Rome the privilege for myself and successors as Presidents to wear the Cappa Magna. I had been long thinking of preparing a paraphrase of the Epistles for the Sundays in English. Bishop Hedley had promised to do the Gospels and to try to get this adopted for reading in place of the English version of the Epistles and Gospels. As the Bishop said, when we were discussing the matter, the present exact translation is almost impossible to understand and one might almost as well read it in the original Greek. In May 1901 I was able to send the Bishop the first part of the prepared paraphrase and (in acknowledging the packet) he wrote: 'I have read with interest the specimen you sent me. I think it is very well done and I feel certain it will be useful and popular. In reading your specimen it is borne in upon me how useful would be a treatment of the whole New Testament in this same fashion. It would be better than any commentary for the ordinary Christian.'

In 1886 I was elected on the Council of the old Camden Society at which I met many leading writers of History. We used to meet once a month in the parlour behind the office of Nichol the publisher, and which has now disappeared in the changes of Great Parliament Street. After the business of the meeting was finished it was our custom to get round the fire and have a general talk on any interesting matters. We had amongst others Rawson Gardiner, James Gairdner, Dr. Hunt, Mr. Epsworth, etc.

In the spring of 1888 I spent four pleasant weeks at Ushaw College to which I had been invited by Bishop Wilkinson to give a course of talks to the elder students, on History. I had already gathered the material for the chapter on Catholic England proposed by Lord Acton for the Cambridge History, which was published this year in a separate book under the title of *The Eve of the Reformation*. Dr. James Gairdner, reviewing it, said: 'There is much in it that will not meet the approval of non-Catholics, but whether they like it or not they will be forced to come to hold the same view if they are honest men.'

We English Benedictines held our Chapter in 1904, in which I was re-elected President. Amongst other matters which came up for consideration at our meeting, was the question of serving Westminster Cathedral. Cardinal Vaughan had spoken of the possibility, but I had thrown cold water on what I looked upon as out of the question. My view, however, made little impression upon him apparently, and at a Downside dinner held on June 27, 1894, Cardinal Vaughan, replying to the toast of his health, enlarged upon the work of the new Westminster Cathedral and expressed a wish that the English Benedictines would serve the Cathedral church as their predecessors had served so many of the old Cathedrals and in particular the metropolitan church of Canterbury. Especially he declared his desire that the monks of St. Gregory's, Downside, would undertake the work, and that their life and work would be of great profit to the Church in England and especially in London.

It was possibly in view of the Cardinal's dream that after his death the Chapter of Westminster proposed two Benedictines as possible successors.

[Henceforth it was not enough for Gasquet (to use Shakespeare's words) to 'live in a nook merely monastic.'

He lived in three London residences while working at the British Museum and Record Office. He also acted as Chaplain to the Cave family at Ditcham Park (Petersfield) from 1893 till 1903. And awhile he lived in a Religious House at Dulwich.]

IV

EDMUND BISHOP
'Carissime Episcope'!
(GASQUET to BISHOP)

This emaciated figure, this angular and broken gesticulation, this
vinegared voice—made one imagine the presence of one of those
agitated Sibyls with lined, cracked, parchment face on the ceiling
of the Sixtine.

HENRI LECLERCQ (*Dict. d'Arch. Chrét.*)

NO memoir of Gasquet would be satisfactory without a pro-
longed mention of Edmund Bishop. He was not only his
closest friend but the guiding power in his scholarship. It is just
to say that Bishop made and inspired him as a historian. Great
partnerships are not uncommon in literature or research, save
that one name is often subdued to the other. In the case of Liddell
and Scott none could distinguish the persons or separate the compilers of the Greek Lexicon. Edmund Bishop's meticulous work
slipped into Gasquet's broad paragraphs. He became his *aide-
mémoire*. His name was added to Gasquet's in *Edward VI and the
Book of Common Prayer*, and in their edition of the *Bosworth Psalter*.
According to the Downside tradition Gasquet wrote the first at
the dictation of Bishop striding up and down his room. It was
Bishop's book as every liturgist was bound to recognize. Gasquet's
book on the Monasteries proved accurate, for Bishop had verified
it throughout. Bishop also wrote important sermons for Gasquet
and letters to *The Tablet*. He was never so superb or unselfish as
when he wrote as a ghost.

Amongst scholars devoted to the curious science of litur-
giology, which is the dissection and ascription of ancient Prayer
Books and Devotionals, Bishop stood first in his time. The hidden
prince of an obscure science, he has received Abbot Butler's brief
laudation in the *Dictionary of National Biography*. But he stands
on a level (in some gradations, higher) with Henry Bradshaw,

4

the prince of Cambridge Librarians, and Montagu Rhodes James, with whom died much mediaeval knowledge. From books dead and buried like the bones of Elisha they could extract the magic of meaning, the spark of life.

From their standing and achievements the rank of Edmund Bishop may be gauged. In that trinity of great-souled and erudite Christian scholars Bishop could be placed first, on the strength of the papers which he left to Downside. He had not the happy conversational style in which James and Gasquet could popularize learning. Like Bradshaw he was content to excavate the bricks and mosaics with which others built. Never was there a more generous and unselfish partner.

His arrival in Gasquet's life was decisive. It has been compared to the meeting of Vinogradoff and Maitland, when one scholar was inspired by the utterly unsuspected researches and resources of the other. Gasquet was a busy Prior in 1880 when he received Bishop as a visitor to Downside. Their meeting might be commemorated in design like that of St. Francis and St. Dominic. They fell upon each other's desks. It was an influence upon Gasquet's whole life and marked renewed scholarship in the Anglo-Benedictine Order. Gasquet recalled that historic occasion after Bishop's death: 'I had heard from him before and had been astonished at the replies he had given me to certain queries I had put to him. But I was unprepared for the evidence he gave me, on our first meeting in the old parlour at Downside, of his extensive reading, his astounding memory and his balanced judgment.' Intimacy began when Bishop returned as a Postulant in 1885. For various reasons, including inability to rise early, he never became a monk. He loved laborious nights.

It was due to Gasquet's admiring appreciation that the book on *Edward VI and the Book of Common Prayer* made a fortunate preliminary to the open conflicts on Anglican Orders. The early editions of 1891–2 'quickly went out of print and no copy has been in the market for many years,' wrote the Cardinal in issuing a third and revised edition in 1928. Every copy had been absorbed in the rising disputes on Liturgy. Perhaps no book by a Roman author had been read with such intimate interest by Anglicans since Newman's *Apologia*. The beauty of the English Prayer Book was dissected historically like a flower by ruthless botanists. The text was written in the terse, pigeon-holing style—almost entirely quotations—while erudite footnotes betrayed the hand of Edmund Bishop.

They brought back Cranmer from his ashes, using MSS. marked in his actual script such as the famous Royal MS. in the British Museum whose 'marginal notes tell a curious tale.' The rare chance was afforded of comparing Cranmer's Commonplace Book with his Common Prayer: his written notes with the printed book. Cranmer's fears, hopes and compromises can be traced even in the underlinings. Here is a grim comment: 'Cranmer's erasure of St. Babilas from the Calendar is doubtless explained by the story of this martyr scarcely according with the Tudor idea.' It may be added that under Henry VIII a book had been suppressed because the account of John the Baptist threw a shadow on a king who had out-Heroded Herod in matters matrimonial.

Gasquet and Bishop explained the *two* Prayer Books of Edward VI from which Anglican duality has been derived to this day. The First remained fairly Catholic with the 'Communion commonly called the Mass,' candles and vestments. The Second was largely Lutheran though much remained translated from the Latin liturgy.

The First was accepted by Bishop Gardiner 'in order to secure at least the maintenance of the Mass.' It was a compromise, dear to the English mind and, had Cranmer met Gardiner in the right spirit, the Church of England might have kept the intent of real Mass and valid Orders. Unfortunately the only answer made to Gardiner was the Tower. The Second Prayer Book was far less English, because the Continental fanatics had overwhelmed Cranmer and their prejudices had been respected.

Gasquet brought out that every point which Gardiner had accepted in hope that the old Belief remained in the First Prayer Book, was swept away or altered in the Second. It was a duel between the gallant Gardiner and the craven Cranmer which Cranmer won.

What happened may be illustrated by a recent revision which the Anglican Church of Ireland made of this same Church of England Prayer Book in 1870, expelling Apocrypha, muzzling Athanasius, forbidding even the Sign of the Cross. This made a parallel with what happened in the sixteenth century.

The High Churchmen of Ireland had believed they could still maintain a Catholic interpretation of their Book, but this ceased with all symbolism thereof after 1870. They were forbidden to use even 'substitutes for incense' (whatever they may be). Once again fanatics had routed the moderates.

In Edmund Bishop, Gasquet won a friend and a co-operator such as the greatest might have proudly associated with their writings. In England Edmund Bishop was unknown. The most effete Don at the Universities, the feeblest columnist in a Church paper was more celebrated. Yet here was a scholar esteemed by Mommsen. England would probably have been astonished to hear that she contained a scholar admired by Waitz, Wattenbach and Liebermann except that she had never heard of them either. Henri Leclercq could only compare him to an oracular Sibyl.

Gasquet proceeded to explore, even to exploit, his good fortune. Bishop had been a clerk in the Education Office for twenty years, spending his leisure and salary on works of research. He read vastly and, as is often the case, his storied memory became too cumbersome or colossal for him to use himself: but he poured it forth into chosen channels, of whom Gasquet was the most choice. He worked steadily with Gasquet and even spent years with him in Great Ormond Street in close touch with the treasures of the British Museum (1894–1901). Bishop's illness sundered them with sad results on Gasquet's historical work: but they came together to edit Gasquet's splendid discovery of the *Bosworth Psalter*. There were visits to Bishop's home in Barnstaple and happy liturgical picnics when they visited the churches of North Devon in a carriage and pair.

Bishop set his mark on Gasquet's two first famous productions. He inspired the reversal of popular opinion as to the English Monasteries which was achieved by sheer publication of facts and papers without the assistance of guess or theory. To the work on the old English Prayer Book Bishop was bound to add his name, for he had practically supplied the content.

What manner of man was Bishop? A would-be recluse and Benedictine, he had been kept in the world by ill-health, family considerations and his method of work. He loved to lose himself in libraries. It was not enough to read a book and index its contents in his memory. He must pierce its pedigree, for he realized devotional books and liturgies are not suddenly born of genius, but made up by a long succession of saints and collectors. Karl Marx's evaluation of Property as Theft could more simply be said of Liturgy. Like a detective, Bishop followed the pious thefts leading to the first origin or originator of a Collect or Saint in the Calendar. He liked to describe himself as 'a devourer of Prefaces.' Certain minds can be revealed by favourite novels. Needless to say *John Inglesant* was Bishop's, a taste he shared with Mgr. Hugh Benson and Lord Halifax. He read that edifying patchwork annually.

He could not assemble his own books but he helped others to build out of his own stores. His knowledge was used by others in the manner that Roman Princes quarried their private palaces out of the greater Colosseum. The book on Edward VI and the Prayer Book was little more than Gasquet's arrangement of Bishop's material.

Bishop was Gasquet's consultor. Together they launched powerful combination into ecclesiastical research. Jealousy or divergence there could be none. Each found a divine gift in the other. Bishop received the loving care and admiring affection of Downside, which cheered his lonely and unplaced existence. On the other side Gasquet and any inquiring monks could fall back on 'the accuracy of his judgements upon men and things, and the sureness of his prodigious memory. It was like having a living Ecclesiastical Encyclopaedia always to refer to.'

Bishop was self-trained except that he had once acted as a secretary to the great and dismal Carlyle. From this distant contact he bore no traces. His view how History should be written was certainly different: and happily he did not inspire Gasquet to write of the fall of the English Abbeys in the style that Carlyle devoted to the fall of the Bastille. In the Catholic Church Bishop had found the 'everlasting yea.' No University had assisted Bishop upon his chosen path of learning. He had educated himself by threading every reference and every authority used by Gibbon in his *Rise and Fall of the Roman Empire* in order to estimate the value of each writer in turn. No one ever attempted this so thoroughly except Dr. Montagu James, who once made a list of the mistakes and misprints in Gibbon's references themselves. Bishop's feat would have commended itself to Cecil Rhodes, who commanded that the same survey should be carried out by a band of translators at a cost of seven thousand pounds!

Probably no one in Christendom, certainly no layman, knew Migne's collection of the Greek and Latin Fathers as well as Bishop. It was difficult for him to find channels for his pent-up learning, but Gasquet was one and the *Downside Review* proved another. His six-and-thirty contributions made it one of the few English periodicals prized by foreign liturgists. His solitary contribution to the *Monumenta Germaniae* won the esteem and gratitude of scholars in that country. Who else could have found a path over the morass of the first ten centuries and traced the tradition concerning the Roman Canon of the Mass, whose wording after all was not revealed to Apostles nor settled by the earliest Fathers? Like much else in the Church the Mass has been subject to the laws of Evolution and to variation of species. As a small instance, Bishop established that the *Memento* of the Dead formed no regular part of the Mass until the ninth century. No one else in the world could have made that kind of discovery. And when did the Mass pass from Greek into Latin? How came the *Kyrie Eleison* to be a borrowing not a survival? And the Last Gospel and the Elevation, when were they introduced? Bishop was one of the few who knew, but these are questions which do not trouble the faithful.

It is true he disclaimed collaboration with Gasquet except over the Prayer Book. But how many hints, suggestions and avenues he had opened on his way. Others had also profited, whose books bore the same clear evidences that certain pictures ascribed to certain Schools bear of an unseen Master in the background.

The Queen of Sheba would have found him even wiser reading than King Solomon. Solomon astonished her by his knowledge of tree and plant. Bishop could turn aside from a liturgical talk to verify some rare British butterfly such as a silver-spotted Blue once visiting the terraces of Downside. 'He was that sort of man,' quoth Abbot Horne, the last link with the legend of Edmund Bishop.

Typically he had collected a large scrapbook of unedited Papal Letters, which he gradually disposed to other compilers until he had to confess half-ruefully: 'The last piece of the *Spiceligium* is gone!'

Yet he was no dry fingerer of the dust. He had a magical power of raising dead scribes through the medium of their own manuscripts. This sense of divination was based on tremendous powers of memory. No one but Bishop could have written, without using book or note, a twenty-four page list of all the best-known guides to Sacred Liturgy. This amazing feat he once accomplished at the request of Abbot Amelli of Monte Cassino.

He left as many avenues open as he had compassed. The great work on the Roman Psalter was unfinished. He had not completed his majestic surveys upon the Spanish Councils or the Greek Liturgies or on the English Divines. But he had approached clearness on the history of Transubstantiation by investigating the philosophical meanings of *Essentia* and *Substantia*.

Friends and disciples could believe he was inspired in his struggles to find the light in obscure points of Liturgy, Philosophy or Antiquity.

He cast an uncanny insight into a Manuscript. In his own words:

Take Ethelwold's *Benedictional* and the *Bosworth Psalter*. Years ago I had the opportunity of being able to examine the *Benedictional*, to contemplate it for a couple of hours. How gorgeous and splendid! *Here* is Ethelwold himself figured in the dead page of script and gold. When first I saw the *Bosworth Psalter* and had leisure for six weeks to scan and meditate on it, it was the same. Here are the two men, Ethelwold and Dunstan, still today under their own very hand, portraying themselves

before one's eyes. For me I must own *Bosworth* is as surely
Dunstan as the *Benedictional* is Ethelwold—a portrait by the
artist himself.

Gasquet's triumph in discovering a unique Psalter of pre-
Norman origin was followed by a liturgical orgy from Bishop
printed by the patient nuns at Stanbrook Abbey in a volume
while the MS. became MS.37517 in the British Museum. By
dissecting the Calendar Bishop's learning proved the date thus:

It contains the feast of St. Dunstan but not that of St. Elphege.
The cultus of St. Dunstan began almost immediately after his
death in 988 and soon became general; St. Elphege was mar-
tyred in 1012 and his relics were translated from London to
Canterbury in 1023. The Calendar falls between 988 and 1023,'

and thus proved to be the only survivor belonging to Canterbury
before the Norman Conquest.

The Abbess of Stanbrook who printed the *Bosworth Psalter*
wrote:

Edmund Bishop was an amazing man and a dear. It was a
liberal education to listen to him and he was most generous in
sharing his scholarship. A good way of approaching him was
to make an intelligent mistake in one's queries. I once did that
and extracted from him in reply eight quarto pages of his
beautiful handwriting—a real treatise. He was delightfully
jealous if one anticipated a *find*, as I did twice: 'Dear, dear, why
didn't *I* find that?'

Take such minute traces from the past as those clock circles
found scratched beside old church doors. According to the sun,
if a dial is inserted, they always mark nine o'clock. Why? The
simple explanation in Bishop's words was: 'the general hour for
Mass in Catholic England.' Many an old fabric bears this sacred
signal upon its stones regardless of centuries of Protestant
services.

Bishop died in 1917, but his companionship and guidance had
for health reasons been largely withdrawn as early as 1901.
Certain mistakes and untenable theories in Gasquet's work were

the result. Had Bishop remained at his side, he would have checked his historical apprehension and insisted on certain corrections being accepted even when offered by hostile critics: *fas est et ab hoste doceri.*

For instance Gasquet had put forward in a lecture printed in the *Dublin Review* the theory that the Wycliffite or Old English Bible was the Old Catholic Bible. As the Reformation controversy had turned largely on the Bible, this was too good a point to be abandoned, although Sir Frederick Kenyon, Director of the British Museum, wrote to prove it was a chimaera and a dream. Gasquet clung to it and called on his friends for support. Alfred Pollard wrote (November 17, 1898): 'By the way I owe you a bad grudge for your papers on the Wyclif Bibles. I have got to write on English versions of the Bible for Chambers' Encyclopaedia and I find the problem a little more insoluble than that of the authorship of the *Romaunt of the Rose.* But you have certainly knocked the ordinary Protestant case into a cocked hat.'

When Canon Pennington of Lincoln criticized the idea, it was Edmund Bishop who wrote the answer for Gasquet to use as his own. It is an interesting instance of their work in common.

Bishop wrote in a covering letter: 'You see it is utter rubbish. Only one thing deserves notice, if indeed that does. I have looked at the texts in the Old English, the Douay and Authorized Versions and think the second perhaps may be (if there be a choice) the most Protestant of the three.'

Pennington had denied Gasquet's assertion that the Old English could have been the work of Catholic translators, pointing out that 'Hebr. IX, 27 is directly against the doctrines of Purgatory. The same applies to Rev. XIV, 13. Again if we refer to I John I, 2 we shall find that no mention is made of the Saints. Ephes. II, 8 is against the Catholic doctrine of good works.'

Bishop's comment was:

Canon Pennington adduces the Old English version as 'passages which directly condemn the doctrines' of the Catholic Church: and he asserts that they are evidences that the version

cannot have been the work of orthodox sons of the Church.
Your readers would gather that there is something specifically
Wycliffite in the translation. This is not so. They are neither
more nor less Protestant than the renderings of other versions.
What Canon Pennington really means is that these verses are
in his opinion irreconcilable with Catholic doctrine. The fact
that Wycliffe commented in Sunday sermons on the Gospel is
no argument that Wycliffite preachers or Wycliffe himself first
translated the Epistles and Gospels of the Missal. Canon
Pennington is convinced the truth will prevail. But he must
excuse a few plain words. If he is to understand the value of
arguments relating to the Old English Scriptures, it is necessary
to have a much wider knowledge of practice and life, ecclesiastical and civil, in the 14th and 15th centuries than he seems to
have any notion of.

All the last is nastyish: but you'll settle it down. It isn't
French! It is bad temper. *Ita testor* E. B.

Later Bishop tried to help him by a note connecting Catholic
frescoes with Wycliffite texts which showed that the orthodox
used them on church walls—'The *Western Antiquary* for Sept.
1885 has a notice of frescoes in Barnstaple Church with texts of
"Wycliffe's Version" of the Scriptures. The frescoes of XV cent.
or thereafter. This may be useful to note. The text (mutilated
now) is given in the Article.'

When Bishop read the bitter attack made by the *Nation* on
Gasquet's scholarship he scribbled (Nov. 30, 1912): 'This is
surely a *pity*. But I cannot be *surprised*—alas!'

This was a subject on which Bishop could not help him further
against unanswerable criticism. Sir Frederick Kenyon replied in
Our Bible and the Ancient MSS, writing to the present writer later
(May 27, 1945):

'The most serious point and the most difficult to explain
satisfactorily is, to my mind, the fact that after his mistake had
been so unquestionably exposed, Gasquet repeated his statement
in a later edition of his book *The Old English Bible*.'

This can only be explained by Gasquet's hope to recover
evidence, for which his correspondence shows he was continually
in search. For instance, he appealed to the authority of Aldis

Wright (Fellow of Trinity, Cambridge) who answered (January 3, 1906):

> I endeavoured to read all that had been written on both sides about the English translation of the Bible attributed to Wycliffe but the impression left upon my mind was that the case against the received tradition was not proven. Mr. Pollard has called my attention to the Dublin MS. to which you refer and it is my intention when I have more leisure than I have at present to investigate thoroughly Purvey's supposed connexion with the second version. If this investigation should lead me to change my opinion I shall have no hesitation in saying so.

John Purvey was the disciple of Wycliffe who revised the first version from other versions. No doubt the old Catholics made and read cribs to the Vulgate, which were regarded as orthodox by loyal sons of the Church. The Church permits Bible-reading to the laity (without pressing it), as though the Bible were the matrix rather than the matter of Faith. There let that controversy lie.

During the controversy over Anglican Orders it was Bishop who pointed out that the key to the question would be found amongst Cardinal Pole's letters in the Roman Archives: a shrewd intuition which touched the vital documentary evidence on which the final decision turned.

When the struggle was dawning, it was to Bishop through Gasquet that Cardinal Vaughan appealed (September 22, 1894):

> I think you or Mr. Bishop have made a particular study of Anglican Orders. I want one or two of the strongest and most manifest reasons, put in the briefest form to send in the letter I must write. Also reference to the clearest popular exposition of the case on the Catholic side, *i.e.,* the names of the one or two works which you may consider to be the best. My letter may get a wide circulation and therefore it is important.

Bishop died in the obscurity which he adorned. Neither Church nor State was competent to reward his peculiar learning. Armed with a method and a memory he could face such French scholars as Duchesne and Batiffol. He recalled Browning's Grammarian who 'settled *hoti's* business' during a life's work without fame or reward. Bishop worked on higher levels than the Greek particles. He settled the Gregorian Sacramentary, and the History of the Cope as part of the vesture of the Church. No scholar could have done more. Henceforth the tides of Western Liturgy appeared to flow to and from St. Gregory's Mass Book as excavated by Bishop.

Bishop's achievements did not appeal to his fellow-countrymen. The *Dictionary of National Biography* omitted his name in the brief extract dedicated to Gasquet, whose *altera anima* he had been. Frail of body, he carried his wonderful working brain intact to the grave. Emotionally he was delicately tuned and sensitive to gratitude or the reverse. Simple villagers in a village procession brought him to his knees sobbing. He was not puffed by that learning which he never forgot. Almost unaccompanied, he had penetrated the Serbonian bog of early Liturgy. He was perfectly content to spend his life in long laborious hours, long library vigils and to give his discoveries to others. Without degrees or decorations, he felt amply rewarded when his companion received the Cardinal's Hat, to which he himself had contributed some of the brightest tassels. Only England could have produced Edmund Bishop. Only England could have ignored him.

Abbot Ethelbert Horne preserved a vivid memory of Bishop's most dramatic achievement:

It was really Edmund Bishop who put Gasquet up to looking for this Ordination question. Some three or four years before the question of Anglican Orders came up, Bishop (who was living here) said to me one day that he could settle them in five minutes, if he was given certain documents. He explained this to Cardinal Vaughan, and it was this information that enabled him to get Leo XIII to give him the order to search the Holy Office Archives, which those in charge strongly resisted!

When Cardinal Pole became Archbishop of Canterbury, under Mary Tudor, Bishop saw that he must have been in a most difficult position with old valid priests and the new

Reformed parsons under him. He would not have dared to settle such a question as the validity of these Reformed Orders himself, but would have sent to Rome for instructions. It was those papers that Bishop realized would really settle the question and Gasquet carried out the idea. It was an entirely new line of attack.

Gasquet mourned Bishop's death with the grief of David over Jonathan, recalling industrious and happy days, 'full of instruction, intellectual refreshment and inspiration.' They were Pentecostal gifts for a layman to offer to an Ecclesiast. Sadly Gasquet recalled his own questionings into the unknown and the answers that no one else could supply, and, when a subject seemed sifted at last to the dregs, the sonorous quiet *Amen* that fell from Bishop's lips.

To Bishop's niece the Cardinal wrote from Rome (Feb. 21, 1917):

> For many years Edmund has been a faithful and devoted friend, ever ready to lay aside his own work to give his help in anything I wanted him to do for me: his death has left a void in my life, which must remain. He and I understood each other so thoroughly that it was not necessary to write to express our mutual affection. As you say in the letter you wrote for him [dictated two days before Bishop's death] 'He says that you have had his love so long that he isn't going to send it any more.' This expresses exactly our relations. What I owe to him no one can tell except myself and you may be sure that he will not be forgotten for a single day as long as I live.

Nobly and humbly, Gasquet recognized the dead man's superb assistance and cried over his dead body the words of the Psalmist: 'If I shall forget thee, let my right hand forget her cunning.' They were only too true.

V

ANGLICAN ORDERS AND ROMAN DIARY OF 1896

Of violent birth but poor validity.

SHAKESPEARE

A prudent Pope, availing himself of the powers given to him by the Council of Trent, would not find it difficult to effect a reconciliation between the Papal See and the Protestant Church of England. The extremes are beginning to bend to the circular form.

GODFREY HIGGINS in *Celtic Druids*, 1827

The Church of England—I said seeing that Mr. Inglesant paused—is no doubt a compromise.

J. H. SHORTHOUSE

THE Church of England for a century has swung admiringly or at least imitatively towards the Church of Rome. Though the High Church has called the Banns, any Reunion of the divorced Churches has failed. Something vital was lost in the process of the divorce engineered four centuries ago. During 1894 and 1895 the question of Anglican Orders was whispered in the corridors of the Vatican and more loudly in the councils of English High Churchmen. The question seemed simple and apparently ripe for solution: were the Holy Orders of the Church of England historically valid like Holy Orders in the Church of Rome? Did the Pope and the Archbishop of Canterbury share the mystical and far from mythical Succession from the Apostles? The answer proved simpler still.

They did not. Each possessed Orders excellent of their kind but different in intention and practice.

When Anglican laymen brought the question to the Holy See, there was much inquiry, some controversy and finally a Papal pronouncement that Anglican Orders were 'null and void.'

This decree of Leo XIII roused the Archbishops of Canterbury and York to protest, angered and disappointed the High Church and relieved most Churchmen, Broad or Low, who could not wish their Orders to be declared the same as those of 'sacrificing priests' of Rome. Old-fashioned Protestant clergy would have been horrified if they had learnt that in reading the Communion Service they could have said Mass! Likewise devout Romans would have been shocked to learn that the consecrated bread and wine in Protestant churches might be the Adorable Host. The sanctity and beauty of the Anglican Rite all liturgists would allow. But it was not intended to be the same as the Roman Mass. This would depend on the validity of the Orders alleged by High Churchmen and their Gallican allies, which again depended on the doctrine of Intention.

The delays, worries and controversies consequent on Lord Halifax's appeal to the Pope were resolved by a Commission, which advised the Pope after discussing both sides. Needless to say, Gasquet led the English team which signally defeated the distinguished French clergy, who believed or hoped it was possible for Anglican Orders to be recognized as the genuine brand.

For three hundred years Roman practice had re-ordained convert Anglican parsons. Rome had forgotten her own Decrees and reasons for this practice. High Churchmen now hoped to be re-ordained *conditionally*. This would save their face and make moral reunion possible. The question seemed an open one. The High Churchmen hoped against hope and in the course of controversy against charity as well.

Cardinal Vaughan and his advisers, Gasquet, Mgr. Moyes and Mgr. Merry del Val, were naturally in some anxiety, when the Pope and Cardinal Rampolla received the Anglicans kindly and perhaps indiscreetly. But the Pope was anxious to show that he was the Father of Christendom and undoubtedly shared in Lord Halifax's dream of Reunion. The question for both sides was: at what price?

'Conditional re-ordination' was the price proffered by the French allies of Lord Halifax. News of startling intrigues reached

Gasquet who passed them on to Cardinal Vaughan, for whom Mgr. Moyes replied (December 1894):

> His Eminence charges me to thank you very fervently for the information contained in your letter. He will write to Rome and will proceed there as soon as may be. And personally state the case to the Holy Father. What mischievous, meddling madcaps these Frenchmen can be! One really begins to ask if these Roman people are demented. Do they expect Lord Rosebery to run a Bill of Reunion with Rome through the Commons and the Archbishops of Canterbury and York to support it in the Lords? I have urged His Eminence to make them understand that the masses of the English people are still thoroughly Protestant.

Lord Rosebery was then Prime Minister.

Early in 1895 Gasquet arrived in Rome to consult with Cardinal Vaughan. Meantime he had consulted with Edmund Bishop, who with perfect intuition put his finger on the spot whence light and authority could be gleaned from the past. How deeply Bishop felt appears in a typical letter contrasting the uses of different languages in controversy and challenging the Frenchmen, who had taken up the Anglican position much to the surprise of English Catholics (August, 1894):

> I was the other side of the Channel. The spirit was alive. I felt equal to Dalbus and Duchesne together. I did want to patter with the tongue: after all French is the only tolerable language. English is essentially the language of shyness and reserve and awkwardness; German is grovelling; in French one can at once establish a pleasant footing by the most atrocious compliments not merely outwardly uttered but inwardly felt with all the sincerity of conviction. And what is better still they are taken, swallowed, bolted down with thorough and easy appreciation like so many 'natives' [oysters]. And then when we come to the grilling process, that's so much pleasanter in French than in any other tongue. I don't know the Italian lingo but when proper I should think it is too oily: and if sharp, then not neat or proper. But French is sharp and proper.
>
> This is all no good: *Dalbus did not come* but there was some interesting talk in his regard only by way of impression derived

from my Lord [Halifax]. Impressions one don't put on paper—
too volatile. But I'm sure of 'em. Lord Halifax is very pleasant,
amiable and intelligent; and as the Cardinal was not present,
I did a sort of pontifical second to Canon Moyes. . . . That pink
of Ultramontane perfection the *Moniteur de Rome* is on the
Dalbus tack, Gallic vanity is at it. There is nothing to be done
to stop 'em. Clear the stage, let the Gauls perform, unhampered
by any considerations of sense, any knowledge of the actualities
of fact, *pas de deux, pas seul,* wreath, applause (*la claque*). There's
no stopping them now they have begun. Let them play the
farce out to the end, and then perhaps it may dawn upon them
what sort of figure of fun they have been making. . . . But I
must be quiet and think away in the country about quite other
things than this wretched Anglican business which really
interests me more than I care for, for it is the subject you know
which calls up one's whole life and being and exhausts it. . . .

Dalbus' particular avoidance of all Catholics is a very unpleasant feature. But it doesn't matter a straw. I would not
wish a single one of 'em not to have their full fling. It is all a
part of the French play. And you must remember the Anglicans
will, in mere light-headedness of delight, do something
'tolerably foolish' as Calvin assures us their great forefather in
the faith did [Cranmer], as witness the Book of Common
Prayer.

Duchesne and the Frenchmen had little idea what was revolv-
ing in the mind of Edmund Bishop whose liturgical instinct told
him that Anglican Orders must have troubled Cardinal Pole,
returning under Queen Mary and finding many parsons had been
ordained by the new rite. This he must have dealt with as the last
Catholic Archbishop of Canterbury. The key to the situation
must lie in his correspondence surviving in the Holy Office.

Gasquet brought Bishop to Rome as his 'constant companion
during all this period.' As a result Gasquet promptly found Paul
IV's Brief referring to Julius III's Bull of 1555. The Brief explained
the words *recte et rite consecrati* and he knew he had found a 'very
important document.' The next day (February 20, 1895) he found
the Bull of Paul IV called *Praeclara Charissimi.* All was moving
with lightning speed, for two days later Cardinal Vaughan

brought him the Pope's permission to examine papers in the well-guarded Holy Office of the Inquisition. The Holy Office found this permission most unusual and there was a long delay, until April 20 when the Pope himself moved. Gasquet wrote:

> This evening I had a message to go to the Pope. I reached the Vatican about 6 o'clock and was received by the Holy Father immediately. I had for weeks been waiting to get access to the papers of the Holy Office for which I had obtained his permission. For one reason or another I had been constantly put off, and somewhat losing patience, I had written to the Vatican to know whether the Pope wanted me to see the papers or not. The reply came in the form of an order to come to see the Pope. He had himself sent for the papers and had arranged for me to have a room in the Vatican in which to examine them.

This was a dramatic victory over the Holy Office, especially when the Pope handed Gasquet the key to the room in which he could examine the papers. The Inquisition is not often brought to bay.

These documents proved vital and even sensational. They included summaries of Cardinal Pole's work in England, upon which the Bull *Praeclara* rejecting Anglican Orders had been based.

Rome had spoken in those distant days with knowledge of Edward VI's *Ordinal*, of which Gasquet found extracts in the Holy Office. So the question was as good as settled. Rome could hardly revise her own three-centuried practice, which she had forgotten.

Behind the scenes Edmund Bishop had settled it unobserved. It was typical of his modesty that his name was scarcely mentioned. His book (with Gasquet) on Edward VI's Prayer Book had not touched Anglican Orders. It was purely liturgical and historical.

His touch upon the documents had proved sufficient and he returned to his studies in England in May.

Gasquet was enjoying tremendous luck, for on the way home he stopped at Douai to examine Cardinal Pole's Register in the Town Archives. The result was all he could have hoped.

May 13: In the afternoon I found a copy of this Bull *Praeclara Charissimi* entered in the second volume together with the attestation of Cardinal Pole that he had received it, dated September 22, 1555.

So that was that. The very dead seemed to rise in order to testify.

The waters of Canterbury and even of Rome were beginning to be troubled by self-chosen angels like the Abbé Portal and Lord Halifax. They hoped the Pope would recognize Anglican Orders, perhaps conditionally. Like Jack o' Lanterns many phantoms began to slip about. The Gasquet group held tenaciously that Anglican and Roman Orders differed and that comparatively the Anglican were void. But many great authorities were weakening and even the Pope under Lord Halifax's filial persuasions appeared neutral. Portal was begging His Holiness to write to the Archbishops of Canterbury and York, who would have been puzzled how to reply.

There was no knowing what might happen. The English Catholics felt the ground was being cut from under their feet. Cardinal Vaughan wrote to Gasquet (August 7, 1895):

> I am writing a strong letter direct to the Holy Father confining myself to the point that mischief beyond words will be done if any decision as to Anglican Orders changing the practice of the Church for 300 years, is made without the fullest investigation and without the co-operation of the representatives of the Catholic Church in England. I ask for a full investigation and a Decision, but protest against this being attempted behind our back. A letter from the Bishops may come later if needed. . . . In my letter I remind the Holy Father of his promise to me in this matter and say we are preparing to be ready for the winter.

There were stalwarts like Mgr. Moyes who wrote:

> It will be a great point won if you can put Gasparri in the right path, and open his eyes to the vitiation of the Anglican Rite. He does not seem to be half-bad and ought to be open to conviction.

At Rome the lynx-eyed Merry del Val wrote (July 29, 1895):

> I go through moments of terrible anxiety at times when I
> see the ups and downs of impressions received and misleading
> actions of those who are quite strangers to the whole question
> and to the situation in England. We must pray hard.
>
> *August* 20: Things have taken a more favourable turn and,
> though there is some danger still, I think we are pretty sure of
> getting the question properly sifted when it does come on. My
> last interview with the Holy Father has been satisfactory: I
> think he quite reckons with you now. At all events he and I
> are most thankful you came to Rome, for this has been the
> corner of the wedge.

It was disturbing that Cardinal Rampolla, Secretary of State,
and the future Cardinal Gasparri were friendly to the Anglican
claims while Portal and Duchesne were out-and-out supporters.

The *enfant terrible* of the time was the charming and irrespons-
ible Lord Halifax, half a saint and wholly a busybody. He played
the tremendous part of a privileged Anglican will-o'-the-wisp.
He was the spoilt child of both Churches. Anglicans, including
bishops, gave way to him in perpetual anxiety of losing their
leader. The Roman Curia allowed him access and all possible
consideration in wishfulness for his conversion. His Lordship
played the intrigue of his life with the highest motives and without guile. He had managed to misquote Gasquet and Gasquet
wrote to *The Times* concerning the famous statement by Pope
Leo about leaving unedifying events out of History.

> Sir,—Lord Halifax's relation of a story, on my authority,
> at a meeting of the English Church Union once more raises
> the question of the expediency of publishing matters of private
> conversation without leave of, or any communication with,
> the person chiefly concerned. As both versions given in your
> columns are inaccurate, I venture to ask your indulgence to
> state what I told Lord Halifax. It was to the late Cardinal
> Manning and not to me personally that the Pope made use of
> the expressions incorrectly reported. The late Cardinal told me
> that his Holiness's words were to this effect: 'It has been too
> much the fashion in writing history to omit what is unpleasant.

If the historians of the last century had written the Gospels, for example, we might never have heard of the fall of St. Peter or of the treachery of Judas.' The way in which Leo XIII really emphasized his desire for honesty in historical matters, whilst more forcible, is not open to the unpleasant construction suggested by the versions given by Lord Halifax.

Lord Halifax wrote privately (July 3, 1895):

I am afraid from what someone has told me of a letter of yours in *The Times* that I have annoyed you. If I have, I am extremely sorry. The speech of the Pope which I repeated as I thought you had told me, was just what would please everyone and give the sort of impression of Leo XIII which would be good. I quoted it solely for that purpose, it certainly *never occurred* to me that there was anything in it which could do mischief or that you could possibly object to being said— indeed I think someone beside yourself had told me of the Pope's remark, implying, as I thought, that it had been said to you. However this is making a mountain out of a molehill but I wanted you to know how the thing had happened and how sorry I should be to do anything which you might dislike.

Whatever Halifax touched, exploded into misunderstandings, but everyone except Mr. Kensit loved him, not least Leo XIII.

Merry del Val always kept Gasquet in touch with the Pope's sentiments as well as with the danger of Gasparri, Rampolla and others taking loose views about Anglican Orders. He wrote to Gasquet in England (December 15, 1895):

The Holy Father is anxious to begin this week, though of course in spite of my unceasing efforts to counteract the impressions he receives from wild and foolish reports, he has only an imperfect grasp of the religious situation in England. You are quite right in saying that the mischief has been done here and is almost exclusively due to Cardinal Rampolla, who has acted without seeking and very often in spite of information and warnings received. It is all the more sad that it is difficult to speak too highly of his right intentions and high qualities. But facts are facts. Still I can assume that we have to be thankful that matters are not worse, for we have had some hairbreadth escapes in the last few months. I wonder that my hair has not turned white, for it has only been at the last minute and by speaking directly to the Holy Father that some things have been stopped.

January 5, 1896: You and Canon Moyes will probably be sent for at the end of this month or at the beginning of February. The Holy Father asked me this morning whether you had seen Gasparri's work *De La Valeur des Ordinations Anglicanes* which has just been published. He would like you and the English Commission to read it. He is evidently much impressed with it. He gave it to me yesterday and asked me today what I thought of it. . . . I pointed out some of the weak points which had struck me in Gasparri's historical acquaintance. . . . I have just read Halifax's letter to the *Guardian* on Primacy and Jurisdiction: I am going to translate it for the Holy Father. I hope he will be convinced I was right some months ago when I assured him that Cardinal Rampolla was mistaken in asserting that Halifax believed in the Primacy as we understand it.

February 6: I have touched on all the points of your *Mem* and if the Holy Father reads them, he will see that there is plenty to be said in answer to Gasparri. The Holy Father as yet is unprepared for a technical discussion, so that arguments fall rather flat. When he does go into the matter it will be different. It is important for many reasons however that he should be on his guard and be informed of the issues and that there is another side of the question. The 'validity' is to my mind quite out of the question. No decision will ever say that. But great efforts are being made to prepare the way for a *sub conditione*. . . . I pointed out to the Holy Father this morning that Gasparri's note in which he asserts that motives of expediency might induce the Holy See not to presume in the matter, seemed to show that the writer had forgotten that it was a question of reiterating a Sacrament and that if the Holy See were convinced of the validity of Anglican Orders or of a reasonable doubt in their favour, it would be a duty to declare it. This is a trying time.

On the same date Gasquet noted:

Canon Moyes had a letter from Merry del Val saying that we should hear very soon now and that *he* had been appointed

Secretary to the Commission. Nothing could be better possibly.

Bishop and I spent much time in the correction and alteration of the Latin proofs of our documents.

Gasquet reached Rome on March 20, 1896, with Mgr. Moyes and Father David Fleming as adjutants. The Pope had decided on a Commission with Merry del Val as secretary. Great were the names thereon—the future Cardinal Gasparri, the great historian Duchesne, with Cardinal Mazzella presiding.

On March 23 Gasquet and his friends were received by the Pope, who said the question had been forced upon him by Frenchmen acting for Anglicans. 'The Pontifical Secret,' he said with a laugh, 'may not be necessary for Englishmen who can hold their tongues, but others perhaps are more *légers* and would talk to journalists.' Bishop noted: 'The Pope must have been told that the *secretum* had in fact been broken.'

The Commission set to work and Gasquet adduced the precious documents from the Holy Office. Gasparri very fairly arranged that everything should be shewn to the Anglican representatives, who had arrived in Rome, the Rev. Mr. Lacey and Mr. Puller.

(April 15.) A talk with De Augustinis the Jesuit who expected the result would let down the Anglicans easily by declaring the Orders doubtful and give the *sub conditione* solution. He thought it would please everyone.

Bishop noted, 'How S.J.!' When Gasquet told him nothing could be agreed to 'that could not be made to square with the facts, Bishop added, 'How British!'

By June Mr. Lacey was lobbying Cardinals with 'a brochure *de Re Anglicana*, in my opinion a very twisted account of the Reformation history.' Suddenly like a dead voice from the remote past appeared a letter in the papers from Mr. Gladstone, who had not fussed ecclesiastically since he attacked the Infallibility in 1870. It was like the tocsin of the Tractarians.

Cardinal Rampolla had persuaded Abbé Portal that Gladstone must not address a letter to the Pope so he had given it to the papers.

It was amazing how many people were drawn in, even Irish
Archbishops like Cardinal Logue, though Orange processions
must have been more familiar to them than Apostolical processions claimed from Canterbury. Curiously, the Protestant Church
of Ireland claimed Orders from the Marian Bishop Bonner,
though this was kept as a skeleton in the cupboard. The English
clergymen left Rome after attending the Pope's Mass. They were
followed to England by Moyes and Gasquet, leaving the Commission to study the evidence.

From that moment private correspondence and intrigue played
their part, while the ecclesiastical world waited in a growing
fever of interest, stirred by an ephemeral called the *Revue Anglo-
Romaine*.

The part played by Duchesne was peculiarly Gallic and not
very scholarly, though he became the greatest historian in the
Church after the death of Acton. Edmund Bishop conceded as
much: 'I share Duchesne's general view and lament the prevalence
of the legendary school among the French clergy.' Bishop was
the one scholar of whom Duchesne stood in awe. They differed
by a century as to the date of introduction of the Roman Liturgy
into Gaul. 'Any little differences between Duchesne and myself
arise only from the fact that he committed himself to a definite
theory before having examined the documents . . . only three
MSS. are outstanding, one at each, Pavia, Prague and Mainz.'
This illustrates methods and once again, hopelessly this time,
Bishop found that Duchesne had committed himself to the
Anglican theory without knowing there were documents! When
he did reach them, it was too late. As Bishop used to remark of
other questions: they had been 'obscured by the people who
prefer war-cries to investigation.'

Gasquet's great opponent was this portentously learned Du-
chesne who 'talked against all old traditions.' His fervent ally was
Merry del Val, Secretary of the Commission. He kept a careful
diary of events in Rome between March 16, 1896, when he left
London with Moyes and Fleming and his return at the end of
June.

During four and a half months he was battling over the

question of Anglican Orders. The story has been told by himself and by many who participated in the controversy.

The English team met some French opponents who were impossible to dissuade from belief in Anglican Orders. The Italians were neutral but open to persuasion. They all held firm ground, for the Pope had insisted on an unprejudiced trial. Roman officials had much to learn about 'High Churchmen' especially about those who 'admitted the supremacy of the Pope in a completely un-Catholic sense': the first Parson in Christendom, etc. Cardinal Ledochowski at the Propaganda had to be coached on this point. Suddenly Archbishop Stonor, a Papal bulldog out of the old aristocracy, brought the dire news that 'Cardinal Parocchi quite believed in Anglican Orders.' Cardinal Mazzella the President warned them against Frenchmen 'quite ignorant of the history of the question who act and think afterwards.' Edmund Bishop's view was that 'the Anglicans had been befooled by the Frenchmen.'

The President Mazzella was Pope Leo's own creation and, when he had made him Cardinal, people all asked, Who is he? and he had replied: You will soon know. The future Cardinal Gasparri was on the Commission but knew no English: 'Yet without this knowledge such a study is absolutely impossible.'

On March 23 the Pope had received the English. 'He said he was determined to give a decision on the question and that the French had taken him in (ce Portal! he said more than once) and he said that the Secretary of State was instructed to write his displeasure of the way things Anglican were being treated of in Paris. It was really the Gallican spirit again.'

Gasparri asked that the Anglicans should attend but Mazzella pointed out this was outside their functions. Then a member of the Commission, De Augustinis, turned out to have 'no notion of the Low Church,' thinking all Anglicans held the Catholic view of Orders!

March 25: We made an examination of De Augustinis' paper—bosh!

March 27: The Pope has given leave to get into the Archives.

(It remains to be seen if we shall do so.) Merry del Val said that Lord Halifax had communicated with the Pope that if an adverse decision were given, there would be an end to Reunion for sure. In this view the Archbishops of Canterbury and York and our Bishops had agreed!

March 28: Mgr. Stonor says the Von Hügels have been very busy and in particular the Baroness.

Palm Sunday: The *petitio* of Pole found by us in the Archives now makes the *Bull* perfectly clear in its meaning.

April 1: Pressure has been put on the Pope presumably through Card. Rampolla by Von Hügel and the [Wilfrid] Ward lot to say there is another view not held by us that ought to be represented out here.

April 7: Gasparri proceeded with a lecture on the Bull and Brief of Paul IV. Putting one view, then another, then objections and answers in a way that made it evident, if the whole thing was to be conducted on those lines, we should be years at it. De Augustinis defended *quod egregie dixit Mgr. Gasparri* at a perfect shout and declared boldly that *omnes Theologi* always taught that *nullitas* was same as *illicit* and that the words used only meant that the Orders had been given by heretics.

April 8: Mgr. Gasparri came in the morning and argued for about one-and-a-half hours.

April 11: What strikes one very forcibly is that the French people have no respect at all to the decisions of the Holy See and freely reject and criticize.

April 13: A good deal of time wasted by an attack upon us led by Mgr. Gasparri. Card. Mazzella tried several times to put a stop to this which he had really invoked. . . . Duchesne was about as captious and nasty as it was possible.

April 14: Duchesne had been to examine the Holy Office Papers and had admitted that the Decree of 1704 had been founded on full knowledge and not on the Nag's Head story at all.

April 21: All about Barlow [supposed link in the consecration of Anglican Bishops]. Duchesne stuck to it that his consecration was as certain as any fact he ever came upon, 'clearer than the noonday sun.'

May 2: Gasparri held that *formaliter consideratus* the Anglican rite was quite susceptible of a Catholic interpretation and that there was nothing on this side to make Orders received invalid! Duchesne believed that the *Preface* [in the Prayer Book] made it quite clear that the authors intended to perpetuate Orders in the Catholic sense!

On the whole it was the most painful meeting we have had. It was impossible to believe that four Catholic priests could have calmly accepted full-blown Protestantism as they did today. Mazzella spoke with great emotion and evidently from Gasparri's attitude afterwards the speech created consternation.

May 7: Duchesne said that if a thing wasn't in the Old Ordinals, it was clear that it could not be essential but even if something was in all Old Pontificals it didn't follow that it was necessary. He produced with great triumph a telegram to say that the mandate for Barlow's consecration had been found. The telegram was to Lacey in Rome and came from Mr. Wood in Cambridge. He seemed quite surprised when we didn't think that mattered in the least. [Reverend E. G. Wood, Vicar of St. Clement's Church, the leading Canonist in the Church of England.]

May 8: Duchesne told someone that he was entirely satisfied with the meetings and that, did the Archbishop of Canterbury know how he had fought for him, he would give him a gold medal.

May 13: Father David and I worked away at the Papal letter and Canon Moyes to Archives. Puller and Lacey were at the Archives. They had been introduced by Duchesne, following up all my references [*i.e.* Edmund Bishop's].

May 18: A printed letter from Lacey to Cardinal Mazzella about the document said by Duchesne to be the mandate for consecration. It turns out to be merely the *significavit*, but Lacey has filled it up as he thought it ought to be. His letter is a specimen of a trap to catch those who have no particular knowledge of documents.

May 27: At Monte Cassino Puller and Lacey had given out that Puller had been sent by the Archbishop of York, who had blessed him and his mission and that Bishop of Salisbury had done the same for Lacey. Asked whether any recognition of Anglican Orders by the Pope would do them any possible good, Lacey instanced what happened at a Reunion meeting in the North of England when someone at the back of the hall called out: Does the Pope of Rome recognize you as a priest? He said he could not answer the question and the meeting were so determined that this was a vital question that practically they refused to let the proceedings go on.

May 30: Lacey at Monte Cassino had expressed his surprise at something he had overlooked, as he said, namely that one of the early Elizabethan reformers had spoken of the authorities in Mary's reign *re-greasing* those who had received Edwardine Orders which meant that the anointing only was supplied.

June 3: Today the papers containing Gladstone's Letter on Anglican Orders were to hand in Rome and caused a great deal of comment. The general verdict that as usual Mr. Gladstone had contrived to say little or nothing in a very long letter. It is an attempt to prevent any decision, should it turn out to be against the Orders.

June 11: There was a panic in St. Peter's during the procession of the Sacrament. The procession broke up and Card. Rampolla went off with the Sacrament into the Sacristy. The Church was packed. There were many hundred sailors from the English Fleet.

June 16: The *Revue Anglo-Romaine* says that Portal with two English priests (Lacey and Puller) had the pleasure of being present at the Pope's Mass. The *maestro di camera* being asked how this had been allowed said that he had no notion the two were Anglicans. Portal had come to him and he had given him leave to be present at the Mass and he had then pleaded for two other priests!

June 18: We had an audience with the Holy Father. He said that it would have to be more than a mere Decree and, though guarding himself with an 'if,' [if] the conclusion is against, then he seemed not to contemplate the possibility of any other issue.

June 21: Rampolla studiously avoided speaking about the chief matter. He said 'Oh, I do not occupy myself with that kind of thing.'

To Fr. Ethelbert Horne he wrote (May 3, 1896):

Of course I am tongue-tied as to our business. It is not unlike a tedious lawsuit. Rome is full of parsons and Lacey and Puller are here to watch events. Report says that they have been told a great deal they ought not to have heard. In fact they told

Barnes as much and implied that they had a quasi-official position on the Commission. This is an absolute lie of course, but I have reason to know that the French party promised to get a representation of the Anglicans upon it but herein they failed.

It was what Cardinal Manning called the Vatican Council, 'a running fight.' It was incredible that Rampolla and Gasparri held Anglican Orders were valid. Gallic learning was behind them. How hard the Anglo-Roman party were pressed appears in the letters of Merry del Val. If Duchesne claimed he merited a gold medal from the Archbishop of Canterbury, Merry del Val deserved the See of Westminster, of which he was one day frustrated.

Mgr. Merry del Val's letters accumulated. To Moyes (June 30, 1896):

> *Private*. After bidding you goodbye I found the *Anglo-Romaine* with the first of a series of articles by Lacey on the Unity of the Church. The impudence of Portal daring to publish . . . I lost no time in putting the whole before the Holy Father, for I felt sure he would be alive to its importance and that this was my opportunity. He was very much annoyed, indeed quite roused and gave immediate orders to Cardinal Rampolla to admonish Portal and stop the articles. . . . I also spoke of the way in which Puller and Lacey had managed to attend the Holy Father's Mass and then announced it in the papers. The Holy Father was really distressed. He ended by saying '*scrivete tutto a Moyes affinche stia attento*' . . . The *Rome* this week alludes again to Duchesne becoming a Cardinal and I heard yesterday that Poincaré said openly in Paris that he wished it '*pour introduire une nouvelle sève dans ce sacré Collège*' [new sap in this damned College!] and he could reckon on Duchesne. A flattering certificate! . . . I have just received Gasquet's telegram telling me that the summary of the Encyclical appears in all the London papers. *Stefani* telegraphs that it has aroused violent feeling. [The *Satis Cognitum* on the Papacy.]

Merry del Val wrote (June 27, 1896):

> Every effort is being made to save Portal and his mischievous work and unfortunately he has still the favour of

Cardinal Rampolla. If anything transpires of what the Pope is doing or preparing in the matter of decision on Anglican Orders, we shall have a deal of trouble. They will move Heaven and Earth to stop an adverse decision.

On July 16 the Cardinals made a unanimous report to the Pope who reserved his Apostolic decision.

July 10, 1896: Our Lady of Mount Carmel is sure to help us. The Holy Father is deeply interested in it and I am preparing some notes for him. The Cardinal will tell you of an attempt and danger of a delay in the publication of the decision. I am trying my utmost in every way to prevent so great an evil. Every month that passes confirms people in the idea that the Holy See has acted lightly in the past, since even now the Pope hesitates or seems to hesitate. Moreover many will not believe the Pope is in earnest in his Encyclical if the second bomb does not soon burst.

While Portal and Lord Halifax were explaining away the Encyclical, and Gladstone was trying to soothe the Pope into nullifying action, Gasquet's team-work never ceased. Letters and memoranda were written day and night. Out of masses in Gasquet's script (apart from his Diary) we select:

Mr. Barnes[1] told me last week at Downside that he had seen some of his Anglican friends in London. Asking them what would happen were the Pope to take Lord Halifax's advice and Mr. Gladstone's letter seriously and in the event of not being able to satisfy Anglican claims as to Orders to keep silent; they replied that of course all would declare that the Pope was quite convinced of the rectitude of their claim to Orders, but refrained from saying so for fear of stultifying the previous actions and declarations of the Church for three centuries.

In Rome Merry del Val kept watch (August 3, 1896):

Halifax is using every means in his power, fair or foul, to protect the *Romaine* and defend Portal here, and alas! there is one here, as you know, who is only too ready to listen to him and believe in him.

[1] Arthur Stapylton Barnes, later Monsignor.

Cardinal Vaughan wrote (August 6):

I have just received your note and have sent a long letter to M. del Val to read to the Pope. . . . Meanwhile the new phase of the Protestant heresy is spread and establishes itself. The Encyclical is passed over, and the poisons concentrate upon Church services and devotions that imply sacred Orders and the people are more and more accepting the situation. Surely if ever the Pope is to pronounce judgment on Anglican Orders, now is the time. Reunion is not even on the most distant horizon. The one effect of this new heresy is to get their Orders quietly tolerated until the people take them as valid as those of Rome. I had intended to speak on the Education Question: but I hear that if I give a lead on this question, the Archbishop of Canterbury will go the other way, so some of his friends tell me. Under these circumstances I propose to take the Encyclical and to answer the objections raised against it categorically. I think Harnack may be made to render valuable services. Will you give me what help you can? You will have points I daresay that have not occurred to me. One point may be made that whatever they say, who reject the Encyclical, they have no claim to continuity with the Church of Canterbury during its first ten centuries of existence. I am rather the more willing to take up the theme, as I hear the Holy Father is anxious that the Encyclical should be defended.

Merry del Val wrote (August 10):

If one had not to deal with such absurdly sophistical opponents there would not be much trouble. I have pleaded that the document or at all events a portion of it should be submitted to you. In a matter so serious every precaution should be taken and you will be able to give a valuable judgment. I have not said anything to you as yet of the famous *Feria V*, a great day for us. I am waiting to do so until I see you. The secrecy of the Holy Office has not been laid upon me. . . . The reserve maintained by the Cardinals of the Holy Office is a blessing: but in this case there is something providential in the general way in which the whole thing has passed unnoticed.

August 22: I have got so knocked up that the Holy Father

has settled that I should leave at once for England. . . . The
Holy Father yesterday evening when making these arrange-
ments said '*salutate mi Gasquet e Moyes e Fra David se lo vedete.*'
I shall be so glad to see you again.

August 29: Do not hesitate to say quite freely what you
think might be taken off, added or corrected in the document.
I hope Canon Moyes will not be angry at his old friend Barlow
being left out in the cold.

Barlow was the Bishop under Henry VIII whose consecration had been the matter of much antiquarian dispute. Mgr.
Barnes used to point out that, if he could not be proved the
Father of the Anglican Hierarchy, he was at least their Father-in-
law, so many of his daughters (no less than five) had married
Bishops! Was he a real old Catholic Bishop? Was his consecration of Archbishop Parker, Queen Elizabeth's Primate, as valid
as his daughter's marriage to Parker's son? There was the rub.
But now, as Carlyle would have pointed out, his phantom was
allowed to drop into the abyss.

Gasquet was at Rouen on the yacht of his friend and convert,
Mr. Cave, when the draft of the Document reached England
from Rome. He telegraphed his whereabouts to the Vatican and,
'Later I had another wire from Merry del Val to say that I was
to send remarks in Latin or French to Vatican.' His instructions
were then to destroy the copies. He accomplished his work and
on September 10 at a happy and exciting dinner in Ormond
Street, Merry del Val, Father David and Canon Moyes arrived
together. Merry gave an account of the famous meeting of the
Holy Office on July 6, when the Pope himself had presided while
Rampolla remained absent.

The Pope was very pleased by the clear way in which the
universal condemnation was expressed. Curiously, though
there was such a large meeting, no idea of its purpose appears
to have leaked out. Merry says that Cardinal Parocchi had
evidentially last year committed himself with Halifax and
Halifax had written him a long and angry letter. Cardinal
Rampolla had also received two long and angry letters from
Lord Halifax about Portal. It is quite certain that the unfortunate

Abbé has at last been shut up. He is very angry at Portal being sent 'to other spheres of usefulness.'

Cardinal Signa apparently tried to do much harm by going to the Pope and representing what would take place in England, were the Orders condemned—how it would stop Reunion!

The Pope had grown impatient and as Duchesne said 'at the age of 86 he does not like to be referred to over distant futures.'

On September 11 they met to finish translating the condemnatory Bull *Apostolicae Curae*, as it was called.

At Downside on Monday, September 14, where I was for Father Jerome's funeral, I gave the Cardinal a copy of the Bull to read. He hadn't seen it before.

Merry del Val tried to amend (September 13, 1896):

If there is time perhaps you can touch it up. I note in the first sentence a certain rhythm which seems to suggest the swing of some of Gilbert and Sullivan's ditties, principally I fancy by reason of the proximity of share and care:

> No small *share*
> Of that Apostolic *care*

my idea would be to take the sentence somewhat differently, etc.

On Friday, September 18, Gasquet received perhaps the most satisfying telegram of his life—'*Bull Ordinationes Ritu Anglicano actas irritas prorsus fuisse et esse omninoque nullas.*'

The British Post Office were receiving some Latin practice in those days, but the real shock came, according to Grant Duff's *Diaries*, when nervous investors rushed to inquire if as the result of the Pope's ruling British postal orders were null and void! Reassured on this point, the British Public did not care twopence whether their parsons were valid or not, provided they were good fellows.

September 19. Memorandum: The week past has been one of great anxiety as to the publication of the *Bull*. Letters to Merry

6

del Val from Rome were delayed and it was not till Thursday night that I got a telegram from him to say all right. The Cardinal telegraphed to del Val to come up and we spent the afternoon in going through and correcting the document as printed in English and later here.

Merry del Val never ceased (September 28, 1896):

I have been very hard at work writing all I could tell the Holy Father of the first impressions produced by the Bull in the public press. . . . I hope the Cardinal may even strengthen a passage in his speech tonight showing how the Anglicans waited on the Pope and had not sufficient words some time ago to praise his judgment, fairness and competency. The Bishop of Salisbury's preface to *De Hierarchia*, the sayings and doings of the Archbishop of York, our friends Puller and Lacey, and Halifax's article in the *XIXth Century* are there to show up the falsehoods of the *Church Times*. . . .

It is your turn for reports now. You are to be a Cardinal, poor you!

October 7: . . . Of course, as you say, one cannot technically assert that 'the Anglican Church,' which like *la France* in the mouth of a Frenchman may mean himself, the nation or nothing at all, has appealed to the Pope on Anglican Orders. But it is barefaced to say that Anglicans have not appealed to him and Anglicans, who professed to speak the mind of the *sanior pars* of the Establishment.

October 15: . . . You will have seen Lacey's wretched and unfair reply in the *Guardian*. . . . It is of course injurious to the Pope to say that he has been influenced in this way by anyone. If your reasons appealed to him and to the Cardinals more than those given by Puller and Lacey, well, it is the fault of the reasons. There is some irony in the fact of Benson being buried in 'continuity' the first since Cardinal Pole in Canterbury Cathedral. And then how strange his dying just *now* in that *way* and at that *place*.

These were dramatic days, for Archbishop Benson, while a guest of Mr. Gladstone, died suddenly in Hawarden Church. His son, the future Monsignor Benson, then an Anglican, was summoned and Communicated the Grand Old Man. When he seceded later, the *Church Times* remarked that the Archbishop would turn in his grave. Others thought otherwise and perhaps Cardinal Pole from the other end of the Cathedral was able to comfort him.

Gasquet wrote in November:

> It is suggested in Rome that the probable explanation of Cardinal Rampolla's approval to Abbé Portal arose from the fact that the General of the Lazarists called on Cardinal Rampolla. . . . Cardinal Rampolla said that the Holy Father wished the Abbé Portal by no means to give up his work for the reunion of the Churches. This probably got out and was interpreted into another approval.

On Friday, November 13, came a telegram from Canon Moyes to say that the Cardinal had had a Brief from the Pope dealing with the *Revue Anglo-Romaine*. Father David's letter gives the feeling in Rome at this time:

> *November 4*: Our Commission has cleared the atmosphere of Rome for many years to come. All have made kind inquiries about yourself and Moyes. . . . It is quite secure. There is no hope for the other side. In fact the whole Ecclesiastical public opinion is on our side. The Frenchers are utterly routed . . . yourself and Canon Moyes ought to come out for 'hats.' I just see that Creighton is Bishop of London. Canon Moyes will have something to do in watching him *de près*!

And so the mighty discussion ended with the Pope's decision. It was Gasquet's finest ecclesiastical hour. Thanks to Edmund Bishop and to Moyes and Merry del Val he accomplished an issue of more than academical interest to all Clergy serving the Holy See in the British Empire or English-speaking world.

What had it proved?

English parsons had not been ordained 'sacrificing priests' by the Ordinal of King Edward VI. Their Mass was invalid according to the Roman Rite.

Cranmer had done his work only too well. The intent of Oblation and Sacrifice had been removed from the new Communion Service. A memorial service of prayer and praise, beautiful in tone, had taken the place of the old Mass. Protestants were not displeased though High Churchmen were incensed and the Archbishops of Canterbury and York enjoyed the unusual distinction of replying to the Patriarch of the West.

The controversy with lapse of time resembled a storm in a rectory teacup. A Papal Commission and Decision seemed hardly needed to confirm an ancient practice of reordaining Anglican parsons who wished to become priests under the Latin Rite.

The Pope left the old condition of things as Cranmer and Pole between them had left them three centuries before. The last thing he did was to insult the Church of England, to which he yearned with uninstructed love. It cannot be said that he denied Anglican Orders as such. He only laid down that they were different from Roman Orders. Purely as Anglican Orders they were not null and void. They were perfectly valid *qua* Anglican, but they were not Roman and they did not confer the power to Transubstantiate. Nobody, not even their own Bishops, could prevent Anglicans saying Mass, but the consecrated elements of bread and wine, though worthy of reverence, could not touch the tremendous sense laid down by Roman theology. This was a relief to all good Anglicans who were loyal to their Common Prayer and common sense. Everybody now knew where they stood. The disappointment was due to wishful believing on the Anglican side and wishful hoping on the Roman—now scattered like chaff.

On the appearance of Lacey's book in later years Gasquet wrote to Father David (November 27, 1910):

Moyes is the gentleman who comes in for it. *We* hardly appear. It is full of ill-natured stories supposed to be told by Duchesne of what went on in the Commission but which are mostly quite false or falsely put. Duchesne appears to have been posing to Lacey as *the* great *Deus ex machina* of the Commission, telling him how he had made this point and the other, how he had sat upon Moyes and insulted him. I shall have to add some notes to deny what Lacey says Duchesne told him. Moyes is worked up and I believe has written to Merry del Val to have a release from the *Secretum*.

One assertion made by Lacey is that a vast amount of time was spent by the Commission over Barlow! Just fancy, actually we spent less than *three* hours and that was all Duchesne's fault. I am bound to put some denials into *notes*.

Bishop noted in Gasquet's *Diary* 'the fond belief held in Anglican circles that good Leo XIII would have recognized Anglican Orders but for some Blackamoor, who by and by succeeded in persuading him *from* his good intent and *to* his naughty Bull.'

One of the stories which gave Anglicans hope at the time was that whenever Gasquet tried to bring up a point unfavourable to them—the Pope turned aside with a prodigious sniff of snuff! This use of the Papal snuff-box seems to fascinate Protestant writers, who always repeat the fable that Pius IX blew away Newman's chance of a Bishop with a good sneeze!

The events during the Commission seared Gasquet's memory. He now realized how little Italians understood English matters. Eight years later he delivered in an American Seminary a vivid lecture, which to his surprise was published in the *New York Sun* soon after he left the country (December 4, 1904).

The Pope then commissioned me to begin an investigation of all the evidence in the case and report to him when the work was completed. I accepted the commission, but requested that I should be allowed access to all the documents bearing on the subject that were preserved in the Archives of the Holy Office. The Pope readily consented and signed an order giving me full liberty to study all the bulls, letters, pamphlets, &c., on this question of the validity of Anglican Orders then in the Holy Office.

I presented myself and the order from Leo, the next day, to the director of the Holy Office, Mgr. Ségur.[1] He received me very cordially and told me to come back the next week.

I returned the next week, but only to receive the same answer. This went on for seven weeks. My patience became exhausted and I concluded that I was not going to be allowed to see the documents I had asked the Pope for.

---

[1] This should be Mgr. Salua.

I wrote a letter to Merry del Val in which I said that despite my signed permission from the Holy Father I was unable to get into the Holy Office to examine the papers I wanted to see. Merry del Val read this letter to Leo. The following day I got a message that the Pope wanted to see me at once.

I went to his apartment, and when I entered his presence he came towards me and taking me by my cowl shook it nervously, saying at the same time in an angered tone:

'Abbot, why do you get angry at the Holy Father? Don't you know that no one should ever become angry with the Pope?'

Here was my chance, and thinking I might just as well be reprimanded for a severe offence as a trifle I said:

'I have been ordered to do this work by you and I cannot carry it out without certain documents in the Holy Office; and, notwithstanding your approbation, I am unable to get all these essential materials.'

The Pope laughed outright, and walking from his seat to the extreme corner of the room he drew aside a tapestry, revealing a large box containing the documents. Still holding the tapestry with his left hand he directed my attention to the box with his right, saying at the same time:

'You shall have this room to yourself, and can work undisturbed, taking your own time in doing the work I have commissioned you to do. When you have finished, bring the key of this room to the Cardinal Secretary of State.'

The very next morning I began work. I was surprised to find upon the top of the box of documents the signed order from the Pope to Mgr. Ségur[1] on which was written diagonally across the reasons why I should not have access to these documents! One can see that my constant going to the Holy Office brought the matter directly to the Pope, who in his final order to have the documents brought directly to him, again marked his 'O.K.,' as you would say in America, on my privilege to examine them.

My first step in the investigation brought me to the Secretariat of Bulls. I supposed that the question of the validity of the Orders must have come up shortly after the break with Rome, and so I began to examine the pontifical Bulls of Paul IV.

[1] Salua.

I found fifty-two volumes of Bulls. After reading carefully five volumes, I became curious to know what was in the last one, just as one might look at the last chapter of a novel. Then, too, I thought that by working from both ends of the fifty-two volumes I might chance on the particular one I desired more quickly.

I took up the fifty-second volume and when half way through it I found the Bull of Paul IV treating of Anglican Orders. In this document two classes of Ministers are very clearly distinguished. In the first class are those who were ordained according to the old Catholic Ordinal, then lapsed into heresy, and again returned to communion with Rome. The Orders of such Ministers were not renewed.

In the second class are those who received Orders in heresy. When such Ministers applied for admission into the priesthood of Rome, their Orders were conferred from the beginning.

Now a document of such importance naturally suggested that there must be other papers bearing on the same subject. I went to the Secretariat of Briefs. There I found a pontifical Brief of Paul IV, explaining still further the principles laid down in the Bull. From here I went to the general Archives of the Vatican and there discovered three sets of documents of the same period.

In the first set was a series of questions proposed to the Holy See for settlement; in the second set these same questions were put in the regular form for use with the Congregations, and in the third set these same questions were found with their answers, and in every case a distinction was made.

Armed with these five documents I came to Leo. He was delighted and kept them all, while I waited further orders from him.

A few days later the Reverend Father Brandi, the Jesuit editor of the *Civilta Cattolica*, had an audience with the Pope, who was still joyful over his discovery. He showed them to the learned Jesuit in his moment of happiness, and Father Brandi, with his newspaper instinct, obtained them long enough to publish them in his next issue.

The news was at once cabled to London and the editor of one of the leading London Dailies, commenting upon the important discovery, said that while the Bull of Pius IV was undoubtedly an important discovery, still it never had been promulgated, for, if it had, it would have been found, not in the secret Archives of the Vatican, but in some of the Archives of London or elsewhere.

I was very much impressed with this strong objection from the London Press, and I determined, if possible, to find some corroborating evidence. On my way home to England I stopped off at Douai, where my Order has a monastery and college. There after three days of work I came upon the exact copy of the Bull of Paul IV. Added to this document was a statement by Cardinal Pole, the Pope's legate in England, that he had promulgated this Bull to all the Bishops of England.

When I got this I returned to Rome and presented this evidence to Leo. He then appointed the famous Commission on Anglican Orders, consisting of all the Cardinals of the Holy Office, fourteen in number, under the presidency of the Pope himself.

Canon Moyes, Father David Fleming, the English Franciscan, Abbé Duchesne and myself were also in this Commission. Merry del Val was appointed Secretary. This was the first time in one hundred years that all the Cardinals of the Holy Office assembled in solemn council under the presidency of the Pope himself to settle any question. Every one was vowed to secrecy even more solemn than the confessional.

For this Commission Duchesne had written a long disquisition on the consecration of Parker by Barlow in England, and for the sake of argument I conceded the validity of the consecration. I then went on to prove that the decision of the Holy See from the very beginning was that those ordained in heresy were not ordained at all, and when they applied for admission to the priesthood of Rome the Orders must be conferred from the beginning.

I also proved that the heretics in their adaptations of the old Catholic Missal in 1549, 1552 and 1662 respectively, had excluded every word that conveyed the idea of sacrifice. Priesthood means sacrifice, and without it there can be no priestly office. As they had excluded in their official manuals every allusion to sacrifice, how could they have the intention of conferring priestly Orders? How, therefore, could Orders conferred in heresy be considered valid by Rome?

The decision of the Cardinals was unanimous against the validity of Anglican Orders.[1]

The other part of this, the most famous interview that Gasquet ever gave, will be found in the chapter on 'American Visits.'

Concerning the drafts sent round preliminary to the letter *Ad Anglos* (April 1895), Edmund Bishop noted later:

> I wonder whether it will be said that these drafts were the basis of the Pope's letter *Ad Anglos*. *I* of course know that they were not and (with F. A. G. now of all alive, *alone*) I know how this letter *Ad Anglos* was drafted and composed (the original drafts, the successive drafts now among F. A. G.'s papers at Downside can bear unimpeachable witness in this matter).

Presumably, as the Pope felt quite at sea in Anglican and English matters he gave the drafting to those who knew not only better but best: and the two friends combined to write *Ad Anglos*.

The Times managed to publish *Ad Anglos* before it was issued to the Cardinals! 'By some mistake,' wrote Gasquet, and Bishop chimed: 'This was a blunder between Cardinal Vaughan and *The Times.*'

At the back of Leo's sanguine mind was the belief that the Church of England could be approached like an Armenian or Coptic Schism. He might just as well have angled for the M.C.C. or the Carlton Club. The Italian admires but never understands the English.

---

[1] *New York Sun*, December 4, 1904. This *Sun* article contains a very inaccurate order of much that was factual but no doubt represented Gasquet's memory of his clash with the Holy Office and his intimate talk with Pope Leo. The Bull *Apostolicae Curae* was issued Sept. 1896, the letter *Ad Anglos*, April 1895.

VI

THE SUCCESSION TO WESTMINSTER IN 1903 AND GASQUET'S MEMORANDUM

Remember that there is Providence to reckon with.

ABBOT GASQUET

Yet they, believe me, who await
No gifts from Chance, have conquered Fate.
Thou waitest for the spark from Heaven.

MATTHEW ARNOLD

THE vacancy in the See of Westminster proved a momentous and agonizing chapter in Gasquet's life. Cardinal Vaughan died and the Chapter selected a *terna*: the grand old system whereby the Canons picked one worthy, one worthier and one most worthy. The Pope chose one of the three or as in Manning's case selected an outsider. The good Canons were in a mood for an experiment. They chose a Cockney Spaniard and two English Benedictines! As a result they fell between three faldstools. Gasquet came within an ace of the Archbishopric, which by devious but no doubt providential ways came to Francis Bourne.

While Cardinal Vaughan was dying, Gasquet wrote to Father Fleming (June 2, 1903):

The Cardinal still lingers on, meanwhile the chaos is naturally getting no better and people are asking themselves what next? Of course it is a very critical time and one cannot help feeling that we might get a worse man than Cardinal Vaughan in his place. Bourne's name I am told is freely mentioned, but this would be very unpopular in the diocese and his notion of Education is too *foreign* to please most people. However, the great thing to remember is that there is Providence to reckon with.

Providence indeed was about to reckon with a handful of candidates including Gasquet himself!

The death of the Cardinal led to this exciting episode in Gasquet's life, his approach to the throne of Westminster. His whole attitude was covered by his exemplary words: 'There is Providence to reckon with,' which was his happy-go-lucky reaction to most crises in life. After Gasquet saw Cardinal Vaughan for the last time he wrote to Edmund Bishop (June 15, 1903): '. . . weaker every day; but how long he may last it is impossible to say. He wished me goodbye when I left, as he didn't expect to see me again on my return from the North.'

Neither dreamed that one would come within a tonsure's breadth of succeeding the other. The Cardinal died on June 19.

From Stonyhurst Gasquet wrote (July 10, 1903):

As to rumours; of course they are only to be treated as such and personally from my heart I hope they will not come true. It is too dreadful to contemplate and were it not for the fact that such an appointment would be the deathblow of the anti-regular idea I should certainly ask to be excused. Of course I know nothing; but the report is that I was the choice of the Canons. If so, it is wonderful. I certainly was before the Bishops at their subsequent meeting as one of the Bishops told me so. Bishop Burton also implied to me that they had sent up my name tho' he would not of course say as much. He told Mgr. Gadd, however, that he took it as certain I should be appointed.

And from Ushaw (July 15):

The old Bishop [Wilkinson] on telling them I was coming said: You had better behave yourselves as he is going to be our new Archbishop and there is no doubt he thinks so. I cannot believe that the danger is serious tho' at times the thought comes back as a nightmare.

The results of Vaughan's rule were not pleasing to those who had wished him to follow in the steps of Manning and a clear change was indicated. He had supported licensed vintners and opposed Irish Home Rule. The Canons of Westminster chose a *terna* of three candidates: Archbishop Merry del Val (a Spaniard

of Irish descent who had been born in London) and two Benedictines, Bishop Hedley and Abbot Gasquet. Before their names
reached the English Bishops for approval, the Duke of Norfolk
had applied his *veto* to Merry del Val on the ground that he was
a foreigner, though believed to be the dead Cardinal's choice.
The Bishops approved the *terna*, but added the name of Bishop
Bourne by one vote so as not to bind the Holy See to a choice
from one Religious Order. At this juncture Cardinal Moran
arrived from his See of Sydney in Australia and, as a member of
the Propaganda Committee selecting Bishops, declared against
putting a Benedictine into such a Primacy. He had himself
succeeded a Benedictine and a Vaughan to boot and, as Cardinal
Vaughan's life describes, there had been a lively squabble chiefly
over the return of Archbishop Vaughan's body to the home-
land. Cardinal Moran had been left with a smouldering feeling
against live Benedictine Archbishops. Perhaps he remembered
when he had been cut out of the Archbishopric of Dublin by
the direct action of an Archbishop of Westminster—Cardinal
Manning—in favour of Archbishop Walsh. Rome had solaced
his Irish pride with a Red Hat. He now solaced himself by a half-
hour speech which knocked Gasquet out.

Amid the newspaper excitement over the Westminster Succession, the *Daily Chronicle* played a sinister part. Their correspondent, an ex-student of the Beda and a Modernist sufficiently
to be considered 'a dangerous man,' opened ironically enough by
announcing that 'Cardinal Moran's sympathies are in favour of
Abbot Gasquet, being something of a historian himself.' This was
an unlucky shot for the following day, being Monday (August
24, 1903), Bourne was chosen. Cardinal Moran had arrived
on the Saturday night. Eleven Cardinals under Gotti had elimin-
ated Merry del Val for reasons understood, Hedley for his old
age and Gasquet as lower in rank to Hedley, but there were
reasons given in mischievous newspapers and the discussion would
never have become historical if the *Daily Chronicle* had not published a startling speech of Cardinal Gotti regretting that 'two
candidates on the *terna* had not shewn themselves free from
tendencies of the Liberal Catholic party.' *Modernist* had not been

coined as a word, so Propaganda seemed to add insult to injury in rejecting the two English Benedictines. It was of course an attempt by a Liberal Catholic to add two unwilling martyrs to his cause. Gasquet immediately wrote to Gotti, who furnished a total denial (September 7, 1903):

> All is a sheer invention without any foundation. No such expression of opinion, not even such an idea was uttered by me, not a single phrase or statement there reported was used by me. The whole may be denied in the most explicit and absolute manner.

When Bourne had been elected Gasquet wrote to Bishop (September 7, 1903):

> We have passed thro' a queer time; but I am thankful to say that I have apparently felt it less than other people. All the time 'the superior point of my soul'—as spiritual writers of the school of St. Francis of Sales have it—was quite free from excitement and I am as right as a trivet. It certainly was a narrow escape from the burden as finally the voting at Propaganda was
>
> Hedley 2; Gasquet 4; Bourne 5.
>
> I hear on the best authority from Rome that Bourne would have been nowhere but for two things: 1. The Newspapers. 2. Cardinal Moran.
>
> The Newspapers frightened people with the idea that I was the candidate of the 'queer party' and Cardinal Moran's arrival brought a strongly determined man to prevent a Regular. Moran is an aged Cuckoo, who having got possession of a Benedictine nest has always tried to ignore the work of his Benedictine predecessors. . . . I am very sorry for Bourne. He wrote me a letter that was all and more than could be expected from anyone and I believe that tho' he will never be brilliant, he certainly won't be narrow-minded. . . . *He* knows that his name was only sent up to Rome by a bare majority and it was the *bottom* of the bench against the top, some of whom spoke against it as they told me themselves.

Gasquet fortunately left his own version amongst the papers which he no doubt intended to appear in any memoir. The

Chronicle had hit him hard, for he was sensitive to Liberalism used as a taunt or taint when applied to his Catholicism. It has since been realized how little articles in the secular Press count in Ecclesiastical affairs. In fact 'Special Correspondents' as a race have received their motto from the Vulgate—*Dixi in excessu meo!* and can be discounted under those words. The 'Frenchers,' whom Gasquet had routed over Anglican Orders, had successfully endorsed the candidature of Bourne.

In the end the exacter truth is discovered by the historians. Gasquet's *apologia* for himself survives in the Downside Archives.

MEMORANDUM OF ABBOT GASQUET ON THE ELECTION OF THE ARCHBISHOP OF WESTMINSTER, 1903

I have been urged to set down what I know about the facts relating to the election while they are fresh in my mind.

On the death of Cardinal Vaughan most of the papers mentioned mine as one of several names as likely to succeed. I paid no attention at the time, treating it as mere newspaper gossip and thinking it most improbable that as a *Regular* I should be in the least likely to be selected by the Canons. I had heard from Rome that it was almost certain that this time the voice of the Chapter would be respected.

About the time of the meeting of the Westminster Chapter to elect their *terna* it was rumoured that Dr. Bourne, the Bishop of Southwark, had acted in one or two ways as if he were almost certain to be the successor to the late Cardinal. At this time I was away from London giving some Retreats at convents, and so heard little or nothing of what had happened until the meeting of the Catholic Truth Society in Liverpool in the second week of July. Here I was given to understand by several of the Bishops that my name was certainly on the *terna* and that the other two were Dr. Hedley and Mgr. Merry del Val. I was also told that the Duke of Norfolk had written to the meeting of Bishops to object to Merry del Val as a foreigner and also saying that he was writing to Merry del Val himself in the same way.

The Bishops approved of the *terna* sent in by the Chapter of Westminster; but somewhat endorsed the objection of the Duke of Norfolk against Merry del Val. On the proposition

of one of the Bishops—understood to be the Bishop of Portsmouth—it was carried by a majority of *one* that to afford Rome
a greater selection the name of Bishop Bourne should be added
to the *terna*. Three Bishops, it was said, did not vote either
way.

What happened afterwards in Rome is common property.
There was I am told much canvassing on the part of the French
for Bishop Bourne—'absolutely indecent' was the expression
used in a letter sent to *The Tablet* as to this French action. The
Abbé P—— told me that the French regarded its result as a
triumph for the Seminary system and worked for that end. I
had already heard that the French were working a great deal.

What really happened at the Consistorial Congregation
will probably never be known. There seems little doubt however that it was Cardinal Moran's arrival that decided the
election. He spoke against a Regular being placed in such a
position as Archbishop and according to a subsequent report
at the same time said that *I* was certainly worthy of being in
any Ecclesiastical dignity.

As regards myself, I can honestly say that the result was a
great relief, as I had been expecting the burden, after what I
had heard. What, however, is serious is the position I found
myself in after all the whole matter had been discussed by the
Press. And especially in consequence of what Cardinal Gotti
said or was reported to have said by the *Chronicle*. What people
say is this. Here are the Canons of Westminster—seventeen
men who may be supposed to know their business—go out of
their way to elect a Regular. Their choice is ratified by the
Bishops and then their view is set aside and one they did not
want is put over them and the Church in England by the vote
of a single Italian Cardinal, who could not *know*, at the instance
of an 80 year old Cardinal from the Antipodes!

F. A. GASQUET.

Private letters allow hints and peeps behind the scenes. It
appeared that though Gotti took a rigid view of the Secret
observable on such occasions, a good deal escaped. Cardinal
Martinelli had spoken at length in favour of Bourne while
Cardinal Satolli had supported Gasquet. The Duke of Norfolk,
not content with making the candidature of Merry del Val

impossible, appealed directly in support of another which the Cardinals tended to resent.[1]

Father Fleming wrote in wild disappointment (August 28, 1903):

> Cardinal Moran upset everything. Some stupid fellow asked him to assist you there. He went *and did the contrary*! Hedley's being on deprived *you* of two or three votes.

From his own Gasquet received loving sympathy. Abbot Cuthbert Butler wrote (August 28):

> I must send you a few lines of condolence at being hung up in so uncomfortable a way. The *Chronicle* report . . . is too preposterous to be untrue. If you and Bishop Hedley are Liberal Catholics, who is not? English Catholics will no longer regard the term as one of reproach. Hitherto there has been no real Liberal Catholic *movement* in England. Cardinal Gotti has created one. Whatever happens, it will always remain the pride of your life that you are the elect of the Canons and Clergy of Westminster.

Father Fleming sent (October 22):

> *reliable authority* that Cardinal Gotti never said anything about your Liberalism. Gotti was certainly in favour of Bourne and Moran backed him up. Besides Moran simply objected to you as *Archbishop of Westminster* but he added that he would not be against you being made *Cardinal*. This I have from one of the Cardinals, a great friend of ours, who assisted at the *Congresso*. You may take this as *final*. Of course, it is well known that some of the silly lot who *call themselves* Liberals claimed *you*, as they try to claim others. . . . As far as I can gather, the only point in Norfolk's letter was the exclusion of Merry del Val. Did he write, when Cardinal Vaughan died (as I take to be morally certain), about Bourne, is more than I can find out. Merry del Val's appointment—a touch-and-go sort of thing, took everybody by surprise. Oreglia got him through. Many Cardinals are most dissatisfied. This is not looked upon as a good sign in regard to progressiveness. . . .

[1] Gasquet MSS.: Downside Archives.

I hope we may be able to do something under the new Pope. You may rest assured that you have not the reputation of being a 'Liberal' in the bad sense of the word in official circles here.

November 6, 1903: I think the rumour about the Duke is not without *some* foundation. He wrote to Stonor informing him how pleased he was at the appointment of Bourne. Merry del Val got there at last! Cardinal Oreglia bore down all opposition and carried his man through in the face of tremendous opposition [as Secretary of State to the new Pope Pius X].

Oreglia had refused to allow his own name to be proposed as Pope.

The *Chronicle* also announced that the Abbot Primate Hemptinne had opposed Gasquet's nomination. This the Primate decisively repudiated, writing (September 5, 1903):

I cannot understand how people could be either so light-hearted or so mischievous as to publish such statements so utterly false and so much calculated to pain and create mischief.

October 20: I was pleased to know that you did not believe the unqualifying news which came from Rome in connection with both your election and my interference with it. It is really painful to witness such proceedings and your note did much towards comforting me.

Later Gasquet was mentioned for the empty See of Southwark and his champion Father Fleming wrote (February 16, 1904):

I have not much hope though I sent in your name. Merry del Val *could* help but he does not seem inclined. I am afraid the choice will lie between Fenton and Amigo. The English Bishops gave us no help. The anti-Regular bias of Propaganda has always to be reckoned with. The Holy Father is very nice and very intelligent but he is new to everything. . . . I see that Archbishop Bourne has given up any alliance with either party in British politics. Well, that is a *sane idea* at last! I look upon the attempt to engraft the Sulpician system on the Catholic Church in England as a calamity. The experience of France is not very encouraging.

Gasquet received consoling correspondence. Dr. Casartelli wrote as Bishop-elect of Salford (September 1, 1903):

> If the wish did not sound rather an impiety, I could almost desire that Cardinal Gotti might have held me 'suspect' of Liberalism and other dreadful things, and so have spared me this most unwelcome burthen. Is it not too bad to take off a student—and we have so few of them—and turn him into a very incompetent, perhaps unsuccessful bishop? However, the *fiat* has gone forth, and we must humbly submit and obey. It is a consolation that I have your sympathy and prayers. Please continue to remember me and my future.
>
> I had fully expected that I should have had to write and congratulate you, or rather the English Church, on your nomination to the Metropolitan See. I felt that you were the one man in England to take up the grand tradition and add lustre to it. *Dis aliter visum.* I cannot honestly deny my disappointment, and I venture to think it is pretty general.

Sir Francis Burnand, Editor of *Punch*, wrote (September 14):

> *A Mon cher élève*
> *qui était le petit François chez*
> *les Oblates ou les omelettes.*

> I see you were very nearly being made Archbishop of Westminster (which would have taken you from your studies and literary work and *ours* would have been the loss) and subsequently you would have been (as in time you will be) an *Eminence.* Now permit me—are you not the very Frank Gasquet (was it not 'Frank'? youngest brother of Dr. Gasquet) who was in the choir of St. Mary's of the Angels when I was there as a sort of ecclesiastical student giving lessons to Cyril Forster from Xmas '57 to Easter or Whitsuntide '58 when I quitted the Hospitable House? I am uncertain as to exact dates. But am I not about right? When they make my pupil Archbishop and Cardinal, I trust he will not forget his ancient *magister* and confer on him some such distinction as Protonotary Apostolic or any appointment semi-ecclesiastical that may bring me some loaves for everyday and fishes for Friday.

The new Archbishop, Dr. Bourne, wrote in answer to Gasquet's congratulations, a letter most creditable to both (August 30, 1903):

> I am deeply touched by your letter, and I am most grateful for the promise of the help that, in certain respects, you alone can give me. I have always greatly valued the friendship that you have been good enough to show me, and I believe that on most points of importance we think alike. Nothing has pained me more during this last terrible week than that irresponsible people should have tried to place us in antagonism to one another. I have felt deeply for you, and I wanted to write to you, but I hardly knew what to do in a position of such delicacy. I am very glad that you are writing to Cardinal Gotti. No one, who knows him, can suppose for an instant that he used the words imputed to him, or indeed accept any of the reasons assigned in the Press for the decision of the Holy See.
>
> I know well your loyalty and devotedness to the Church and the Holy See, and you may be assured that, in the terrible position in which the Will of God is placing me, your reputation will be safe as far as my influence extends. The lies about myself in *The Times* of the 17th, and again in the *Chronicle* last week, are small matters compared to the suspicion so gratuitously cast on you, but I should like to say that never, directly or indirectly, has the idea of the appointment of an Apostolic Delegate been brought before me in any shape or form.
>
> Once more thanking you from my heart, and earnestly begging your prayers, your help, and your friendship believe me,
>
> Your devoted and affectionate servant in J.C.
>
> FRANCIS, Bishop of Southwark.

Nearly fifty years have passed since those days when the Church suffered a kind of general change, reminding readers of the game of 'Musical Chairs.' Gasquet's future was deeply affected. He had been rather unkindly put aside for Westminster, in fact, as in 'Musical Chairs,' he was 'man out.' This he accepted with exquisite composure. Having left his story to posterity, he turned to the tasks which attracted him in the Order of St. Benedict.

He little realized what parts would be played in his future by the new Pope. His patron Leo XIII was no more and by a lightning Veto, flashed by the Austrian Cardinal in Conclave, Leo's Secretary of State, the sagacious Cardinal Rampolla, had been deprived of the Papacy. Gasquet's close friend and colleague Merry del Val was Secretary of State to the new Pope with lasting results upon France and Modernists. It was largely due to Merry del Val that Gasquet received his Hat in this Pontificate. It was also due to Merry del Val that a humble secretary under Rampolla was moved from the Vatican to the Cardinalitial See of Bologna which he occupied as Archbishop de la Chiesa until the last days of Pius X, whom he succeeded. Presumably de la Chiesa took advice too often from his old master Rampolla who had also been relegated to the background. Merry del Val was conducting the new Pontificate with a new broom. The broom was turned on Modernists and many of Gasquet's Liberal friends. Geniuses like Tyrrell and Loisy were lost to the Church. It is interesting to read what Gasquet had once written of Loisy to von Hügel in 1893: 'A wonderful thing to find a man speaking out so boldly and perhaps from what we know of the narrowness of our teachers in England at least—to have a man who is allowed to speak as he does. But then Loisy speaks as a master.'

Loisy, who had wanted to be Bishop of Monte Carlo, lost the terrible gamble to which his opinions exposed him. Von Hügel, thanks to his mystical fidgets, always avoided excommunication but the unequivocal Tyrrell fell into his own pit.

So much for so-called 'Catholic Liberalism'!

VII

AMERICAN VISITS IN 1904 AND 1913

AMERICAN visits made variety in Gasquet's life: once to São Paulo in Brazil and twice to the United States. In 1904 he decided to sail on the *Oceanic* to the United States on a lecture tour. He received an interesting letter from his old ally the new Secretary of State. Cardinal Merry del Val wrote (July 14, 1904):

> The Holy Father sends you his blessing and wishes you every success in your expedition to America. I shall be much interested to know what your impressions are. Cardinal Satolli is over there now. As far as I can judge, they are running him as an advertisement in favour of the present administration and in view of the Presidential Elections! Things in France are as bad as they can be. We shall have another fight soon and it is quite possible that it may be the last, and end in a definite break-up.

Cardinal Satolli, the bewildered Delegate of the Pope, found himself being exploited by President Roosevelt's friends in the Hierarchy. Archbishop Ireland certainly induced Catholics to vote Republican as well as Democrat. The Satolli mission resulted in a Delegation of the Holy See in Washington.

In a diary Gasquet described his send-off on August 10 from Liverpool with Mgr. Nugent. At Queenstown he landed to see the new Cathedral. On Sunday Mgr. Nugent said the prayers in both Classes. The Bishop of Albany did not turn up, but the Anglican Dr. Grosvenor, of New York, arrived with some good stories. One of his stories told how the Puritan Fathers 'first fell on their knees and then on the aborigines.'

When not taking notes in the Record Office Gasquet's pen collected the odds and ends of conversation.

Another story told of an Irishman found cursing the Italians. His sister remonstrated: 'But remember that the Pope is an

Italian,' to which he replied: 'Sure don't I know that: but he isn't half as infallible as he would be, were he an Irishman!'

Gasquet landed at New York on August 17. He noted:

> In the afternoon we went to the Hotel where Archbishop Ireland was staying and had a long talk with him.
>
> *August* 18: Went round the City with Father Doyle of Paulists—and to their establishment, Archbishop Redwood of New Zealand staying there [the Centenarian Marist]. They tell me they can always get an audience anywhere in the States. In some places non-Catholic pastors have shut their Chapels for the people to go to hear the priest.
>
> *August* 19: To the top of the highest building (25 stories) in New York.
>
> *August* 20: From Albany to the Paulist Summer house on Lake George (St. Mary of the Lake). This place is most beautiful. It is the original Lake of the *Last of the Mohicans*. The lake was originally called *Lac du Saint Sacrement*. They do a lot of camping out on an island, all returning here for the Sunday. Free and unconventional. All look quite robust owing to the fresh air they get during the two months. We had long chats with the priests [on such devotions as] *Nine Fridays, St. Anthony's Bread*, etc. They have my views. In their opinion the Jesuits of this country are more foreign in their type than those we have in England.
>
> *August* 23: Left Lake George by steamer. The Paulists came out in all their boats, 11 in number, to give us a send off.
>
> *August* 29: Cliff Haven on Lake Champlain. Explored this wonderful place. Dr. MacMahon the President most kind in every way.
>
> Some stories. The snake who grew so tame and fond of his master that he saved him one night from a burglar by sounding his rattle for a policeman.
>
> A Pessimist is one who, of two Evils, chooses both.

September found Gasquet in Canada and at Windsor he saw the strange sight of 'The Archbishop of Canterbury [Davidson] in the Church of Notre Dame', unless mistaken.

> *September* 9: Heard a good deal about the Knights of Columbus. Once any Catholic interest is declared to be paramount,

all, whatever political party or nationality, have agreed to act together.

September 10: Arrived at St. Louis. Called on Archbishop Glennon—very fine man, young and vigorous. [Cardinalized by Pius XII.]

Gasquet felt encouraged to speak some chaff to the Press:

For nearly a generation I have spent half of each day rummaging in the British Museum for material and perhaps the Fair will give me a chance to catch up with the times.

As for the Benedictines in France, he said:

The Order is banished. Leases were annulled with a wave of the hand. At Douai we educated none but British subjects on property held by leases signed by President Carnot, yet in a twinkling the School was seized.

At St. Paul Gasquet gave a Retreat to the Seminary after long and profound talks with Archbishop Ireland on Social problems in America.

Have found him most sympathetic and by no means too strong. The relations between him and the late Pope [Leo XIII] were cordial and intimate. His description of great harm done by condemnation of the Benefit Societies for Catholics. Constant differences of the Archbishops of America, 14 were in favour of the Societies, 2 neutral and 12 against and giving no reasons. These Societies were condemned by Rome. Archbishop Ireland calculates that at least 50,000 Catholics were lost to the Church by this. The labour of many great concerns is directed by these organisations and so need for Catholics to belong.

One danger to Church at present day is the raising of the peasant element to the Cardinalitial posts in place of the great families who no longer enter ecclesiastical state.

This is remarkable as an opinion coming from America, but all Archbishop Ireland's views were original.

It was interesting that the three great Ecclesiastics in time came, all three, within reach of the Sacred College: Gasquet completely, Glennon only in the last days of his life, while Ireland (the greatest of them all) was only deprived of the Red Hat by unlucky intrigues on the part of his friends and perhaps because his health could not have survived the Great War.

Meantime Gasquet's Cathedral lectures at St. Paul were a great success:

Lecture on France and Vatican. Very crowded, between 2,000 and 3,000.

October 3: Dined at Mrs. Hill's with Archbishop. Miss Hill told me that a Unitarian Minister had announced the Cathedral lectures and advised people to go to them.

James J. Hill was reckoned with Archbishop Ireland as one of the two great Empire-builders of the West.

October 7: Wonderful day, arrived late at Denver and was met by Knights of Columbus, drove round City and lecture in evening.

October 9: Omaha. Met on train W. J. Bryan the former candidate for President [defeated by Theodore Roosevelt and Taft].

October 17: Notre Dame (South Bend) wonderful place! Father Zahm showed me round.

October 19: My astonishment grows. Wonderful collection of portraits of Bishops and memorials of early American Church!

October 28: Washington. The position of the Catholic University here is impossible. About 3 years ago the Arch-bishops handed over the whole management of the secular part to the Sulpician Fathers.

October 29: Had interview with the President of the United States [Theodore Roosevelt] at White House.

At Rochester Gasquet met the famous Bishop McQuaid and inspected his famous Seminary.

November 8: From Rochester to New York with Bishop McQuaid. In evening Mgr. Lavelle took me to see Election scenes in the City. Good-humoured crowd everywhere.

November 9: Roosevelt declared elected.

November 12: Philadelphia. Archbishop Ryan told me of his connection with Archbishop Polding and how he had intended to go out to Australia.

November 13: Archbishop Ryan preached a very fine sermon in every way. The Archbishop is a grand man full of humour in everything. He reminds me of the pictures of O'Connell.

November 16: On board the *Oceanic*.

November 18: The Log entry is strong gale and terrific seas.

One of his lectures given at the New York Seminary about Anglican Orders caused a sensation when it appeared in the Press. The late Father Fenlon recalled in a letter to us:

> I remember that he lectured at Dunwoodie on the negotiations at Rome for the recognition of Anglican Orders. The lecture was extremely frank and revealed the ignorance and misconception of the Italians concerning the Church of England and the narrow escape from giving Papal recognition to the validity of Anglican Orders. The lecture was reproduced very accurately, I was told at the time, by the young priest who brought him out to Dunwoodie, D. J. McMacken. The lecture could not help being offensive to the Romans and Gasquet gave a diplomatic denial of its accuracy; but auditors told me it was a very fair report. The lecture took up a column of the *New York Sun*.

It is interesting to quote (December 4, 1904), as no doubt it expressed the Abbot's real feelings about the Commission on Anglican Orders, which haunted his whole life. His account offended the *Curia* as well as Canterbury, but Rome always realized how filially he had obeyed and saved Leo XIII from a brilliant blunder. The lecture stated:

> The Abbé Portal came to England with Lord Halifax to witness, examine and judge for himself the ceremonies, rubrics and customs of the High Church party. He was carried away with them and his enthusiasm knew no bounds.
>
> The next thing to happen was that the Abbé Portal went to Rome and through the French Ambassador was presented to Cardinal Rampolla, then Cardinal Secretary of State, who secured him an interview with Leo XIII. The Abbé Portal gave the Pope a very encouraging description of the High Church party in England and gave the Holy Father to understand that

if he would write a personal letter to the Archbishops of Canterbury and York they would at once submit to the Holy See.

Leo at last saw the dream of his life realized and the unification of the Christian world under his rule a fact. He promised to write the letters at once.

The Abbé Portal telegraphed the news at once to London. The stir it created among the Church people on both sides was amazing. There was a hurrying hither and thither and private talks were indulged in, and then everybody sat back to await the personal letters of the Pope to the Archbishops.

At this time there was in the High Church.party a very warm and close friend of mine, who came to me and said:

'Gasquet, is this true that Leo is going to write a personal letter to the Archbishops of Canterbury and York asking them to come into the one fold and submit to the successors of St. Peter? I, for one, know positively that the Archbishops of Canterbury and York have as much intention of submitting to Rome as I have.'

'I know nothing about the affair,' I said. 'But to assure you in the matter I shall go to Rome at once and find out myself.'

To Rome I went at once, and through Merry del Val, then Private Chamberlain to the Pope, obtained an extended audience with Leo. At first the Holy Father began to reproach me for the unsympathetic attitude of the English Catholics toward the High Church party, saying:

'They are ready to come into the Church, and the great obstacle to their entrance is the fact that they receive no encouragement from you.'

I endeavoured to speak, but the Pope interrupted with emphasis by continuing: 'Am I not right?'

After a pause of some minutes, as I did not wish to interrupt him again, I said:

'Holy Father, since you ask me, I must, in conscience, say that you have been utterly deceived. I do not say that the Abbé Portal has deceived you intentionally, but he certainly does not understand the situation in England.'

The Pope faced me full, I said:

'To my mind, Holy Father, it would be the greatest

blunder you could make to write a personal letter to the Archbishops of Canterbury and York before making a more
accurate investigation of the matter.'

At this juncture the Pope's face became covered with displeasure and the colour came to his cheek as he said.

'Who am I to believe? You tell me one thing and the Abbé
Portal and others tell me another.'

I replied, 'Archbishop Walsh of Dublin is in Rome at
present. I suggest that you send for him and ask his opinion.'

The Pope said he would and I was dismissed. Archbishop
Walsh confirmed everything I said the next day, and he had
barely left the Vatican before a messenger was on his way to
me with a message asking me to come at once to the Pope.
When I came into his Holiness's presence, he began by saying
in a most peaceful voice:

'I have come to the conclusion that the situation is not such
as has been presented to me. However, as I have promised to
write this personal letter I feel that I cannot entirely go back
on my word, and since the question of Anglican Orders has
been brought up again some action might be taken to settle it
definitely.'

After some further consultation with me it was decided that
the whole question should be reviewed again. The results
arrived at from the investigation, after a special Commission
had been appointed by the Pope, should be formulated in such
a manner that the Pope could, in a general letter to the English
people, give forth his views, thereby fulfilling his promise to
the Abbé Portal.

Gasquet felt that his lecture had been coloured by his reporter
and wrote to Father Fleming in Rome (February 16, 1905): '*The
Tablet* has printed an absurd account of a talk I had at the New
York Seminary. It is so absurd and untrue that I have written
to protest.'

To Father Fleming he wrote (December 31, 1905) on other
matters:

Since coming back from America I have been considering
what a very dangerous game the *Curia* is playing in regard to
the English-speaking races. There are (counting England,

Ireland, Scotland, Canada, Australia, Africa, United States) hardly less than 20 million Catholics with life and grit and the hope (I think unquestionably) of the Church in this world. Yet all this vast body is looked after by a set of men in Propaganda as a mere department of the entire Congregation. Such a vast body ought to have its own Government. It is amply big enough for one Congregation.

Do you think you could bring the matter before the Pope in some way? It is absurd to continue a government that was intended for missionary places and has to do also with the Eastern Rites.

A correspondence developed with one American priest as a result of Gasquet's travels.

From Father Ryan of St. Bernard's Seminary in Rochester interesting Church gossip arrived, too good to be lost to history (March 7, 1912):

> Since reading Ward's *Life of Newman* a testimony of Bishop McQuaid recurs to my memory. Once at our table some were discussing Newman and one said to the Bishop: 'You knew him personally, didn't you, Bishop?' He answered: 'Aye! and I could have fallen down at his feet and kissed them, I was so touched at the combination of humility with genius that I found in him!' His visit to Newman was paid on his way home from the Vatican Council when Newman was *under a cloud*. It is the more remarkable because Bishop McQuaid was always an Infallibilist . . . though Manning during the Council was a little fanatical on the question at issue and not very learned in theology and though aiming at lofty and noble ends was not troubled by scruples as to the diplomacy which he used to attain them.
>
> Cardinal Cullen, so his nephew Dr. Verdon told me, came home from the Council with the conviction that the History of the Church was much more necessary for a theologian than scholastic theology. If he had known that truth 15 or 20 years earlier, he might have been able to value Newman more justly.
>
> Bishop McQuaid always said of the anti-Papal agitation of 1850 that it was the work of Italian refugees from Rome who after the re-establishment of the temporal Power fled all over

the world . . . the real cause of the American Revolution was not the Taxation Acts but the rage of the Protestant Ministers at the concession of complete religious equality to the Catholic Church in Canada [the Quebec Act]. I am surprised Lord Acton did not know it. The American Catholics should be the last to attack England.

I was amused at [Sir George] Trevelyan's attempt at a reply to you—first by assuming that you said of him what you did not say, and then by making an answer, which is not an answer. His book would be creditable to an American as his uncle's book would be creditable to a Dutchman [Macaulay's History].

The Editors of the *Catholic Encyclopedia* have just been privately warned that there is a German-American conspiracy to get the *Encyclopedia* condemned. German jealousy has been irritated by Reviews which compared the *Encyclopedia* with the *Kirchen Lexicon* to the advantage of the former. I am glad something has occurred to prevent the coalition of German and Irish on anti-British lines that has been worked for some years. The Irish now will be anti-German.

Gasquet was one of the first to realize the immense power and importance of the Catholic Church in America. He also realized the value to British diplomacy of dissociating the German from the Irish Catholics. In a very few years these questions reached world-effect.

In 1913 Gasquet made another visit to America, to collect funds to continue his work on the revision of the Vulgate. Cardinal Merry del Val gave him 'an excellent letter recommending the work in the name of the Pope.'

On August 24 he sailed with Father Philip Langdon as secretary on the *George Washington*.

On September 1 they arrived and were met by Benedictine monks and Knights of Columbus. Their journey became a succession of visits, interviews, lectures and, happily, subscriptions.

Gasquet called on Cardinal Farley of New York and on President Theodore Roosevelt, now in retirement at Oyster Bay. He spent five days with Cardinal Gibbons at Baltimore. Visits to

America left him with an endless string of good stories. A speaker said of him that he would make 'a tidy American, if it were not for his aggressive English accent,' which delighted him.

Mary Anderson described him as a *raconteur* on his return from America, how:

> One afternoon on reaching a Western town in which he was to speak, he went to the hall to see what the acoustics were like. There he found a local professor lecturing on a recent trip he had made to England; he was speaking disparagingly of the English: 'Why, you never saw such dull-looking people as I saw in the London streets; there was a look of settled melancholy upon their faces—entirely unlike us: we are alive, we are animated, when we see an opportunity we seize it!' This naturally nettled Father Gasquet. In the evening, when we walked on the platform, he saw the professor sitting in the front row of the large audience; he bowed to him and began by saying that he had heard his lecture that afternoon, and, while regretting that he could not see eye to eye with him about the settled melancholy on English faces, he entirely agreed about the lecturer's people seizing an opportunity when they saw it— 'Yesterday in the train, I left my umbrella in the compartment and went out for luncheon. On my return the umbrella had disappeared: someone had seen his opportunity and seized it!' Everyone laughed, including the professor, and before Father Gasquet left the town he was presented with a fine gold-headed umbrella.

Though he collected his funds, he had to work for them. Ecclesiastical lectures are not valued outside the pulpit and once he found himself scheduled to speak between a lady pianist and performing dogs! It is related that the great Italian actress Duse once burst into tears in her declining days when she found herself advertised between performing dogs and a hypnotist!

Gasquet delivered the Advent sermons in St. Patrick's Cathedral, New York, while Father Philip took his place on the lecture tour. The Governor-General of Canada, H.R.H. the Duke of Connaught, invited him to lunch, but this he was compelled to decline for reasons of health. In Washington he was entertained by the Papal Delegate, Archbishop Bonzano.

His most interesting meal was partaken with Edison, whose praises he uttered in public. Mr. Edison in turn, speaking of the Abbot, said, 'He has a big job. It's too big for me. I am glad I do not have the task in front of me that is assigned to him. No, I would not like to tackle a job like that.' A Vulgate, collated or corrected by Edison, would certainly have electrified the Church.

The wizard gave the Abbot a concert with his latest invention, a disc-record phonograph. After the concert the conversation turned to the work of Palaeography.

Mr. Edison was greatly interested in the restoration of ancient manuscripts, and the processes used, as explained to him by his guest. He was deeply impressed with the invention which enables the Benedictine scholars, through a perfected photographic process, to read the writing in the negative. The dinner at Glenmont was planned by Mrs. Edison, as a surprise to her husband, for Mr. Edison did not know of his distinguished guest's presence until he came home from his laboratory that evening.

It was difficult to make Americans realize that they were helping in a work which like a Cathedral could not be finished in a lifetime, but Gasquet had a way of interesting them in the detail of his immense task whose completion was bound to be posthumous.

In his lectures he mentioned:

In this collection already have appeared the two old Cassinese Psalters, edited by Abbot Amelli, fragments of the old Latin Bible from the margin of the Leon Bible, a manuscript found by Dom Donatien de Bruyne in Spain, and the Tours Pentateuch, edited by Dom Henri Quentin.

The Commission set to work to gather together a collection of all the Biblical texts already in print. Progress has been made with this collection.

The importance of making notes of every possible circumstance connected with the different manuscripts will be seen when it is known that a few torn-out leaves in a manuscript of St. Paul at Monza aided in clearing up a disputed point of great importance. The men engaged in this research work do not allow a single point even of apparently minor importance to escape them.

The research work of the scholars engaged in the revision of the Vulgate brought to light many of the ways in which precious manuscripts were destroyed or badly damaged. In the old times when new texts were produced, there was no hesitancy in using the old manuscripts for binding purposes or for the sake of the parchment. In this way many of the manuscripts that would be of incalculable value today went out of existence.

At Worcester in England a precious fragment of a manuscript was found to have been used for binding purposes. It is thought that this fragment may be leaves of the Bible presented to Worcester by King Ethelred in the tenth century.

So that it will be seen that the work of even preparing for the revision of the Vulgate was no easy task. But we have been very successful. We have brought together a wonderful collection of manuscripts, and when these have been collated there is no doubt that we will be able to produce a fairly accurate version of St. Jerome's text. Few of those who are engaged in the work today will see it done, but when we drop out, others will take our place.

Bringing home some 10,000 dollars, Gasquet returned to find a momentous year ahead of himself as well as for Christendom, during which his Biblical studies were sadly disrupted and postponed.

VIII

GASQUET AS A HISTORIAN

'Tis no sinister nor no awkward claim
Picked from the wormholes of long-vanished days.

SHAKESPEARE

Coulton tells the Cambridge youth
That Roman Catholics doctor truth:
While Abbot Aidan Gasquet cries:
Your English History's packed with lies!

Cambridge Squib

It becomes not me to draw my pen in defence of a bad cause
when I have so often drawn it for a good one.

DRYDEN

PRIOR, schoolmaster and builder, in 1885 Gasquet turned aside from a life of administration to consider rebuilding his own health. The historian emerged like a winged moth from the broken cocoon. In his dark robe, enclosed in choir and cell, he resembled one of those hidden larvae whom the Creator evolves to unexpected shape. He took dusty flight to London and applied to Cardinal Manning for relief from his busy life. The Cardinal instantly arranged for him to pass from one activity to another— from the laboriousness of choir at Downside to the isolated industry of the British Museum. It seemed the best way to meet heart and diabetic troubles. The British Museum was the compromise between the Monastery and the Infirmary.

He was provided with a ticket to the famous Reading Room, and a home in Harpur Street, with a Benedictine companion or two, while the Pope's blessing descended on his historical studies. For twenty years he became a familiar figure under the dome of the Museum. A second time in his life he buried himself alive.

Gasquet found himself moving and studying amid that queer and pathetic company who toil in the Reading Room, the dredges

8

and drudges of literature, the 'ghosts' of real writers, seated in their numbered desks like the convicts of Research. Included are many of independent powers, writers of ability and achievement, but the herd laboriously slave for others. Amid the seekers for a pittance or cranks in pursuit of some missing link, men have passed upon the road of fame. Here Marx plotted the disintegration of Capital and Lenin fashioned a new Society for the Western world. Here controversialists of every sect scrape up their thunder. Here religious apologists chew the inky cud. Here the enthusiast finds lost Gospels, and the Baconian traces secret cyphers in the Sonnets of Shakespeare. And here Catholic and Protestant bottle their powders to blow up each other's theories in the outer world.

Gasquet became a *habitué* of this immense hive of the dead, enjoying to the utmost that impartial hospitality provided by the English taxpayer.

Catholics have always provided a trickle among the readers. Some like Coventry Patmore served on the staff, but Gasquet became the most familiar and famous of the students on the side of Holy Church. After his departure the Benedictine tradition was solidly maintained by Dom Henri Leclercq, who seemed to consume his own weight in books every day. When that portly Benedictine finished his work on Christian Antiquities, he died, but for regularity and industry he exceeded even Gasquet.

There has been a choice Catholic company since the days when Richard Simpson lighted in a manuscript upon the only possible lines written in Shakespeare's script, the most exciting discovery ever made. Here Francis Thompson toiled in glamorous poverty. Here worked the Jesuit Thurston and the antiquary Mgr. Barnes, hunting for data on witchcraft, mediaeval ghosts, the Man in the Mask, St. Peter's bones, the Holy Shroud, Stigmatics and all the Catholic flotsam and jetsam. Side by side James Gairdner the Anglican and Gasquet the monk sat down to sift the dust of years and to analyse the English Reformation.

For years Gasquet toiled his quota of hours with Edmund Bishop hovering like Ariel at his side. Gasquet became a favourite of the staff and a Quarto Monastic Breviary was placed at his disposal so that he could always turn from work to prayer. He soon became the 'Abbot of the Reading Room,' just as in later years he was known as the 'Cardinal of the British Museum.'

Gasquet also worked in the Record Office. Before the reforms of Maxwell Lyte it was a corner of old London worthy of Dickens' pen. Tattered and eccentric searchers delved in the huddled records. Amid the confusion moved giants like Stubbs and Maitland, while Horace Round, who pursued Freeman as Coulton pursued Gasquet, undermined pedigrees with a venomous fang. Round showed there was no continuity of the old Mass in the English Service. Gasquet and Stevenson were the first priests to break into this unindexed and uncharted sea.

Gasquet's task was simple. It was to study the fall of the English Abbeys and the dissolution of the English Orders in the mouldering Registers and records. He worked like a pioneer in the clay and sometimes a flint sparkled on the tip of his industrious pick. Gasquet was the first Catholic historian since Lingard to handle documents and to copy out the endless references.

Gasquet had not the learning or the lifetime of leisure which the perfect historian brings to his task. He had to build up in middle age the knowledge out of which his book could be shaped. Leisure was given him for the first time in his life because he had broken down at tasks which his Order placed first.

The great English historians had the advantage of being their own masters. Their prejudices were on a majestic scale and from glittering but biased pyramids they looked down on the centuries. They achieved gigantic pamphlets. Gibbon had exhibited Christianity as the corrosive which rotted the Roman Empire. Macaulay had rewritten English history to the greater glory, not of God, but of the Whigs. On a minor scale Froude had whitewashed and glorified Henry VIII. The nearest to an impartial historian still lived—Lord Acton—who had spent a lifetime collecting his bricks without building a temple to the History of Liberty. It was not clear that either Popes or Reformers would fare well at his hands.

Though Gasquet belonged to no school of History, his Liberal British mind turned towards Acton no less than Acton turned later to him and invited him to share in the *Cambridge Modern History*.

For the time Gasquet had been set to challenge the popular account of the English Reformation. He had developed Edmund Bishop's love of forgotten facts. He could not help favouring his natural partiality as a Religious by his selective power. Even so, Bishop made him hold the balance. It was clear that if the popular view of the Abbeys was false, only the truth could cause that view to dissolve, but the truth includes both sides.

In the immense web of Religious Houses covering the land, like the Stately Homes which usurped their place, there was much waste of leisure and resources. There were real black sheep, who would have been forgotten if the Church had not registered them. Thousands of blameless lives passed down the centuries to oblivion. They produced no more mention than the simple Annals of the Poor. History prefers records of criminals—and rarely of Saints.

Gasquet's achievement ended in definitely disassociating the old Religious Life from the story of complete and wanton stagnation, which alone would have justified Wolsey and Cromwell. He retold the tale, in mingled haste and horror, of the great Spoliation. Henceforth the old monks and nuns did not taste so bad in the mouths of modern Englishmen. It was a manner of life they have no wish to bring back but, while it lasted, it had helped and honoured the national life. It had bequeathed some very beautiful ruins, and the old monks had been very human and English like themselves.

Gasquet had shewn that monks were good and respected as landlords. There had been no extremes of poverty or wealth on their estates. 'Everyone knew his neighbour and everyone was his brother's keeper.' As for delinquencies he granted that any 'literary *chiffonnier*' could fill 'his basket with the soiled rags of frail humanity.'

Any tradition, unkindly called myth, when buoyed by a series of printed books copying and distorting each other, can be riddled by reconsideration of the records. It was fairly certain that during two years of research Gasquet would find much in favour of the

Monasteries which had been ignored and omitted. Green and Seebohm assigned about two-thirds of the monks to slackness or scandal. Gasquet proved this was a gross exaggeration. It is true he ignored and omitted in his turn. He may have been inexact in his views of the lay population of the Monasteries or in the social effects of suppression, but he brought a Creighton and a Gairdner to favour monastic practice as a whole. The ideal remained the brighter for controversy.

It could be pointed out that hundreds entered religious life without any real vocation in the manner that uneducated drones enter the Teaching or Civil Services today.

Gasquet will be remembered as the pioneer in challenging the accepted Protestant tradition and in bringing about more impartial views towards the old Abbeys and Monasteries, whose ruins lay like a massive query across the land.

A more accurate and specialized school of writers has followed him. Mediaeval Studies flourish greatly in England today and still the fair name and social utility of the monastic system survive the constantly edited scandals. All that 'the muckraker' (Gasquet's phrase for an embittered assailant) could do, has been done. The Church suffered by her very records, for it was the laxities and failures which found their way into the ecclesiastical 'police news,' and later became so soothing to the consciences of confiscator and destroyer, prude and Puritan. The vast number of Religious left their records in a Book which Tudor Commissioners or subsequent historians were never likely to ascertain.

To champion thousands and tens of thousands of dead and forgotten English men and women, who had lived conscientiously and fruitfully according to mediaeval standards, Gasquet wrote his historic apologia.

He did not ignore the blots nor did he wallow in whitewash. He simply studied and copied the manuscripts touching the fall of the Monasteries and in a monk's clear script collected hundreds of items, sentences, glimpses, names, figures from the records. His book caused a sensation. Cardinal Manning, no particular admirer of the Religious in the past nor their episcopal friend in the present, was convinced. But most prized of praises was a letter in the quavering handwriting of Cardinal Newman (May 8, 1888):

> We have been reading with great interest in our Refectory the important work you have sent me. We thank you for the instruction it has given us, and feel how unworthy this letter of acknowledgement for it is. I am sending you [indecipherable] . . . by the feebleness of my fingers.

Most gratifying were letters (also from Birmingham) which Bishop Ullathorne wrote to his fellow-Benedictine. His was truly a voice from the past: the voice of the venerable monk who had once served as a Chaplain in Botany Bay and helped to destroy the hateful convict system.

Ullathorne wrote (January 25, 1888):

> I have read your first volume and congratulate you upon it. It has taught me a great deal more than I knew in detail both of Wolsey's actions and Cromwell's villainies. You have made it clear that Wolsey was the real originator of the whole mischief and that he was the trainer of the monster Cromwell. I had no notion of the mass of evidence that still exists, and of which you have made such good use. It is the most melancholy history I ever read. Still it was necessary that it should be written. How the whole history of the Reformation hangs together by one string of revolting and most cunning injustice.
>
> There is a phrase which you sometimes use, and which I take the liberty of pointing out, which the educated converts point out as limited to us old English Catholics, brought by us from France but not English, and refer to the phrase *in their regard*. The moment a convert comes upon this phrase he says: Here is an old English Catholic. The English equivalent is *with respect to* or *with regard to*. How annoyed Canon Estcourt used to be when he met with that phrase, and quite recently Father Pope of the Oratory complained to me of a piece of writing, that it still clung to the old *in their regard*. Excuse this tedious remark upon a trifle but it is taken as a symbol of our past education in France.
>
> Though saddened, I have been much instructed by your volume and thank you for writing it, as well as for sending me a copy, and praying God to bless you and your work. . . .

Ullathorne wrote a year later (February 27, 1889):

I thank you for the second volume of *Henry VIII and the Monasteries*, which I have read with great interest. The exposure of what has been so long buried from sight is now complete and the Catholics of this country owe you a great deal as well as the Religious Orders. You have brought out Henry's character into a full flare of light, especially in his letters about the Rising in the North and his conduct towards Robert Aske. I had always been under the impression that the greater Monasteries had been suppl. . . .

Here the old man broke off what was the last letter he wrote on earth.

His faithful secretary Joseph Parker added (March 13, 1889):

From his deathbed our venerable old Father and Bishop bids me send this unfinished letter to you with a last loving blessing. A grand old solid Saint, in full possession of his faculties, he is humbly, yet calmly and fearlessly, awaiting the summons from the Divine Master he has served so well. Always grand, he is grander than ever in the hour of his death: and to not a few will his noble example be a help when their own turn comes. It will be a comfort to his friends to know that he is dying from weakness of the heart's action and not from what has been his cross for 19 years.

So passed the last of the Vicars Apostolic of England, blessing the work of the rising star in his Benedictine Order.

This two-volumed treatise on the dissolution of the Monasteries remained Gasquet's masterpiece. It was an achievement to have launched upon the tossing sea, whereon few, save a Brewer or a Gairdner, could keep afloat. All three buoyed themselves upon vast collections and survive by pure industry.

Gasquet gave England back her Abbeys and monks as a happy memory. Once the Abbeys had been the glories of the land and a visible link in the national progress. There was no reason that Englishmen should continue to foul their own nest by pointing to monastic ruins with the holy horror with which local antiquarians recall Hell-Fire Clubs. The monks of England could henceforth be considered respectable as a whole. Popular history ignored the bitter protests, the widespread distress and social insecurity which followed the fall of the Abbeys. The Pilgrimage of Grace remained in Protestant books like a road-sign pointing the wrong way. Gasquet noted that the weighty expostulation of Aske, the leader, had never seen light whereas 'the filthy scribbles' of the King's agents, had been printed and reprinted for centuries.

Gasquet kept his pen passionless and as far as possible impartial. He had only to reproduce surviving documents to make a story as grim as he could wish. He had no need to paint Wolsey and Cromwell licking the hands of the tyrant. Wolsey had taught the King how to bully Popes, suppress monasteries and confiscate Church revenues, but Wolsey had tried to rebuild the proceeds into modern colleges. Cromwell was only the King's burglar. Royal lechery needed constant funds.

The grey letterpress seldom breaks into humour. The much bruited 'amendment of the Monasteries' allowed Gasquet one of his rare chuckles by comparing it to the act of the Devil, who mended his wife's leg by breaking it to pieces. Another instance follows Bishop Latimer's reference to a 'bloody abbot' which Gasquet explained 'probably means that he did not agree with him in his reforming tendencies!'

It is typical of Gasquet that he did not feel capable of mixing the purple patch. Scenes flash through the darkness such as the condemnation of the 'Holy Maid of Kent' or the burning of Queen Katherine's confessor Friar Forrest, but his most moving paragraphs were borrowed from writers who were not Catholic, such as Froude's beautiful tribute to the Carthusian monks preparing for execution: or Canon Dixon's sentences describing the ruin of Furness Abbey. Aubrey's later collections lent a delicious reminiscence of the nuns in Wiltshire coming out with their distaffs in the meadows. The mental agonies suffered by Abbot Hobbes of Woburn reveal their piteous tale at the last.

Occasionally Gasquet delivered a telling phrase. He gathered a good deal of history when he wrote: 'The Monasteries stood alone. Singly they were attempted and singly they fell.' The

pervading reasons why they fell he left to history, to the candid
reader and to his multitudinous extracts. There was no one reason
why their fall should have been so facile and fatal. The Black
Death of a previous century and a half was insufficient. The Great
Schism, the Wars of the Roses, the weakness of the Barons, Tudor
statecraft, the greed of the new aristocracy, the King's quarrel
with the Pope, which was really a duel with the Emperor—
all had their share. It remains to say that very ripe and rich fruit
fell for a little shaking of a top-heavy system.

The Abbeys suffered the disadvantages which have befallen
the Stately Homes of England in later days. They made easy
plunder. They were expected to be indulgent landlords, providers
of hospitality to great and small, and to maintain road and bridge
and dyke. They were saddled with pensions which opened the thin
edge of confiscation. They accumulated prestige and privilege,
but they upheld and ruled the countryside like the recent Squire-
archy. When they fell to envy and malice, the Crown lawyers
found ways to undermine them. Gasquet does not mourn
material losses, which fell equally upon Church and poor.
Occasionally he mentions some superb church now lost to
Christendom and to disappointed tourists, such as the Priory at
Lewes or Glastonbury Abbey. Occasionally he refers to some
exquisite antique like the Regale of France on St. Thomas Becket's
shrine or the jewel which King Ethelred had presented to St.
Albans Abbey. These were all trash and junk but it was the good
name of the old monks and the honour of the helpless nuns which
he set out to establish. He combined the historian, the antiquarian
and the old English gentleman in his chivalrous quest.

After the execution of the Holy Maid of Kent, the King was
not likely to spare holy women of any degree. Gasquet gave her
a cautious chapter, but never hinted at her sanctity. Yet grave
ecclesiasts, who kept conscience free, believed in her, above all
the saintly John Fisher. Archbishop Warham accepted her though
she exceeded the bounds of religious ecstasy. With her visions and
speech of the Virgin, she might have remained a 'Bernadette';
but like Joan of Arc she passed to political prophecy and certain
death. She rebuked the King as the Baptist rebuked Herod, and

her destruction and defamation became essential to the royal plans. Her trial, forced confession and judicial murder at Tyburn were of the type which Russia has since made familiar to the world. A prophetess, who dared forbid the King's divorce as a result of her traffic with a holier world, must be 'a hypocrite nun.' Any nation but the English would have reversed the stigma as France reversed that upon Joan of Arc. Gasquet gave the facts without enthusiasm or exaggeration, but sufficiently to upset the common English view that Elizabeth Barton was a weak-minded epileptic. She was as brave and orthodox as Sir Thomas More and John Fisher, and merited to share their honours as well as their fate. All writings in her favour were destroyed and her name left under attainder. It was part of the immense conspiracy to make Tudor statecraft and persecution appear as the normal flow of English history. To reverse this was Gasquet's steady aim.

Naturally the Protestant view could not tolerate total reversion, but Gasquet was content when writers began to accept his facts as possible. If the monks were not always worthy, their spoilers and investigators were foully unworthy and for motives that England has learnt to execrate in modern times.

As for the so-called 'Black Book' which Froude believed had sent a shudder through the nation, Gasquet modified the national shuddering by pointing out that this record of monastic horrors was non-existent except in the minds of those who guessed that it had been destroyed during the Marian reaction!

The first result was to place Gasquet among historians at one bound. He attracted the attention of Lord Acton and an important correspondence followed from which Gasquet quoted in his Autobiography.

During eighteen months I had been occupied in studying the position of the Catholic Church in England just before the Reformation, in view of writing a Chapter for the *Modern History of Cambridge*, which had been projected by Lord Acton on his being appointed Regius Professor of History at Cambridge University. In June of 1890 I had so far settled what I

proposed to say that I submitted a draft to the Editor. I had a
letter from Acton (June 12, 1890).

'I did not quite accurately explain to you the thing we aim
at and I fancy you have thought of a review article more than
a permanent and rather too pretentious work. Would you
permit me to ask you to rewrite and consider the Chapter
from that point of view, of strictly scientific treatment. I do not
allow my friends to manifest their own views and standpoint.
Sometimes you seem to adopt an attitude of contention and
argument, which I entreat you to discard in the interest of the
whole. I want you to make your points clear without thinking
of contradiction or of people who have written otherwise, as if
the Chapter was composed by Frederick Harrison. Your profound erudition is the one thing that should appear and as much
as may be. You would, if you kindly accept this petition, give
its character in that way to the book.'

I replied that I quite agreed that History was History and
that the idea of a Protestant or Catholic view of History was
repugnant. I could not undertake in view of much work I had
to do, to rewrite what I had written, but would bear in mind
what Acton had said.

In September of this year returning from Douai I met
Acton on the boat and we had a long discussion on the matter
and on returning to London I sent him the following letter:

'I have been thinking over the Chapter which we discussed
on the boat on Friday and which I received yesterday, and I
really think the best plan would be for you to cut it out altogether. I quite see your position and that it would never do for
you as a Catholic to give me, a Catholic, more "rope" than
you allow to others. It is in my opinion impossible to write on
Catholic England without at present seeming to be more
Catholic than people would like—that is, if I am to write what
I hold to be the truth and set down what in time people will
have to come to, whether they like it or not. Still I quite
believe at present people are not prepared for this view and
would look on it probably as Catholic special pleading. This
from your point of view would be a mistake and my only wish
in the matter was to serve you. There is really no right understanding yet of the position of the actual state of the Church of
England in pre-Reformation days as a work-a-day concern. To

me, and I have given a great deal of time and trouble to the consideration in this respect, it was vastly better than people ordinarily think.

'I remember reading somewhere a very sound remark to the effect that "revolutions really occur when things are mending and that when things are thoroughly bad they do not often break out." Now I am gravitating to the conclusion that this is true of the Reformation in Europe, and that its successes were mainly in countries where the religious condition of the Church as a going concern was more sound than in countries where the movement failed. This by the way; but it may help to show why my contribution may appear to be too much like Catholic special pleading. Had I time now, as I had two years and a half ago, when I handed in my contribution, I might have tried my hand at the subject in another point of view, but, I fear, with the same result. Now that is out of the question. For more than twelve months now I have had all my time and energy devoted to a reconstitution of the English Benedictine body. It will take me months still, but it is worth all the trouble, even from *our* point of view—that is if proper historical work is to be done in the future by our English monks. It is work that cannot be delayed and to which I must give my whole time for months to come, as success requires a great amount of personal intercourse. Hence it would be quite out of the question for me to undertake to look at the Chapter, now with the hope that it might be made less—what?

'Consequently I hope you will think with me that it had best under the circumstances be cut out. It does not seem necessary—or very necessary—and after two years and more I should have to try and get back into the atmosphere of the work again, which at present is impossible.

'If you agree that we need say no more about the Bibliography—for about that I have something to say, I have my note books and could empty references with the best of them; but for what purpose? My conclusions from numberless manuscripts and from examining every early printed book I could come upon, are founded upon a general survey and the mere references would help no one.'

In the end I concluded to withdraw what I had written and ultimately the material served me for a course of lectures I gave at Ushaw College to the Philosophers and Theologians, and subsequently I published what I had written in a volume called *The Eve of the Reformation*.

Lord Acton had reached Cambridge as Regius Professor of History thanks to Lord Rosebery. The Liberal Premier promoted the Liberal Historian: but a Catholic succeeding Seeley and Kingsley seemed startling enough. It was a veering of the compass, which would have filled Newman with irony and probably angered Manning. Cardinal Vaughan must have credit for permitting Catholics to attend the Universities and for appreciating Acton's orthodoxy. Manning had pressed him hard after the Vatican Council and called him to account for letters in *The Times*, but Acton had arranged his submission with his own Bishop. He lived and died in peace with the Church, even as a Cambridge Professor!

The later publication of his private letters to Mary Gladstone (intended for the G.O.M.) caused some scandal. If Manning had been Gladstone's political conscience, Acton was his historical guide. He had allowed himself to refer to Carlo Borromeo and Pius V (both canonized) as 'assassins.' These were personal, but not charitable, judgments and they were adequately challenged on publication.

In mollification of Catholic opinion Gasquet was given the delicate task of editing a further series of letters to Richard Simpson, Newman's brilliant correspondent and editor, who was supposed like Acton to have primed Gladstone against the Infallibility. Gasquet edited the letters in *Lord Acton and his Circle* and showed that in 1875 Acton did his utmost to dissuade and disarm Gladstone. Still, the book was a stirring of cold embers and Father Thurston proved to be in a scolding mood. Gasquet was sufficiently nettled to write twice to *The Tablet* in counterpart. Incidentally the brilliant paragraphs in the book about Simpson were written by Bishop.

Gasquet was anxious to keep Acton's memory orthodox without shocking the weaker brethren. In dealing with the letters he allowed himself to modify phrases and Acton's family called for whole letters to be suppressed. It was not strictly historical, but he was anxious to plant Acton's letters on the Catholic shelf without drawing pious recriminations. Some of Gasquet's changes seem amusing as well as innocuous.

For instance he suppressed the fact that Bernal Osborne made a speech in the Commons 'perfectly drunk': and Dickensians may wonder why Newman may not be alluded to as 'Noggs.'

'Lacordaire is unsettled' is a mild version of Acton's original: 'Lacordaire really sees through the hollowness of the Roman system.' A letter of Newman's described as 'abominably malicious' is whittled to 'unjust.'

Acton had called Pope Pius IV 'an ass' which Gasquet changed to 'no good,' forgetful that an ass was good enough to carry Our Lord. Pope Pius V was not to be referred to as 'the type of an Inquisitor.' The Jesuits subsequently restored his character but Acton, when he assumed the bonnet of Liberty, kept a few angry bees therein. In one of the suppressed letters Acton confessed that he had mistaken Pius IV for Pius V 'in the dark recesses of memory.'

This comparison of print and manuscript shows that Gasquet watered down what seemed likely to cause pain at the expense of his own character as a historian. But he thought more about the feelings of strict Catholics. He might suppress or soften but he never lied or deliberately cheated. He took the trouble to rout out a survivor of the *Home and Foreign*, old Wetherell, aged ninety.

Gasquet was anxious to save Acton's good repute, for the great historian had died in Grace. There was no reason why this instalment of Letters should not please Howards as well as Hawarden. Gasquet's position enabled him to lend a hand to so-called Liberal Catholics in trouble. No one tried harder except Father David Fleming to save Mivart when that brilliant biologist was excommunicated. He threw a lifeline to Duchesne when in trouble, and the dead Acton he defended, not as a historian, for Acton was reckoned among the greatest, but as one who merited the proud memory of the Church. Gasquet realized that Acton's prestige in English Academies was second only to Newman's. In view of the big area of Acton's compass he could overlook details which shock the pious but not the historian. To the general historian details should not matter in view of the greater perspective. On the question of the Roman Primacy Acton saw no alternative save the divine right of Kings and a future dim with dictators and clouded by the worship of the State: which has certainly constituted the real trouble of the Church in our times. Was Acton also among the Prophets?

The book on *Henry VIII and the Monasteries* carried Gasquet's name far and wide. Amongst those who were deeply interested was Lord Emly, who later proposed helping Gasquet to found a house of studies on a generous scale. Lord Emly was the William Monsell who had served as Postmaster-General in Gladstone's Cabinet. With Lord Dunraven and Aubrey de Vere he had been one of the High Church Limerick landlords following Newman and Manning into the Church. Gasquet's work aroused his interest and he asked him to prepare a Latin letter to send the Pope on the subject.

If Lord Emly figures as a Patron, the names of Gasquet's coadjutors, Dom Gilbert Dolan, Dom Norbert Birt, and Abbot Snow, must be laudably recorded in any memoir. Edmund Bishop was nearer a guardian angel to him.

Gasquet's answer has survived among the Emly Papers (June 3, 1892):

It has been only this morning that I have found time to do the letter we spoke of. I fear you will think it long; but first it is difficult to express oneself shortly in Latin, and secondly it is a thing much to be wished that the Holy Father should understand what we hope to do. He has so often expressed himself upon the necessity of historical work in these days, that anything of the proposed nature is sure to have his blessing and best wishes. The fact that he has kept me at work for more than seven years shows his interest in England. I must once more offer my best thanks for the great kindness you have shewn me, by aiding me to help in literary work so generously. I hope, directly our home at Dulwich is ready, to be able to write and testify that we have two of our Fathers devoted to research into

the pre-Reformation period of our Church history and claim
your kind promise.

P.S. I may mention that I saw Archbishop Vaughan last
Monday and had a long talk with him about the matter which
has his entire approval in every way.

During his researches into the Old English Bible he fell ill and
was taken abroad by his friends, the Caves of Ditcham Park,
whence he wrote to Lord Emly (February 2, 1893):

I am with some friends here getting ready to start for a trip
to Italy and Sicily. I hope to be able to see the inside of some
foreign libraries before I come back. It is most unfortunate that
this should have happened just when my *socius* Father Dolan
was beginning his labours with me and I think it perhaps better
to set him to some other work till I return. Your kind pecuniary
aid to our researches will thus not be drawn upon except when
we are both at work together. I think it more than likely that
I shall have to move with him nearer to my work in London
as I find the daily getting to Dulwich and back almost more
than I can manage. When I broke down, I was deep in the
question of the English MSS. Bible of the 14th century. I feel
fairly confident that Wycliffe has no title to be considered the
author of the version which goes under his name: and certainly
the version was used by undoubted *Catholics* in the 15th century. However this and a great many other interesting points
must now wait for a short time. As to the *Spectator* review of
the Dean of Winchester's book, the reviewer has taken the
Dean as if he were an authority. When the book first came out,
I wrote an article in *The Tablet* shewing up the point and
stating that the account given was a gross caricature of the
reality. Someone in Hampshire—I haven't the least idea who—
had this printed and circulated broadcast in Winchester. If I can
put my hand on a copy I will enclose it. The Dean's *Introduction*
is wrong in so many points that nothing less than a treatise
would answer it. I hoped to have had another article on it but
was, as I told you, knocked out.

Gasquet's intense interest in the Old English Bible arose in
the British Museum. Day by day he passed a handsome 14th-
century manuscript and stopped 'to admire the well-written page

with its painted border and again and again I have read and re-read this Legend inscribed on a card *The English Bible, Wycliffe's translation.*'

He sent for the manuscript and eventually asked four questions. Did Wycliffe translate it? What had the Wycliffites to do with it later? Were translations forbidden? Was there already a Catholic version?

Many volumes would be needed to summarize the evidence to answer these questions.

If Wycliffe was responsible for the first, certainly Nicholas Hereford produced the second edition and John Purvey completed it. Wycliffe made his peace with the Bishops and died two days after a stroke while hearing Mass. Hereford died a Carthusian monk and Purvey recanted his opinions. So the chief translators ended orthodox sons of the Church. It was possible to criticize conditions in the Church without leaving her. The truth was that both Catholics and Protestants later could have used the book which translated the Vulgate.

As a historian Gasquet was most severely criticized, not for facts and quotations, but for such a theory as 'The Old English Bible.' His answer, whether to the 'serious and courteous criticism' of Sir Frederick Kenyon or to the personal attacks of Dr. Coulton, was practically the same: to republish his article uncorrected. His theory that the Wycliffite Bibles were 'the Catholic versions of our pre-Reformation forefathers' appeared in the *Dublin Review* (July 1894). He met the denials by a lengthy demurrer without withdrawal.

It is difficult to discuss the English Bible without launching into the controversy between Protestant and Catholic or landing upon the shallows of Church *versus* Bible, as if they were not as much part of each other as the Belly and the Body's members. In one period, which Gasquet made his own, Reformers were Catholics and it seemed impossible for Bible and Church to be fundamentally subversive. But Lollards, like Lutherans later, went further and used Scripture to back views destructive of Society and the State. The Lollards were wiped out like anarchists, while the English Bible, which they used as dynamite, survived under

the label of Wycliffe. Gasquet concluded that Wycliffe had used
and his disciples revised old texts made by orthodox sons of the
Church. He jumped at the conclusion that there must have been
an Old Catholic Bible—but in spite of hints and traces there was
always a missing link.

He shed a great deal of information on the standing of Scripture in Catholic days. The Protestant legend that Wycliffe like
Luther suddenly found a Bible and translated it with thundering
results was too easy. Reformers made things far too complicated
for the cut and dry, cut and parry versions of History.

The English Bible was not created. It was evolved by a long
and painful process. Impartial justice will give as much credit to
the old Catholics as to the Reformers. Lollards made it a political
weapon and it later became a religious rapier in Protestant hands.
Henceforth English History became obscured by violent po-
lemics. For long, both sides had shared the Vulgate. In time they
made their own versions: the Catholics with a pious literalism,
choked with controversial notes, the Protestants in a freer text
which had the good fortune to pattern the English language for
three centuries.

Protestant writers used to be annoyed when it was pointed out
that the Authorized version shows signs of the Catholic having
been read without acknowledgement. But Gasquet's overclaim
that the previous Wycliffite version was a Catholic relic caused
indignation. If he did not prove his point, at least he raised a
quantity of dust (not without some fresh air) and left new lines
of research to the historians of the future.

Bible controversies have since taken different directions.
Gasquet was the last of those who entered the old-fashioned lists,
when it was important for Catholics to prove they were patriotic
fundamentalists and that without the Church there would have
been no English Bible at all.

It is accepted that the Church relayed the Gospels and Epistles
in English and that Church walls were coloured with Bible
pictures (and a few Saints and Legends thrown in). The Church
did not object to translations unless they were false and used to
propagate new ideas destructive of the old. Imagine a Bible

edited today in the sense of Karl Marx, or a Communist parody of the Sermon on the Mount? Would either be accepted by old-fashioned Protestants?

The Church could not be expected to produce an English Bible before there was an English language, which only found itself by 1400. Thereafter Scripture must have leaked to the laity. Chaplains, mystics and noblemen valued any portions they could obtain in English. Amateur translations had the disadvantage of cribs, and 'cribs' are always forbidden. Scripture cribs needed the hallmark of the Church. Before the art of printing, Scripture stories were passed from mouth to mouth, for few could afford a manuscript. Thomas More professed to have seen such before they disappeared. Where did the English laity draw their Bible knowledge? What was happening in the last quarter of the 15th century when A. W. Pollard of the British Museum informed Gasquet that there had been fourteen editions of the Bible in German! 'many of them with illustrations, a sure sign that they were expected to go into the hands of well-to-do laymen.' Could England have been so utterly behind Germany in this matter? As a matter of fact the Gospels were known, repeated and believed without need of Bible Societies. Whatever the means, the Church secured the belief. As for certain holy horrors in the Old Testament, the Church kept them hidden in a Pandora's box which was opened at the Reformation.

When Gasquet surmised an Old Catholic Bible which the Wycliffites had revised and palmed off as their own, it was suggested that Thomas More had mistaken one of the two Wycliffe versions for this Catholic version.

If there was a missing link, it was not apparent. Gasquet pointed out the next best thing. There were copies of Wycliffe Bibles which had belonged to such orthodox laity as the Duke of Gloucester, son of Edward III.

All great apologists seek a sign to overwhelm their opponents. The Darwinians sought fiercely for the link missing to Darwin's theory of Evolution. Baconians scour the libraries for connection between Bacon and the Bard. The mystery demands a Shakespearean play written in Bacon's script. Gasquet needed an Old

Catholic Bible in manuscript written and cherished by the laity before the age of Wycliffe. His guess in the British Museum was a mistake.

There is a spirit of vendetta amongst historians as exemplified by Freeman's weaseling pursuit of Froude. Dr. Coulton followed Gasquet with increasing accusations of 'scandal' until he became scandalous himself. His grievance was of inaccuracy and mis-statements. Coulton seemed to pick up hints from greater scholars like Creighton and Kenyon, when they reviewed Gasquet's work. His real grievance, to judge by his Autobiography and pamphlets, was that Gasquet would not enter the ring against him. England still echoed the knockout which Kingsley had received from Newman. Coulton, desirous of notoriety, offered challenges of which no notice was taken. It maddened him beyond words, at least beyond the words that one historian should apply to another. Incidentally the accusation he hurled could have been applied to Macaulay, who like Gasquet, in the words of Father Thurston, was 'regrettably impatient of anything like revision.' Thurston was the Cardinal's strongest supporter, writing to Dom Ethelbert Horne (November 1, 1938):

> I have had occasion lately to read some of the things which Dr. Coulton is continually repeating about Cardinal Gasquet. They are growing more and more outrageous. Of course there is foundation for many of his criticisms, but he comes back again and again to Gasquet's reference to the general Preface of the Wycliffe Bible, describing it for example as 'an assertion of plain fact so patently false that nothing but the most astounding carelessness can explain it,' etc., etc. It seems to me that, though a sentence is most unfortunately worded in Gasquet's Old English Bible, his meaning is quite intelligible and innocent.
>
> November 4: Unfortunately I cannot take the line that Cardinal Gasquet made out his main contention and I also should have to admit that he was often very careless, and that it seems to me regrettable that he reprinted old articles without revision. None the less it is preposterous to pretend that he based his case for the pre-Wycliffite Bible upon a *patent falsehood*.

Many Catholic friends of Gasquet regretted that he had not made corrections or considered Coulton's great mediaeval knowledge worthy of reply. Gasquet disliked Coulton's endless harping on the seamy side of history. He felt a deep family sense of loyalty and decency. The Religious *familia* was more sacred to him than even family honour to the aristocracy. Great families are often proud of their 'wicked Earls' or 'bold bad Baronets,' but it was different with the Religious Family in which Gasquet's ideals had been tempered. Gasquet believed Coulton had cast mud upon the monks and nuns of the past out of proportion. Gasquet had rescued their general good name and flatly ignored their vituperation. He did not mind drawing vituperation upon himself, but he made up his mind not to indulge Coulton in a public duel. The protesting and baffled critic had to write his angry apologia against a dummy of his own creation.

There is a type of history for which Gasquet had no use. Lists of delinquent monks and clergy proved nothing except that human nature is human. A publication of the names of all modern priests and ministers who have been convicted of crime would neither embellish nor degrade the institutions to which they belong.

What is called the 'scandalous' or obscene occupies a certain proportion of all History, literature, journalism and even human conversation, as we know them. The proportion of such in Holy Scripture exists on a smaller but necessary scale. The proportion in clerical history has proved smaller still, but scandals there must be, as Our Lord laid down, though woe be their accompaniment.

The part, however scandalous, must not be allowed to sully the whole. This, of course, is always the offence of partisans and partial historians. Their works are paved with statistics which generate false generalities.

Gasquet may not have been endowed with the exact sensitiveness of a scholar or been able to cast the sweep of an Acton to the horizons of History. Perhaps he was fortunate to rouse an opponent like Coulton, who though minutely accurate, had as little real penetration as himself. They stood facing each other until Gasquet coolly turned his back. Each became the Bee in the other's Bonnet, but History will adjudge to which belonged the honey and to which the sting.

Neither Gasquet nor Coulton seemed to realize the Middle Ages as they were in their own light and atmosphere. Both judged Mediaevalism against a Victorian background.

The Middle Ages were as magnificent and terrible, salutary to soul and uncomfortable to body as possible. Mediaevalism stood deep in darkness and mire but like a Colossus whose head reached into the stars. To apply the standards of prudery, by omission or exemplification, was as ludicrous in Gasquet as in Coulton. Had they returned across time to those centuries, both would have been severely shocked. The old English Puritanism was no doubt rooted in the Catholic past: but hypocrisy and prudery developed with the Reformation until in the eyes of the Continent they became peculiarly English characteristics.

The full and deep history of Mediaevalism can never be written by Dr. Bowdler any more than its shining spiritualities can be appreciated by the professional 'muck-raker.' Muck there was enough to take Dr. Bowdler over the head but Sanctity flourished like the lotus-flower growing out of the mud.

Gasquet's book on the English Monasteries still floats. Its calm dissuasions were accepted by the reading public and after forty years Gasquet claimed that except for many small corrections 'the text is allowed to stand.' After all, Gairdner had declared the old scandals had been dispelled for ever. Coulton worked to disillusion Gairdner, from whom he said he obtained 'a letter of partial retractation' and later hailed an article as 'a general retractation.' But as Gasquet declined to retract his book, the flow and froth of letters and articles drifted away with time. English readers preferred the impartial and kindly tone of the historian who had appealed for fair play from the first.

In this spirit the Anglican Canon Dixon described the book on *Edward VI and the Book of Common Prayer* as 'written in an excellent spirit, conciliatory and calm,' while Edmund Bishop wrote in his own copy: 'There is not even one word which can be read as provocation or as even possibly opening the door to a discussion or consideration of the case on its merits.' Liturgy can be an exact science.

After his resounding success with the Monasteries, Gasquet plunged into unrecorded corners of the 14th and 15th centuries, mediaeval preachers and catechists. What was the preaching, what was the catechising in the years of Faith? His essay on the sermons of Bishop de Brunton opened the first question. The second question he answered in favour of the parish clergy, who had been equally maligned with the Religious. Diligently he collected odds and ends of manuscript and information: Bishops' Decrees and books like Caxton's *Liber Festivalis* (a book of Sunday sermons). He stressed the value of collections by John Filton or John Bromyard. Their sermon notes must have been invaluable to unlearned priests especially when dotted with those good stories which make preaching endurable. Alas! they were often only notes. If only Gasquet could have filled up the 'Note about the man in Bristol,' or 'the woman in London to whom Our Lord showed His Heart' centuries before Marie Alacoque was heard of! Gasquet made his points at the cost of terseness and dryness. He was digging the vast mediaeval midden, and the broken potsherds outnumbered the jewels. There were hollows as well as haloes in the system.

Gasquet never wrote another book, only Studies and Sketches. From Henry VIII to Henry VI he played a Henrican gamut and back to Henry III, whose clash with the *Curia* showed that Rome could be disputed without breaking with the Pope. He was called upon to edit and introduce books, redounding to his virtue of charity rather than his art of history. And this he did gaily.

He sometimes tackled the inaccuracies of others, for instance when the *Annals of Winchester College* described from the Latin a *Vicar* breakfasting at the College with his wife with two boys of his name in the school in 1420! This 'pretty story' Gasquet destroyed by pointing out that the Latin was *Vicecomes* or Sheriff and not *Vicarius* at all!

Picking off inaccuracies is the sport of scholars rather like snipe-shooting to sportsmen. In one letter Gasquet scored an account of a priest's funeral in *The Tablet* which listed among mourners 'the priest's nephew and wife!' Coulton would have leaped on this mis-statement in an old Register as proof!

To the end Gasquet kept up his loving interest in the old English Monasteries, writing about an Anglican critic (August 2, 1924):

> Canon Wilson of Worcester sent me a *tirage à part* of his visitations of Wolsey and Cranmer. The visitations are useful but his comments are very naughty and I have told him so plainly and I don't think he will like my letter. I asked him what he thought some archaeologist three hundred years hence would make out of a set of his household books—the Baker's book and the Butcher's book contain nothing given to the poor! Fancy the wicked old sinner, calmly and without any evidence, saying that.

The nearest to an original work was his book on the Black Death which he believed responsible for the distant decays he described in *The Eve of the Reformation*, though Vinogradoff (a greater historian) has shewn that the great Pestilence had not 'the dignity of a constant economic force.' It was a temporary disaster not a standing catastrophe.

The study of the Black Death deeply employed Gasquet's thought not merely statistically but in the final results on the Church and realm. The records have been exhaustively studied: the movements of the Bishops of the time, the number of benefices vacated and the mortality of priests and people. The Plague was the bubonic plague which swept over Europe from the East. The decimation of England chilled the life of the Church. Whether the clergy and doctors fled in despair or not, an enormous percentage died amongst their flocks or as a result of ministering to the sick. Bishops retired to their country places, but two Archbishops of Canterbury died during the plague years. One half of the beneficed clergy died. Parishes were so reduced that the clergy, if left alive, often retired themselves, but hardly to safety, for no one knew how or where to escape. It was the duty of Bishops like staff officers in war-time to remain in the safest places they could find. Most of them continued and carried on their duties by ordaining new priests. But with the wholesale deaths it was clear that ill-educated and unvocationed clergy would be added to their ranks, leading to a poorer standard and the laity's disrespect.

Such was Gasquet's main theme. His important concluding chapter covered 'some consequences of the Mortality.' He believed that quality as well as quantity had been diminished in the clergy. 'It is a well-ascertained fact, strange as it may seem, that men are not as a rule made better by great and universal visitations of Divine Providence.' It was curious that Boccaccio wrote flashily and fleshily in time of plague in Florence. Possibly the amusing improprieties in Chaucer could be traced to the restless spirit which had also released the Peasants' Revolt and the Lollards in turn. There had come a general breakdown in authority as though the Black Death had weakened the old order. The English Reformation, when it came, was not a bolt from the blue but the result of many side-causes.

In the preface of the second edition Gasquet compared the bubonic plague then raging in India. He lived to see the 'Spanish 'flu' so-called, which ravaged the world during the First World War.

Gasquet kept a dry clear style. At times he was pedestrian but never pedantic. Provided he reached his aim, he never minded how slowly he stepped. He has been criticized for inability to paint vivid passages, but as Adrian Morey has pointed out:

> Gasquet lacked Froude's gift of word-painting, as he lacked his extraordinary bias; if we compare his account of Woburn Abbey at the Dissolution with that of Froude, the advantage, so far as style is concerned, rests with the latter; but Gasquet was possessed of a command over words that was quite sufficient for his purpose, and he could handle a small subject especially with an ease and distinction of his own.' [1]

When deeply moved, for example by the fate of the three Abbots executed by Henry VIII, he had the power of moving his readers by the quiet tide of his words. Abbot Whiting's martyrdom is a good example of Gasquet's style with rare touches of allusion and imagination added to the grim facts.

[1] 'Cardinal Gasquet the Historian,' *Cath. Hist. Rev.*, Oct. 1929.

Thus he painted the scene at Glastonbury:

At the outskirts of his own town his venerable limbs were extended on a hurdle, to which a horse was attached. In this way he was dragged on that bleak November morning along the rough hard ground through the streets of Glastonbury, of which he and his predecessors had so long been the loved and honoured lords and masters. It was thus among his own people that, now at the age of well-nigh four score years, Abbot Whiting made his last pilgrimage through England's *Roma Secunda*. As a traitor for conscience sake he was drawn past the glorious monastery, now desolate and deserted, past the great church, that home of the saints and whilom sanctuary of this country's greatness, now devastated and desecrated, its relics of God's holy ones dispersed, its tombs of kings dishonoured, on further still to the summit of that hill which rises yet in the landscape in solitary and majestic greatness, the perpetual memorial of the deed now to be enacted. For, thanks to the tenacity with which the memory of good Abbot Whiting has been treasured by generations of the townsfolk, the very hill today is Abbot Whiting's monument.

The fate of the Abbot of Woburn touched Gasquet's chords of humanity. A weak unhappy man had been caught in the Gestapo system of the Tudors. Guilt was assumed and confessions were suggested and enforced.

This ample confession, which was evidently made by the advice of Cromwell, pitifully reveals mind and soul and heart in all their perplexities. But the Abbot had also vividly before him the horrors of imprisonment and the thought of a terrible death. Under stress of this fear, before his examination is concluded, he, in accents more pitiful still, admits that he may have been mistaken after all and prays for pardon.

This is but a picture of the anguish of conscience and the sinking of heart in dread of an uncertain end which must have been the experience of thousands in that terrible time. . . . But such a surrender of convictions as that to which Abbot Hobbes had brought himself was all in vain. His prayer for pardon was denied; he was not allowed to live. Henry had passed beyond the stage of compassion for any human weakness, of pity for any living soul. . . . The Abbot was hanged before the gate of Woburn Abbey and tradition pointed to an old oak tree . . . property granted with many other broad acres belonging to the Church and the poor to Sir John Russell.

And so another Stately Home started its career.

For a learned yet lively passage take the account of the bells at St. Edmundsbury playing during the visit of Henry VI at the Christmas of 1433:

> Christmas Day was rung in by four successive changes; first came the tones of the two Londons—the greater and the Holy-water bell: the second and third peals were sounded on the bells in the cemetery, and amongst them Gabriel, the bell rung in thunder-storms, and its companion, *Galiena*. The beginning of the third peal was the signal for the cantors and all the rest of the vested ministers to enter the choir for Vespers, where-upon the younger monks began ringing the bells in the great lantern tower, and then all the bells of the monastery took up the music, and above them all was heard the well-known tongue of *Haut et cler*; and thus, all sounding together, there rang out what the townspeople knew as *Le glas*, which was the signal for the beginning of the Office.

No other writer in England could have written with such grace and exactitude this paragraph of Campanology, as the science of bell-ringing is called.

James Gairdner had been the first leading historian to appreciate Gasquet's work. Gasquet helped him with information in the Vatican Archives, but criticized Gairdner's subsequent use of what he had provided. Gasquet felt like an eagle wounded by the arrow tipped with his own feathers. The two historians, remaining friends and admirers, continued to cross swords over Abbot Wallingford of St. Albans. Froude had wildly attacked the great Abbot on the strength of rumours and Cardinal Morton's proceedings. In his *Lollardy and the Reformation* Gairdner took the view that the Abbot was a villain and a spendthrift. Gasquet quoted Gairdner in full, adding such critical notes as:

1. Morton does not *state* that *he cut down the wood* but that he *hears reports* that he has done so.

2. This is absolutely contrary to the *information* I obtained from the Vatican Archives.

Wallingford was supposed to have averted Morton's threatened Visitation by intrigues in Rome but Gasquet noted: 'This statement is absolutely without foundation. There is no proof that the Visit was not held.'

Dr. Gairdner replied:

You can certainly do me no greater favour than by correcting an error. At the same time—so difficult is it to arrive at truth—I fear I cannot make an offhand recantation without looking a little further into the documentary evidences. Indeed there is even a moral perplexity to me arising out of your view, if it is quite established. For Archbishop Morton surely believed in the dreadful imputations on the Abbot and says in his letter that he had admonished him charitably even before he had received Apostolical authority to bring him to account for the matter. Under these circumstances are we in the 20th century better judges of the probable facts than Archbishop Morton was?

Last night on receiving your letter it certainly seemed to me that I had been strangely misled by Dugdale. That Wallingford was the Abbot to whom Morton's letter was addressed I think you have fully made out. But if he had deserved the good character in the obituary notice, how did Morton conceive such a bad opinion of him? You talk of his 'vague charges' but they were very specific and particularly abominable. . . . I don't think Yorkist and Lancastrian will explain matters. A respectable M.P. would be even more cautious of what he said of a political opponent that might touch his private character than of anyone on his own side. . . . But the charges carefully read do not seem to me to touch the Abbot himself except in the matter of relaxed discipline. And surely it is quite possible that a strenuous man charged with high responsibilities, may have broken down both bodily and even mentally *in senectute*. This I think is the most plausible.

Do you think Abbot Wallingford was a man of private means and endowed the Abbey with property that he might have inherited? . . . gifts that did not come out of the revenues of the Abbey itself. I really want to form a clear judgment of the matter and must apologise for troubling you for what perhaps I could find by a little search. But oh, the number of questions requiring a little search that press upon me now!

Gasquet's notes and correspondence certainly modified Gairdner's strictures. He only asked him to abide by facts and regretted that 'so excellent an historian, to whom the entire world is so much indebted, may stray from the path of history into the realms of romance, once the signposts of facts have been disregarded.'

Their relations form an excellent example of how historians should treat each other in private when differing in public.

Another great historian with whom Gasquet had clashed during the battle about Anglican Orders was Duchesne. It was typical that having won that battle handsomely, he invited Duchesne, when under a cloud, to attend as his guest the International Historical Congress in London. Duchesne answered: '*Il me semble que frappé, et précisément dans mon œuvre d'historien, je serais peu qualifié pour représenter, dans cette réunion la science Catholique. Tempus tacendi*!' This was tragic, for Duchesne was in his work as great and fearless as Acton.

In the same volume in which Gasquet defended Wallingford, he collected old articles on 'Adrian IV and Ireland,' 'Polydore Vergil's History,' 'Roger Bacon and the Latin Vulgate.'

He had concluded that the English Pope did no such thing as give over Ireland to Henry II but the tide of history has gone against his view that the famous Bull *Laudabiliter* was forged. He allowed his article to stand, perhaps as a sop to the Irishry, with whom he was not always on excellent terms in Rome.

The papers on Polydore Vergil, the Italian historian of Henry VII and Henry VIII, and on Roger Bacon's amazing understanding of the lines of Higher Criticism in Scripture, were types of information that scholars welcomed in Gasquet's researches. With his wide access to foreign libraries he filled gaps in English Historical Criticism. In his tremendous zeal and unresting travels he passed from subject to subject, reading papers out of his varied knowledge to Congresses and Societies. But he never settled down to another *magnum opus*. Though his pen never lost its industry, he cast aside the dusty fetters of Museum and Record. He preferred writing articles, introductions to the books of others and speeches as his means of expression. Hurried by manifold labours and mounting duties, he never had time to look back. He became careless and indifferent to contradiction. He left corrections to those who enjoyed making them. His sense of historical criticism, blunt and sturdy rather than subtle, allowed curious lapses from the strict standards which modern scholarship demands. But the bulk of his work remained immensely valuable. The learned must excuse the inevitable bias of selected facts and a certain untidiness in presenting them. The enthusiasts of English historical prose must look elsewhere for glittering outbursts and Shakespearean characters pleasing to national pride. Some of his work is obsolete and may safely be jettisoned. The mighty avenues which he cut into the forest of mediaeval history remain. It is incredible that one pen drove so long and exhaustive a furrow, for he never really had time to be a historian.

The Anglican controversy at Rome he won because he had the trumps in hand, to say nothing of a few up Edmund Bishop's sleeve. The controversy over the Monasteries left him with honours easy. In many of his controversies he won the game but lost the rubber. He lost over the Old English Bible by calling the wrong suit. The discussion on the Black Death was difficult to summarize. He played his facts carefully on the short and obvious scale but he lost to conclusions on the long view.

Adrian Morey must be quoted again in summary of Gasquet's achievement:

> One of the greatest of all the services which the Cardinal rendered was to open up new fields of research among neglected archives and to suggest new subjects for development. . . . Cardinal Gasquet broke a silence of over forty years and restored literary labours to their traditional position of importance among the English Benedictines. If in England today Catholics enjoy a place in the intellectual life of the country far

different from that of the days when W. G. Ward compared
their relations to the Protestant world to those which exist
between barbarians and civilized men, Cardinal Gasquet has
played his full part in effecting the change. In Acton the
Church had possessed the greatest English scholar of the
Century, but his conflicts with ecclesiastical authority had
restricted his influence and crippled his activity. To Cardinal
Gasquet fell the task which Acton in less troubled times would
have accomplished—that of breaking down prejudice and
misunderstanding in the world of Letters.[1]

Strictly speaking, Gasquet was not a trained historian. His
failure to write History in the grand manner was due to a certain
unwillingness to reason or think to a standstill. He was content to
flow between his chosen banks. He took pains without suffering
the pains, which in scholarship as in life bring the great horizons
in sight, when *le pourquoi de sa misère est le pourquoi de son succès.*

When the book on the Monastic Life appeared there was a stab,
perhaps justified, from the Jesuits. Father Birt wrote in anguish
(August 12, 1904): 'The number of reviews is simply prodigious
and *all* more than laudatory *except* the *Guardian* and our friend
the *Month*.' Gasquet's friends suspected St. John Hope of the
former and Father Thurston of the latter. Gasquet was described
as 'overwhelmed with all sorts of occupations both administrative
and literary' which does excuse much of his hasty popular work
in later years, but there were some stabs so bitter that a detective
might wonder whether Dr. Coulton was a Jesuit novice at this
time. Birt arraigned the *Month*:

> Thus we decently stab and inter our friends! I am the more
> furious as Gerard the editor has never received anything but
> kindness from Gasquet. Anyhow in the *Vita Antiquissima* I
> think we managed to wipe the eye of Grisar of that ilk which
> is some satisfaction. . . . I have bided *this* chance since the
> awful life of Fr. Roberts and I can bide some more for the
> agricultural colony near Berkeley Square. *Tout vient,* etc.

The family quarrels between Benedictine and Jesuit are part
of the merry life of the Church, and it is pleasant to note when

[1] *Art. cit.*

they join against a common enemy. In the end Thurston proved
Gasquet's most effective defender. At the time of the *Month's*
assault Gasquet suggested that 'the *Month* with *Thirst-on* should
amalgamate with the *Civilta Cattolica* with *Brandi*!'

No doubt Gasquet wrote conscientious history, and the propaganda, out of which all history is composed, will be found
littering the depths as well as the shallows. The most careful and
accurate transcriptions of contemporary documents leave as much
to the Final Judgment as the pious fraud or the biassed interpretation. Most documents were propaganda in their day before they
sank into the sediment of Museums and Record Office.

Quis custodiet custodes? Who can sufficiently watch the watch-
men who peer into the darkness of the past? Who can adjudicate
the trustworthiness of materials flashing into the historian's ken?
History, when resolved by introspection, is not an exact Science,
however exact the superficial may be in the historian's work.
Gasquet, no doubt, would willingly have commended all his
writings together with the criticisms of his critics to the only
Judge Who can appreciate the pitfalls and blunderings through
which the conscientious historian must find his stumbling path.

IX

LETTERS OF ABBOT GASQUET TO EDMUND BISHOP (1885–1903)

June 2, 1885: The Church is making great progress and in a couple of weeks we shall have the whole ground-plan worked out in stone. The more I see it rise, the more impatient I get to see the choir. It will certainly be the most like one of the old Churches of any in England.

August 1, 1886 (Lochnell House, Argyll): My *Index* is rapidly approaching an end. The *Cromwell* correspondence has been done for some ten days. . . . You ask about the people round about. We have about 24 Catholics mostly belonging to the house and to these I hold forth every Sunday. The rest well! they are nothing. I really believe they have no religion of any kind. The only people who have any go are the Episcopalian lot. Their Bishop Chinnery-Haldane is the beast who said Mass at Holy Sepulchre. He gets his places up just like Catholic churches and it is sad to think that he had already 'taken in' many Catholics[1] who have been left to their own devices. I am looking over Ardmucknish Bay, a most interesting old rock with a buried fort on top. In a quiet way I have been grubbing there. (Photo of) this rock that will fall when handsomest man passes. . . . Then at the foot of *Ben Cruachan* (oh such a dear old mountain with a great heavy base—like a genuine O.S.B. of the 19th century) is Sedaig Moss the site of an old lake dwelling.

September 12, 1886 (2, Russell Road): It was such fun! at Paddington Station when I was seeing Dom Leo off I came 'bolt' upon the President. I think he didn't want to see me, but I had 20 minutes and I had it out. I said: Look here, I want to know what you are going to do about me. If you don't like what Rome

[1] Including a pious Breton innkeeper, who was only disabused by the appearance of Mrs. Chinnery-Haldane!

has done you should write and say so; but if you do not do this,
then you must give some sort of countenance to what I am doing.
I never asked for it and don't want it—though I think it will do
good—and it is unfair to go on as you have been doing. He said:
Oh I could not write after the Pope has said what he has said and
you must go on with the work. I said (wickedly): Would you
like me to write and say you don't approve? On no account, said
the P: it would never do to take this line. Then I think, replied
I, that you should aid and help me, not speak against the thing
as you have done. This however I have cleared up, namely, that
I am to be left to my own devices. . . . Isn't it *Ben Cruachan*! . . .
The fact is very few ever realize what it is to *study* and this was a
dreadful disheartener for me of old. The *habitués* of the Record
Office seemed so genuinely glad to see me back again at that dirty
old place and it was really a pleasure to find that anyone cared
what the d—— you did.

October 2, 1886 (Record Office): I have sent off a roll of MS.
on which you may perform any of the usual simple arithmetical
processes of addition or subtraction. How long is this kind of life
to go on? I miss your valuable self very much. At present I am
engaged at the *Pension Books* and Baigent[1] is very urgent that the
mine should be worked out so I am going through the *lot*. There
are only 30 huge folios and I have got through three! Excuse this
scrawl, written with Record Office mud in the midst of the dust
of ages.

October 9, 1886 (2, Russell Road): Many thanks for your last
castigation after which I felt better. Did you notice my letter in
The Times against Dr. Littledale? The Cardinal [Manning] wanted
me to do it and I never expected they would print it. It is looked
upon as *cheek*! and people laugh about it. Baigent says I am like
the man who wrote a book and then went to the Museum to
look up his facts. Be that as it may I don't see why Dr. L.
should always be telling lies about us [presumably 'Reasons
for not joining the Church of Rome,' but very helpful to
converts].

[1] Hampshire Antiquarian and convert.

October 17, 1886: I am getting through the Patent Rolls of Elizabeth's reign taking three a day. What I am looking for is old 'Barlow' and I am personally satisfied that the beggar was never *consecrated*. I have been doing a little Lambeth also. Old Billy Barlow is called *episc electus* in all the documents relating to S. Asaph. Most of the quotations I make are referred to by Gairdner but not *quoted*. . . . Don't say I didn't warn you. We must hope for some *deus ex machina* but my belief is that Hercules would have to be a fool to him. Nobody but a supreme B.O.S. can hope to do the trick and make the O.S.B. but *magna est veritas*!

November 1, 1886: As to other libraries which ought to be visited they are many—Oxford of course where there is much that Father Stevenson says should be looked up. Also the Belgian libraries, particularly the Burgundian at Brussels and the Lille library. . . . What would be very delightful is if Gilbert [Dolan], you and I could pay a month's visit to the foreign libraries and if my suggestion to the Prior of Lord Bute being invited to pay and what is as important—if he do so stump up—'why should us not' as they used to say in dear old Somersetshire.

November 29, 1886: What am I doing did you say? Well I have written the rough draft of a chapter on 'Suppression Act of 1536' tomorrow I start Chapter ? 'The *Comperta* and other charges' . . . what I do now is to write all the morning and then go to Record Office or Museum for the afternoon, but what I begin to feel is that my collection is getting too big to be within the compass of one volume. *Tres digiti scribunt, totum corpus laborat. Qui scribere nesciunt multum putant laborem.* Oh! it is weary work.

December 12, 1886: For a little Xmas recreation I am going to send you *Souvenirs d'un Journaliste Français à Rome* by H. des Houx. It gives a very amusing account of the Roman officials. It wouldn't do for the weakminded as it puts very strongly what may be called the human argument for the Divine Origin of the Church. I generally go to the Record Office in the afternoon for a couple of hours. On Friday I found the record of the conviction of the Abbot of Colchester and the Abbot of Reading but not Glastonbury.

December 19, 1886: Yesterday I went to help the old parson in his Church of Holy Trinity, Minories, and we hobbed nobbed like two thieves over the fusty tomes. He can't read the old writing well (neither can I for that matter).

December 24, 1886: This is the first Xmas I have spent at home since 1856 I believe. I should have liked to have come to Downside but thought I would stick to work till Sunday when I go to Gillingham and perhaps to Wardour to look at a book, a Quarto of Visitors' Letters. I wish to goodness you were still up in London to pitch into me about your *feu sacré*. It wants blowing up sadly sometimes. Why the deuce, I often say, should I be digging and delving like this and not now enjoying mine ease at my own little fireside like a true *Ben Cruachan* of the good old time. 'Dem it I'll be a body' of Mr. Mantalini is the real philosophy, or the highly moral song I heard at Lancaster Terrace— 'He's *not* going to work any more.' Why should he? This is a serious question which I am sure it would take the collective wisdom of all Anglo-Bs to solve. *Quod semper, quod ubique, quod ab omnibus—nihil!* is my motto. Now to be serious. I have got the Visitors, villains all—Layton, Legh, London and ap Rice done for in the rough and tomorrow I fancy they will be put in the drawer till after Xmas. I shall then be proposing to inflict you with another lot of MSS.

January 24, 1887: From my lofty Eminence of the eremitical state, which as S. Benedict says is the calling of only a few, I may sometimes be allowed a grumble. Wednesday I saw a certain Baron von Hügel, such an enthusiast about work, Greek MSS. of the first centuries and early Biblical matters. He found it so hard to keep up the *feu* without help or sympathy from Catholics. The only people who seemed to care were Protestant friends. He reminded me of you except that his hair stuck up on end. Friday a long talk with Dr. Boligo the Vatican Jesuit, who says Englishmen don't care about serious work. In his view they are all *Ben Cruachans*. Pity he doesn't know a few of ours thought I! His experience in the Museum is that there is work for a lifetime and the only people he has got to care are Protestants. But his learning is very dreadful—Coptic, Syriac, Hebrew, etc., all going at once and it makes one feel what an old owl one is. He says nobody knows what it is to go on without sympathy or help, who has not tried it. This did me good and I nearly clapped the old gent on the back in Oxford Street, but his coat looked so dirty I refrained for fear of making people sneeze with his superfluous snuff. . . . Lately I have been doing work for the *Martyrs* and have not been doing so much of my own *magnum opus*. The work is sometimes very heavy and I wish I had never begun it, but then one feels better for a good grumble.

January 31, 1887: We might have a chance of meeting at Oxford. I thought you would have plenty to look at in Bodley-Liturgies!!! and then you could help me by advice and moral support. Altogether I expect we shall have a high old time, if you come to the work with your usual good humour. One day I should like to make a descent on East Hendred as I see something among the Egerton Papers. *Tunc* on the way back why should we not try the *Registers* of say Worcester or Gloucester? Fr. Stevenson is very urgent to do the thing properly and look at all accessible registers for Visitations. By the way Cardinal Morton was a *oner* at visitations and didn't he wig the Prior of Folkestone! The good Anglo-Benedictine deserved it I fancy, as he had preferred to live in London for 20 or 30 years and would go and do his *three* months in his monastery. . . . Wouldn't I just send you on a mission if I could—writes R.R. *Dom Praeses*.

February 8, 1887 (Oxford): I have just returned from my first day at the Bodleian bringing away 13 closely written pages of Visitations in Diocese of Norwich 1574. Really it is wonderful what a picture these same Visitations give one of the house. All the time I am saying: 'Pon my word how like they were to us! One Prior makes a boast after his *dicit quod omnia bene* that he has saved £2,000. But it is as good as a play to see what the community have to say: Their grub is bad, the bread and beer beastly and the meat unwholesome *quia morbide*. By the way I have quite found out the meaning of *comperta*. It was in ordinary use for all the Visitations and means the *tales* of religious on each other, true or imaginary as the case may be. . . . I find that one can work here from 9 a.m. to 10 p.m. That is if you are able. I find that 9 to 5 is about as much as one can do good at. I often think of what you used to say that there was a point when you would do more by giving up. I know the point now exactly when I feel myself turning into a writing machine. I am quite close on Benedictine quarters, a stone's throw from Worcester.

February 20, 1887: The worst of Oxford is the climate. There is something very depressing and I have felt more 'heart' here than for many months. The *social* requirements are also very much too much for me. Thursday I dined at Christ Church with Canon Liddon (very interesting evening). Tonight I dine with the Fellows of Exeter and so on. It is very dreadful.

March 27, 1887 (2, Russell Road): I went off to see Gairdner almost as soon as I got here and it is too true that Jessopp is bringing out these Norwich Visitations . . . he wants to discuss Layton & Co. and get my ideas. Also I am to take my MS. and show him what a real Visitation is like. . . . I have asked the Cardinal to try and get me access to the Duke of Bedford's Papers. There must be a mine there, neither friend nor foe has ever seen them. The Cardinal thinks he can manage it.

April 8, 1887 (East Bergholt): I think Gairdner has *bitten* about the great value of the Visitations. He has had those Oxford copies of mine for a fortnight and I think we shall see the result in his next preface. Now can you help me to the *pedigree* of Abbot Whiting? I have found in the Museum and in the Record Office a good deal about the Whiting family but I cannot *fix* Richard yet.

April 14, 1887: I quite take your view about help given to others coming back like bread upon the waters and shall, as I have said nine hundred and ninety-nine times, be very ready to help you or any you may think worth helping. . . . I find that

Richard Whiting took his M.A. at Cambridge in 1463. He must have been considerably older, when made Abbot, than the witnesses thought and hard on 80 when executed. I do not think there can be much doubt that he was a descendant of Xtofer Whiting. *They* were Somerset and one of them made Sir Amyas Paulet his executor. The same gentleman gave evidence as to Abbot Richard's age. . . . By the way I found the original depositions against Abbot Marshall of Colchester the other day. They are as fine as anything of that time on the Primacy of the Pope.

May 22, 1887: I have glanced through the *Notes* and approve of all I read but I wonder whether others will. My eye! won't there be a squall. You know I am a horrid coward, and like to be on the top of a hill to watch a fight now. How curious! It used not to be so and I have had my share of fighting. Now I am at work on that much-maligned woman 'the Holy Maid of Kent.' When that is done, I have laid myself out to do Wolsey's *suppressions.* . . . I should like to have a volume out this year to present the Pope!! What do you think of my cheek?

May 24, 1887: Although you certainly know how to damn with faint praise, I am only too thankful to have such a careful critic. Your notes did remind me so very much of what our old lay-brother Francis Rea said of a sermon of which the preacher was rather proud: My dear Sir, the text was excellent. So you think with one or two corrections the first page of my poor production is good not even *excellent*!! I am only joking of course, for I really am more than grateful for all you have done. The only thing I am doubtful of is whether it is quite honest now to put my name at the *end*. . . . I find that Dixon, though invaluable and excellent, still is founded *only* on printed matter. He never read a document in his life and what is more, they told me at Oxford that he couldn't if he were to try. I should like to have started a theory but it is not quite worked out. The more I read, the more convinced that England never understood the Primacy as being *de jure divino*. To most it was the result of convenience, discipline. Christendom required it but the Divines even clearly did not know the Definition of Florence in 1440. Fisher even does not quote it nor Sir Thomas More use it but he studies the question from the Fathers beginning with *Ignatius*. None of the Bishops' Registers with the exception of Nykke of Norwich in 1532 mention that the Bishops hold their see *gratia sedis Apostolicae*. Fr. Stevenson to whom I propounded the theory says he believes that it is quite new and would explain a great deal that has puzzled people about the Reformation. Of course by Elizabeth's reign the Catholic party had learnt by experience that Rome was the only rock on which to rest the faith, but I feel certain that it was not understood before. The attitude of clergy to the Primacy in Henry VIII's days was like that of Gratry to the Infallibility [a French Oratorian at the time of the Vatican Council]. If this be so we can understand them saying let it go awhile, we can get back to Rome when Henry VIII has had his fling.

May 26, 1887: A line to say that I was only in joke in my letter and that I quite understood the spirit which prompted you to 'cut me up' as you did. I am only too thankful for anyone to do it, I can assure you. In the Record Office they have put a stop to the use of ink (d——n). It is such a dreadful nuisance.

May 28, 1887: Now about Hereford. The Registrar was very polite and put me in a room with all the books. Very shocking! but it suited me to the ground. I went through the Registers from 1453 to 1539 . . . all tending to show the Monasteries were looked after and in good order. The most important thing I found was the answer to the stock charge made against the Abbot of Wigmore. You may remember he is charged with having sold the plate etc. of his Abbey to bribe the Pope to make him a Bishop. There is also a letter from one of the Canons there containing a variety of charges against him. Almost the least he has done is murder. Well first I have got the letter of Bishop Booth of Hereford to the Pope asking for the Abbot to be made his Suffragan as he is old and infirm. Then I have the most curious Visitation made in 1537 and evidently after the letter of the Canon. This visitation by Bishop Fox practically shows up the accusation and frees the Abbot.

June 26, 1887: In the Museum I have made great friends with Mr. Fortescue and also the big man Jenner, son of the Bishop [of Chester]. They are both Anglicans and we have great fun at times. I will always persist in calling them Protestants and forgetting that the Queen is not the Head of their Church. They are very nice indeed to me, will do anything for me.

July 23, 1887: I suppose you got the Whiting article I sent you. I had 50 copies but they are all gone but a dozen. Hodges asked me to let him have one and yesterday he said he was reading it when old Gladstone came in. The old boy wanted to borrow the copy but Hodges told him he would ask for another, which I gave for our illustrious ex-premier.

August 28, 1887: I go to Peterborough for one day and then to York for a week's work. Don't you feel tempted to join me there? After that a fortnight's holiday at Bordeaux and Lourdes. Then I shall come with my MSS. to Downside to go through them with you. . . . I have ordered Gairdner's new volume of the *Calendar*. So don't get that. There is lots of Layton's filth in it, but on the whole a fair Preface saying that the reports can't be relied upon. The said Gairdner has hardly been fair to me, as having had my *Norwich Visitations* and my having pointed out to him how many of the Monasteries mentioned in the *comperta* had been visited by the Bishop, he refers to old Jessopp for this information.

September 2, 1887 (York): Yesterday I remained six hours at Peterborough and was very delighted. The West front is a thing to be dreamt of. One great thing is that you are left alone to wander as you like. One thing that struck me was much very late work, same as *Henry VII* or perhaps more like Bath Abbey. The monks must have been very busy for fifty years before the Suppression. . . . Over the great gateway are two statues. One of St. Benedict: lifesize with his hood up and this same hood is ours exactly. In the exhibition of relics of Mary Stuart there is a very curious old chair. It must have been the Abbot's. All the figures carved on it are turned towards the East, I suppose to the Altar.

If so, it must have been on the Epistle side. One of the figures is in a cowl and with our hood.

November 5, 1887: What did you think of Wolsey? I fear some Catholics will be grieved. . . . It is the greatest satisfaction that you have been over the proof. What I do is to read and correct and then get my brother to go through and add his suggested corrections. Then I wait for yours and do ditto. My brother has read the Introduction and thinks it will 'fetch 'em.' Certainly if people will give 7/6 for the Essay on Thomas Cromwell by Fr. Cuthbert they could give 9/6 for mine. At any rate I have put together a great deal of scattered material. 60 copies are ordered through me. 4 O.S.B. have paid.

November 7, 1887: You forget that I am not 'pleading a case.' I quite admit that the 'Holy Maid' might have been made to look much more holy. Still to me there is great force in the fact of Fisher's previous good judgment. His subsequent opinion was like Sir Thomas More's based on the assertion of Cromwell and his crew that she had confessed herself an impostor. In the same way I read Cromwell's anxiety to entrap Fisher, as meaning that he wanted to involve him so as to force him on the King's side in order to save his life.

November 9, 1887: I saw the Cardinal [Manning] yesterday. He looked over some of the sheets of my volume and expressed himself delighted. He read the *ad Pedes* which he liked making only one suggestion to leave out 'by the Author.' It will thus run:

At the Feet of His Holiness Pope Leo XIII this volume, the first fruit of labour undertaken in obedience to His Supreme Command, is, on the occasion of His Sacerdotal Jubilee, laid as a testimony of entire filial devotion.

The Cardinal said there could not be the slightest objection and he was sure the Pope would be pleased . . . some very kind letters from seculars. Only 3 O.S.B. have so far sent in their names.

December 13, 1887: Perhaps my ambition to have a book on the shelves of the Reading Room may be realized by means of it. Who knows?

January 7, 1888: After many days of anxious waiting for the fulfilment of broken promises my first volume is on the table before me. It looks—well I won't describe it, but leave it to you. I am satisfied.

February 4, 1888: I should be sorry to repeat all the Cardinal said. It beats even the *Catholic Times*. He said he had read the whole, every word and a good deal twice. Even as a literary production he spoke in the highest terms. 'There are passages in it,' he said, 'that ring in the ears.' He showed me the notes he had made for the *Dublin Review*. . . . I am beginning my 'cinder-sifting' again on Monday and shall go steadily to the Record Office till Easter.

February 12, 1888: Like a good fellow always put down what you think will do for the coming volume. One has to live up to the *first* now. I have made the acquaintance of Dr. Collett. He is the most splendid old Protestant and with good temper and chaff: we get on splendidly. He says that in the second notice he will say that I have completely proved *my point*. I have had six hours a day at *Minister accounts* this week and am getting on into them. The Record Office people are uncommonly polite to me just now.

February 29, 1888: I do not think you need fear the effect of success on me—at least I hope not. I put it all down to the Cause. Certainly no one could ever have expected the book to have been received as it has been but it's the Cause not me. The Record Office and six hour's dirt and cold is an excellent specific for pride. When you are only *cinder-sifting* and shivering in the East wind during your occupation it is good for the spirit. I read your paper last night to the *Gild* in my very best style as it deserved. All I can say is: I wish I had written and you had read it—that's all.

March 8, 1888: I told Fr. Maurus to tell you that I had got on some splendid Rolls in the Record Office. They are consecutive and perfect accounts of the *plunder* of the monasteries and have never been used. . . . The Dep-Keeper was spoken to by Gairdner and they agreed to aid me in every way. Gairdner has himself been in two or three times to the search room and he says that now he shall only generally work upon the Dissolution history and leave me to tell the consecutive story.

April 19, 1888: A line with a review from Creighton[1] in the *Historical*. It is *nasty* and I fancy that Creighton sees what others have not that the volume really attacks the Anglo-Catholic position and is angry. However I should be glad to know the 'obvious sources of information' I have neglected.

April 22, 1888: It is in all the Clubs I am told and the Carlton has *two* copies on the table. At St. Paul's they have it on the library table and ditto at Syon College. But apart from that what does it matter to me? I have tried to tell the truth for the *public* which does not see the State Papers. Have you seen the Cardinal's article in the *Dublin*? People are already talking of it in Dublin and H.E. Card: Manning's view will do good perhaps at Rome. ... Now I am hard at work copying depositions in the Pilgrimage of Grace. There is much to be learnt from these papers that Froude thought well to leave out. First there are some delightful touches in Aske's *declaration of events* about the good the Monasteries were doing in Yorkshire which will come in *beautifully*. Then there is nothing to connect the *Abbots* with the Rising except that they probably furnished the people with food and no doubt gave them their good wishes. ...

May 13, 1888: I have just finished the Pilgrimage of Grace papers. They are A.1. For my purpose Aske's declarations as to the Abbeys might have been written for me. The language is grand and reminds me of *Shakespeare*. Froude must have seen them but then he left out all that was good—the beast! ... Did I tell you that Cardinal Newman has sent me a few lines?

July 15, 1888: I saw the Cardinal yesterday and he had quite taken your view about my not appearing in the matter of the article *re* Gladstone. At the same time he did not want to put his own name to it, and hence when I saw him, he had sent it with

---

[1] Bishop of London later.

the name of Fr. Bailey who has fathered other things for him. He said he had read it carefully and considered it a perfect answer to Gladstone. He was sure that the *Nineteenth* would put it in. . . . There was only rumour about Persico at Chapter. It will be very interesting to see whether Rome does what it assured several it would or whether it is only Italian *diplomacy*?

October 15, 1888: Of course I might do a great deal more in Chapter I about the *cold-blooded* manner. In the Chapter on the *spoils* I have tried showing what devastation there was throughout England. The fact is that I want you to discuss with most terribly. To most people what I put down is new and they say: good! I had no conception of that. You know more than that.

October 22, 1888: Many thanks for your castigation. I'll be more careful; but you are somewhat hard upon me. I adopted every one of your suggestions as far as I could. . . . I have no doubt that your English is better than mine, but as the sheet stands I do not think it is absolutely atrocious. No doubt I shall be ready for a Liverpool mission and let someone else take up the *cinder-sifting*.

November 6, 1888: I am just off to Westminster to see Dean Bradley from whom I have had a very kind letter.

November 10, 1888: I had a visit from and a delightful chat with Dr. Jessopp. He has promised to lend me some transcripts of the Cellarers' Roll of Ely, which gives all the dinners for a long period in the convent.

December 7, 1888: Rome is going to insist upon our congregation being put on the same *basis* as every other Benedictine body in the world. . . . It is impossible not to see that we have won the victory for which we have contended and suffered these ten years. Our views are declared to be the only sound ones.

December 16, 1888: I quite agree with Goethe about small things in history being everything. Do you remember Macaulay's Essay on History? His thesis is that very thing.

February 7, 1889: I shall have finished the Westminster book (Ain't it lovely? What fools we have been not to have worked on these things before) in about another six weeks steady work but I am determined to get it. Also in the Harley MS. Register of Barnwell Priory there is a lovely piece about the life of the *Canons* which must be worked. Oh, for two hands and ten pens, but they grow. Now as to Henry VIII, he is going off steadily. I have had letters! Oh how pleasant these things are and how enervating they would be had they not been born out of the forty days in the desert with nothing but Rolls and dust.

June 12, 1889: I am at the York MS. What rite by the way did the York monks follow? No doubt you will know all about it but the introductions of long prayers for King and people into the Canon of the Mass after the Pater Noster was new to me. Also the order for the priest to wash his hands after the Ablutions and the communicants after communion at the *piscina*.

October 1, 1889: I saw Manning today. He tells me that his letter to the Pope went off. 'It was as strong as I could make it,' he said, and I do not think they will let the matter alone. This accounts for the milk in the cocoanut. I am looking forward to getting at Cranmer and his Breviary again. It was deeply interesting. Today at the Record Office all I got was an important letter of Gardiner's a few weeks after Henry's death about commissions for the Bishops.

October 14, 1889: I have made out that the *corrector's* hand is that of Cranmer. The Harl MS. of the *Reformatio Legum* is drawn up in the same way and the corrections in the same hand. A note by Parker or Cecil says this is Cranmer's hand.

July 1, 1890: Protestants are beginning to talk and their special wonder is: can it be true that there are documents we have not yet seen after all that has been written?

July 7, 1890: On Friday Christopher Wordsworth came to the Museum and asked to be introduced to me, said many Anglicans were looking out for this book with great anxiety. He added that when Archbishop Benson had heard about it, he said that he 'always felt sure there must be some such documents in existence and would be most glad to see them in print.' I wonder whether they will be so delighted when they have read the story?

July 17, 1890: Really it began to look as if the devils in Hell were conspiring with their printing namesakes to prevent the book coming out. . . . I was amused to be told by an Anglican that they thought we were keeping back the book so as to coincide with the judgment in the Lincoln case. I did not tell him that our great fear has been that the Archbishop would be ready long before we were. Bishop Stubbs has been for a week at work in the Record Office on the papers of Elizabeth's reign.

July 25, 1890: Proofs with changes have just gone off. I had to strike out about the King being present at the Debate because after three hours' hunt I could not find that he was. Donaldson, chaplain to the Archbishop of Canterbury, writes to know when they may expect the book to be ready.

October 24, 1890: Legg has sat up all night and gone right through the volume. He says the facts are indeed painful for Anglicans; but that it is impossible not to feel that we have studiously avoided making them more unpleasant. As to the documents on the Prayer Book he says that it is impossible to exaggerate the importance. He fears Anglicans with small minds will be sad but if the facts are facts they must be faced. I said Amen and told him that if he could show that we were wrong or had expanded any fact we should be very glad to change what we had written.

December 8, 1890: I am sending two reviews. One, the *Freeman*, requires to be read with the brogue. The other, the *Guardian*, has astonished everybody. It is wonderful and would be quite satisfactory but for the fact that it only mentions my name at which I am really humbled and distressed. . . . You don't know how I miss you at every turn and I do not believe I should have the courage to go on working by myself again.

January 18, 1891: Our meeting at Downside was a grand success. Our people came out splendidly. They spoke out like men and the other side behaved no less well throughout. They listened most attentively to all we had to say and they could not but feel that *we* were acting on *principle*; they on mere sentiment and *feeling*. Talk of good temper and fraternal charity I never saw such an exhibition. To me the meeting was the most enjoyable thing I have known for twenty years. I forgot to say that in the middle of our meeting a letter came to me from Cardinal Rampolla saying that the Pope had received with the greatest pleasure the evidence that I was still labouring hard at the work he had charged me with and sent to me and *Sig. Edmondo Bishop suo collaboratore* his special pontifical blessing.

May 22, 1892: I have great hopes that we may be able to do something good before we die. I have come across a most interesting book in the Record Office—two complete years of the household expenses of Abbot Litlyngton of Westminster (1371-3). You have no idea of their great interest or rather *you* will understand. You can follow his journeys—the dinners he gives to nobles and to the tenants. It made my heart beat in thinking of the picture one ought to be able to bring out of its dull pages—and if I can only paint my picture with your help, be it added—the life of a great Abbot in the reign of Edward III.

May 29, 1892: Sunday last I went to call on Lord Emly. I talked to him on what we had contemplated about the 14th and 15th centuries. . . . He was in a position to guarantee £100 a year for three years certain on two conditions, that I would certify that two people were devoted to the work and that I would only take a man who was fitted for it. He said: 'Write me a letter in Latin. I have certain means of getting to the Pope personally and I will take care that he shall know that you are really trying to start a school of historical research in England at Dulwich.'

July 8, 1892: Now for a bit of news. The Archbishop [Vaughan] is to receive the *Pallium* on August 16th at the Oratory. I am overwhelmed to think that on this occasion he has asked me and indeed insisted that I should occupy the pulpit. Now will you help me as you have so often done in this?

July 22, 1892: I send the first portion of the sermon. It is the first draft, so cut it up as much as you will. I have treated the origin rather gingerly for as far as I make out the *Pallium* was rather the natural growth than the original meaning. It is quite clear that St. Gregory meant it to signify St. Augustine's Archiep. power, but he didn't in every case mention it in his letter. Then the oath to Rome was later than the days of St. Anselm.

August 17, 1892: The ordeal is over. It was certainly a sight to upset stronger nerves than mine when I had to face 19 Bishops and about 400 clergy before getting into the pulpit. There was a vast sea of heads stretching right away. However in two minutes I was right and it is over. The *Standard* devotes a leader to my iniquity. *The Times* prints about two-thirds of the sermon. The *Chronicle* promises the attention of Anglicans. So you see the string is pulled. There was a parson just below me who absolutely squirmed once or twice.

August 26, 1892: The Archbishop said to me: Have you seen Fr. Thurston's article? What do you think of it? Rather sawdust, I replied. Oh I am glad you said that, says he, for it made me rather unhappy that this was all that could be made out of it. So you see your instincts were right. I have got the Archbishop to include in the ceremony the presentation of the Archiepiscopal cross with the old formula used at Canterbury as I found in Cardinal Kemp's Register. He quite entered into the idea of the thing and caught up the notion of making it as much like the old English thing as possible.

November 1, 1892: I have promised to write a lecture on Westminster Abbey for Catholic Truth Society. Hints will be thankfully received. Remember me sometimes in your prayers. I am rather in the *cui bono* state again and it requires all my will to keep my nose to the grindstone.

November 5, 1892: Six days continual hard work at the *Formelbuch* in the Museum has done wonders. It has been a mine and has given me a new idea of the social work of the Church, how much was done in the Church that is now done by the police court and higher courts. I had no idea that up to the crash the whole system of excommunication was in full force or that so many things were done in the Church on Sundays in the way of *bonos mores*, correction etc.

November 19, 1892: The Catholic Truth are pressingly anxious to have a small book about the Book of Common Prayer. I said I would consult you. Between you and me, I have had 'Fr.' Maturin[1] all day with me. You know who I mean. There have been such rumours of late that he has gone over to Rome. *A Cowley Father.* I never quite appreciated before what a plaster that book has been to the Anglicans and how dearly they would have liked to smash it.

December 22, 1892: I have been at work on Wyclif. I am convinced that the version attributed to W. isn't his at all. These versions are in use by good Catholics in the 15th century and to nearly all are added a table for use in the Epistles and Gospels of the Sarum use. Lord Ashburnham has the most important books and luckily he came the other day and introduced himself. I see by his catalogue one of the copies is dated in a contemporary hand 1347 and the earliest date given for W.'s bible is 1380.

March 5, 1893 (Naples): I cannot attempt to tell you all I thought of Rome the 17 days I was there. The Cardinal promised to do all he could to further the scheme I suggested. At the Libraries of the Vatican and the Archives I was welcomed with great cordiality. I went on to Monte Cassino for part of three days. I was delighted with the place and Amelli was kind beyond measure. The last week I have spent in Sicily. We saw Palermo and Monreale, enough for a trip in itself. . . . In these Sicilian churches one sees the Lenten veil still in use. Taormina was marvellous but Syracuse beat it hollow. If this doesn't set me up again on my working legs I shall give up. At present I feel as if life was being poured into me every day.

January 1, 1894: Of course you saw Dr. Bright's letter. It would be very easy to answer what he says, but I think for every

---

[1] Died as a priest nobly giving absolution on the sinking *Lusitania*.

reason it is best to keep quiet, especially as he admits what we contended, that he did take the *Pontifical*. His quotation from the preface of the Prayer Book of 1662 about 'equity' hasn't much to say to Cranmer in 1559. Dr. B. either is or pretends to be ignorant of the Lutheran and Protestant notion of the *minister* being 'called' and of the ceremony of Ordination being merely the public recognition of the calling.

September 17, 1894: What you say about Lord Halifax and Dalbus is most interesting and I have no doubt that it is best to give these Frenchmen rope enough. They will in the end find that their Anglican friends have rather made fools of 'em. What I don't like is that Dalbus should shrink from meeting Catholics. It looks as if he could suspect that he was wrong, if he dared. I too am much occupied with the wretched Anglican Orders business and feel quite sure that we ought to attack the question from its commonsense side of cold-blooded fact.

December 10, 1894: What set me on was the following which you had better keep to yourself. Never mind how I got the information. . . .

1. Through the influence of the French in Rome Cardinal Rampolla sent an invitation to Dalbus to come to Rome.

2. Rampolla tells him the Pope is much pleased with the attitude taken by Dalbus and really thinks he is destined to bring about a reunion.

3. On September 12 Rampolla takes Dalbus to the Pope and they have a long conversation. The Pope asked him what step he would recommend and Dalbus (evidently posing as a *Deus ex Machina*) says he believes the best plan would be for the Pope to write a personal appeal to the Archbishops of Canterbury and York. He thought that the Holy Father might write as an old man on the verge of the grave and the sentiment of the English would be stirred up by such an appeal.

4. This the Pope and Rampolla agreed to!!!! But three days later it seems to have crossed their minds that they might be only making fools of themselves so they informed Dalbus that at present this would not do.

5. Meanwhile Dalbus had written in triumph to his Anglican allies in England how he had assured the Holy Father of the real Catholic feelings of these Anglicans. Halifax apparently sounded the Archbishop of Canterbury whether he would consent not to snub the Pope should he write and Benson kindly promised that he would be civil at least.

6. When Rampolla and the Pope concluded not to write to their Graces of Canterbury and York, the Pope to show he had the best desire to consider the Anglican Orders valid said he would appoint Duchesne to study the question and report to the Holy See. He made choice of Duchesne because he had already declared himself convinced of their validity and consequently would be *persona grata* to the Anglicans.

Now all this would be quite beyond belief were it not that I have actually seen the whole thing in the writing of Dalbus himself. The thing was shown to me more or less in secret, but I thought it was too important not to let the Cardinal know in case he was ignorant of what these absurd French fools were doing.

[To this Edmund Bishop added in red ink—'The person (as I afterwards learnt from Lord Halifax) who shewed it to Gasquet was as I gathered from indications afterwards occurring, Wilfred Ward.']

April 27, 1898: I have been getting my thoughts together a bit for Lord Acton's Chapter on *Catholic England*, it's a world of thought and life. At present it is in chaos but it will I think shape into something. One must try and put the *difficulties* that existed straight and I shall like to have a talk.

May 24, 1898: The Dean of Gloucester was delightful. He made me stay for lunch and was altogether evidently most pleased at my visit. Made me promise to go again and told me that 'Henry VIII' had entirely altered his view about the monks. Also that he was the author of the 'Passing of the Monk' which was refused as likely to be unpopular in tone. Subsequently he strengthened his statements and the *Quarterly* printed it.

March 8, 1899: James Gairdner's letter was capital. How curiously it was like what you wrote in many places. . . . There ought to be a chapter upon the Lutheran movement in Germany I think just to show how it was the parent of our English.

March 29, 1899: I have a letter from some barrister who is engaged in the 'incense' case to come on before my Lords of Canterbury and York after Easter. He is against the use and wants to get information. I have written he may come and call next week but that I have nothing to tell him and that I regard the matter as 'nonsense' rather than 'incense.' I had a letter from the Cardinal asking me to let him have a scheme for 34 large paintings for the Cathedral and of course 'at once.' I sat down and wrote out the first thirty-four incidents which seemed proper and today he writes: I am greatly obliged for your well-considered scheme. It is certainly by far the best that has yet been suggested.

May 17, 1899: Father David writes: I was sent for after writing to you and had a long and hot discussion with Cardinal Vannutelli and the Primate. I held my ground and all was *definitely* settled by the Pope next day. You are appointed President of the Commission and the Bull will be out at once. We had the Pope clearly and definitely on the right side. That is certain.

May 25, 1899 (Ushaw): The young men are quite 'hound up' and have been working themselves in the libraries with Wilkins and Lyndwood and Rymer. Mr. Philips, who is enthusiastic in his history work and who is one of the oldest Professors, asks me to ask you about the Stowe Missal, as to whether it was used certainly by the Iona people or Columban monks, whether the Pope is named to be prayed for in the Canon, etc., and what *date* you would give to the book.

June 25, 1899: The reception by the Duke [of Norfolk] of Archbishop Ireland last night was a very brilliant affair. Today I am to lunch with him at the Grand and tomorrow dine at the Athenaeum, so I shall have done my duty to 'old Ireland.' People are wanting tact. Someone told the Cardinal that Gibson [Lord Ashbourne] and Dell (who very unfortunately are I notice coupled together) had been telling it as a great joke that they had succeeded in making the obscurantist Cardinal and the old Tory

Duke do the honours to Archbishop Ireland. Gibson had tried to get me to go down to him. I have politely declined, especially as his invitation was pressed on the ground that people could talk quite freely.

July 1, 1899: I saw a great deal of Archbishop Ireland. He is a powerful man and a man full of life and interests. What, however, struck me more than any other point was his caution. I thought it best to let him know exactly what I thought of the O'Connell and Gibson lot and what harm I thought that kind of free-lances did the cause. To my astonishment he quite agreed. He said that he had told them so in Rome and begged them to hold their tongues and be prudent. His task he said was to put out the useless fires they had lit and he attributed all the present reaction to their imprudence. . . . The Cardinal told me that one of the things our friend the Primate hinted to the Roman people was my 'advanced Liberal views.' At present all our ends are best served by work not talk.

July 6, 1899 (R.Y.S. Alvina): Your letter was the first intimation that the bomb had burst and of its nature. This is of course what we so strongly urged in Rome—make it clear! Really it is something to have lived to have seen the burst up of the old regime. What a blessing it is that we can hold our tongues. Had we not been able to do so, things would or might have been quite different.

July 12, 1899: I have read and re-read the Bull. It is a 'oner' and no mistake. What must certain people feel who have 'mistaken' the Pope's meaning? I have not heard a breath of what people think!

October 23, 1899: The *Eve of the Reformation* is promised without fail for tomorrow. I saw Nimmo and he tells me that the whole edition is subscribed for. The news is turning us all into very bloodthirsty mortals. I found myself joining a chorus of *Rule Britannia* at Waterloo Station on Saturday as a send-off to a train of officers.

August 15, 1899: Meantime I enclose some *proof.* I see I have not got the *folio* marked in three places. If you would look into the Volume I (bound in red) of Early Printed books, it is behind where I sit on the top of the Rolls books near the window, I dare say you could put in the foliation. Will you correct and send to Nimmo. As I always take your corrections it will save time if you will send direct for me.

October 19, 1899: In Tuesday's *Times* there appeared a long letter (2 columns from Mivart) and a leader on it in which *The Times* was hugely delighted at the frank admission of 'one of the most learned and enlightened of English Roman Catholics.' What a pity it is that Mivart can't stick to his 'biology.'

April 3, 1900 (San Anselmo, Rome): Here I am in the lion's den and a very comfortable den it is. They have given me a double room with everything I could want. Yesterday I started our business about Bishops and Regulars. It was lucky that I came when I did, for today is the last *Congresso* before Low Week and at first Budini declared that our matter could not be included. I pleaded that we all wanted the matter pushed through as quickly as might be and finally he promised to help in this. I urged that there was no reason to treat our Statutes as if they were *new* and that they need not go to the Commission of Cardinals . . . to see whether they meet with the provisions of the Bulls. If this be possible, the matter need take very few weeks. Please tell the Prior but tell him to keep my plan to himself as no doubt if the Primate gets word of the thing being settled in his absence he will try to delay it. I find that the Monsignor, who came to Ormond Street, has just been appointed Archivist at *Bishops and Regulars* and a great deal of power to expedite documents depends on him. He was delighted to see me and said he would do anything in the world to repay the kindness he received. . . . I am promised access to the Archives of Propaganda and Father David will see whether he can find any trace of Dr. Barnes in the Holy Office so will you let me have the exact title and date.

May 3, 1900: The Primate returned last week and we had a long interview. He will not try conclusions again and will make no objection to any of our proposals. He was much astonished to find how far I had pushed the Constitutions in the time I had been in Rome. Meantime I am having four hours every day in the Propaganda Archives. They only begin about 1626 and so far I have not come upon anything of great interest for O.S.B. I am taking a note of every document about English matters and there are plenty. One curious letter from Richard, Bishop of Chalcedon in 1629 asks for the removal of Father Gerard from any connection with English College at Rome and a lay-brother porter at Valladolid, because of their undoubted connection with the Powder Plot! The Bishop says he has evidence that the lay-brother was one of the men who made the excavations.

June 3, 1900: The situation here is the following: the Primate has sent in his animadversions on the Constitutions. . . . I had a bad quarter of an hour at *Bishops and Regulars* yesterday and thought that there would be another long period of delay. I told you that both Serafini and the Primate suggested a re-arrangement of some of the papers. They were no doubt right and these portions were very 'jumpy.' I had great work to arrange this and Father Mackey and I were at it for several days. I took a list of these changes and the Secretary said: this can't be allowed without returning the whole thing to the Commission. After arguing for some time he allowed me to sign the document as President of the Commission so it was fortunate I was here. . . . By the way in Propaganda there is a long account of a Commission held under Cardinal Barberini to consider the Greek Ordination Service. As one member was *Bona* and another *Morinus*, you may imagine that the discussion was most interesting reading and I fear it kept me from copying more in my own line.

June 10, 1900: I am sorry to hear that John Vaughan's eloquence has given you a chill. . . . I hope that our affairs will be taken but there is no absolute certainty. The Primate is pushing as well as I and Cardinal Gotti has promised. I feel with you that I am bound to wait and see the end. . . . I have taken notes from the Commission on Greek Ordinal. It is very important for the history of the Sacrament of Orders. One thing is quite clear, that the theologians of say 1638 quite understood that the tradition of instruments was merely accidental. One of the Commission explains the Instruction just as we do today. I hear that Wilfred Ward has written upon the very matter against Gore in the *Pilot*. My informant says he gives the case away. . . . I have made new friends and the one with whom I enjoyed my talks most has been the Archbishop of New York [Corrigan]. He has urged me very much to write something on the *secular* and *regular* difficulties, which monopolised the energies of Catholics in the 17th century. He is sure that it would be a great thing to have a calm statement of the main difficulties at issue, as in the present day the lesson of the past is needed. I have the key to the Bishop of Chalcedon's [Richard Smith] departure from England. On the whole I shall come back not altogether empty-handed.

June 15, 1900: The inevitable hitch has come at the last moment. Cardinal Gotti has thought it better. . . . I have had to write out four copies of the *changes* and send them round. I got them off within 24 hours after the Cardinal had so settled. . . . It is fortunate I was still here. Had I gone, the whole thing would have been hung up over the holidays. Of course this makes it all the more necessary to stay on altho' I confess I am very impatient to get off. Such is life! Another difficulty is the Pope. Cardinal Gotti has not been able to see him for five weeks and as the *vow* question has to be put to him it cannot be got on with. The Primate has been very good and went with me to Gotti to try and induce him to hurry up.

July 3, 1900: You see I haven't got away yet! Saturday did not bring the signed decree as Cardinal Gotti had promised nor yesterday. The delay is simply the great difficulty experienced by all now—even Cardinals—of getting to the Pope. Cardinal Gotti tells me he tried to have his audience and settle our matters but failed. . . . I can only wait and wait. I shall be very delighted to get North for I have found the heat of the last fortnight rather too much. For three nights I could get no rest.

August 26, 1900: It is terrible to think what a monstrosity of a mitre a Frenchman like Pécoul might produce for one but he is

evidently very exalted about the finish of the Constitutions and
the Election. Tomorrow I go to Stanbrook for a day. I suppose
it is really a good thing to let the poor things pour out. 'It never
rains but it pours.' I find myself committed to a sermon at
St. Bede's, Manchester, to celebrate the declaration of St. Bede
as a Doctor of the Universal Church. Dr. Casartelli won't let me
off.

September 27, 1900 (Downside): We have had a really enjoyable meeting, 64 of us—and the sight in the church at the installa-
tion was a thing to remember and I saw the tears running down
the cheeks of several. We kept to the letter what we had talked
about as to the boys, who were there in the Chapter room (the
monks' Refectory) and went in the procession to the church with
us—such a *Te Deum* as I never have heard (and the same the Mass
for Holy Spirit in the morning). The *corona fratrum* stretched from
the lectern right round both sides of the sanctuary to the steps of
the altar. The boys all came up for the kissing of the hands after
the monks had done. I am today quite pumped out as you may
imagine.

November 12, 1900 (Rome): A few lines only. The function
yesterday was prodigious! Thirteen Cardinals assisted and
Rampolla acted as Legate *a latere* for the day and the Mass was
Papal with the Greek as well as Latin. I consecrated the altar of
St. Boniface and said the first Mass on it today. There were
present a dozen or so Bishops and 57 Abbots. The work of
preparation for all must have been terrific and what it must
have cost! Still I think it was worthy of the Order.

November 17, 1900: The English were much to the fore and
today to the astonishment of the Primate and the others I have
secured a special audience to which we are just going. The Pope
has *signed* a special blessing for the Congregation also.

May 16, 1901 (Ditcham Park): I can't shake off my feeling of
'swollen head' but I suppose it will go sometime. Monday I went
to Baigent and had that afternoon and Tuesday morning at
Wykeham's Register with Kirby's print. I was pressed to try and

go back to Petersfield by road on a motor car. I foretold a break-down; but was assured such a thing was now impossible, but the impossible did happen and I was landed nearly six miles from Petersfield with my bag and no means of getting a trap. No more motor cars for me!

June 20, 1901 (Dublin): The Purvey MS. is certainly interesting and had it not been for the *wish to believe* I fancy we should never have heard about it. The Monogram is one of the many scribbles which scribes indulge in and it is certainly not *Pervie* and I believe is *Perive*.

December 16, 1901 (Great Ormond Street): One line to say that I was sorry to find that the inevitable had taken place, when I got back this morning and you had departed. It makes one think of all the years we have lived and worked together and as you say I think we should, on the whole, be satisfied with the results. I feel sure that your move was the right thing for you to do and in every way you needed and need a long period in the sun and air and without the excitement of London life. Don't forget that we shall always be glad to see you when you want to come up to this 'Babylon' for any purpose; but at present . . . who knows what the future will bring.

January 3, 1902: The enclosed will interest you. I told you of our move in Rome twelve months ago and of Father David's and my interview with Volpini and the Pope. You see we have carried the thing and even to Robert Clarke's appointment. I wonder what the S.J. will say!

[*The Times* announced the famous Biblical Commission with David Fleming as Secretary, 'England being represented by the Rev. R. F. Clarke, D.D., of Chiswick.']

My poor brother is very bad and I could only make out a tithe of what he said. My sister the Abbess at Arundel is also worse and has received the Last Sacraments. *Pour moi* I have been going regularly to work this week at the Marini Transcripts in the Museum and my notes on Henry III's ecclesiastical politics are growing and taking shape. Still I shall not be quite happy and settled until a certain matter we wot of is put to rest by an appointment.

January 9, 1902: Father David writes that the Scripture Commission in Rome is highly approved of and equally disapproved of. The great point is to get the Romans to realise there *is* a question. The transcript of Bishop Redman's Register is to hand and I have spent two interesting days at it. The main interest is this: it was not the *Regest. Premonst.* which Peck used and you copied. There is not a document in the Ashmole which is in your transcript. They fit into one another and Peck is the earlier and most important. This raises a very big question of an interesting series of Premonstratensian documents in the two combined. . . . I forgot to tell you that the Syllabus you drew out for me years ago of your transcripts (strung on a bit of tape) came in most useful. My lecture at the Historical appears to have been a success. It was a record meeting—some 300 or so—and they were I think quite satisfied.

February 15, 1902: I have had ten days at the old Record Office. With steady work I have got through the Papal Bulls and have some 60 for Henry III not in Rymer—a good addition. I have also had a turn at the Roman Rolls, which, tho' too late for me, are most useful and instructive. Lastly I have had down some few of the vast number of volumes of Transcripts made for the *Monumenta.* It is too gigantic a collection to contemplate and there is no knowing what lies hidden there. The sight of all these lying in the dust since about 1835 is terribly depressing. Father David writes me that the Cardinal is trying to secure the appointment of a Dr. Burton to Clifton. He is probably a Northerner and not very well affected to Regulars. This is of course strictly between ourselves and as it might be anything but a good thing for Downside, we are trying to 'spoke this wheel.'

April 27, 1902: In the North I heard nothing but good of Dr. Burton. He is in no sense anti-regular in his dispositions, and is the best of friends with our O.S.Bs in the North. He is a capital speaker and a most genial man, a student who loves his books. So I hope that it is all right.

May 4, 1902: I have some news for you. I think I have con-clusively identified the relics at Douai as those of Venerable John Roberts and H. Wilson. I have got at Ormond Street two large bones (arm and leg) from them.

January 8, 1903: My visit to Douai was very useful. I got to the bottom of their tenure of property there. The Government since 1823 has always refused to look on them as *owners*, in the sense that they could sell. It is British and Benedictine but that is all. Further, from the first there were perpetual warnings not to claim to be 'religious.' They were to be content with the name of *Collège Anglais*. Personally I do not think there is any chance of their being allowed to remain tho' the Douai folk can't yet believe it. I fear that they will have to begin again in a humble way.

[On his nomination as Abbot-President Abbot Gasquet left a Memorandum which he entrusted to Edmund Bishop to keep for posterity (Bishop Papers: Downside).]

Today (June 27, 1899) I went by appointment to see the Cardinal. I found that he wanted to tell me about all he knew as to our affairs in Rome. Shortly after he got to Rome he had a visit from Card: S. Vannutelli who said that he was anxious to get the A.B.C.'s[1] affairs settled and that a hitch had taken place as to the appointment of someone to supervise the drawing up of the Constitutions. The Pope had desired to nominate me (F. A. G.) but the Primate had vigorously opposed such an idea and had urged in every way that the present President should be ap-pointed. Card: Vannutelli did not know what to do as he did not like to throw the Primate over altogether. The Cardinal told him what he thought and Vannutelli went away with the intention of making an end of the whole matter. Next day the Primate returned to the attack and Vannutelli told him that Cardinal Vaughan had been consulted and had suggested the nomination of F. A. G. This brought the Primate to the English College. The Cardinal described the interview as very warm. It was so long

[1] A.B.C.—Anglo Benedictine Congregation, not the popular cafés of that name.

that the Cardinal terminated it by saying that really there was no use going on talking as they could not agree. He said the Primate was most bitter against me in every way, saying that I was adverse to S. Anselmo's: that I had made no secret of this and that when in Rome had not gone to stay with the Benedictines and that I had written a certain *Preface* in which I had shown I had no real belief in Benedictine principles.

(Note by Edmund Bishop: 'What a mustard plaster that *Preface* must have been!')

I told him, said the Cardinal, that I had read the Preface and thought that had more people understood the Benedictine spirit as Father Gasquet had shown it to be, there would have been far less difficulties between Seculars and Regulars and that I supposed that what he did not like was that Father Gasquet had shewn in the old days, at least in England, there was far more union than in modern days. The Primate apparently had hinted at other things; but didn't say anything definite; but the Cardinal was quite under the impression that he had got certain tales taken to the Pope and amongst others that I was in opposition to his wishes about S. Anselmo etc.

The Cardinal said he told him plainly that Rome, in his view, would stultify itself hopelessly by appointing ——. The Primate went back next day to Vannutelli to try a last go to get his wish and Vannutelli told him to return later and meanwhile sent for Father David and confronted him and there was a long and angry dispute, as the Cardinal had heard. Cardinal Vaughan had, I gather, a few words with the Pope the same day.

On the next day again Vannutelli says the Holy Father told Vannutelli 'Put in *il nome di* Gasquet' and tell de Hemptinne, if he doesn't like it he may lump it, or words to that effect. Vannutelli told this to the Cardinal the same day and said that the matter was finally closed and would not be again opened.

October 4, 1902: The Oxford celebrations might have been better managed I think and the speeches were beyond endurance, but I was very pleased. I went everywhere in my habit and cross and even processed from Oriel to the Bodleian thro' the streets in it and certainly when I went up as the Vatican representative the applause seemed to be very great. Traube came up and introduced himself. I fear the S.J. were not too pleased. Fr. Erhle had appointed Fr. Pollen to represent the Vatican and at the last moment he found the Pope had already appointed me.

October 28, 1902: I think the [Harrow] nuns were pleased with their retreat. So far in the memory of the oldest nun they had never had any other food but Jesuit Spiritual Exercises and never had instruction on the religious life and virtues. They got nothing else this time and were at first lost as they could not believe a retreat possible without Hellfire and the Seven Deadly Sins.

December 20, 1902: We seem to have gone out of each other's lives altogether. . . . I am going over to Douay on the 30th to meet the Abbot and Council. My letter (in *The Times*) has been received with approval I am told in the Clubs and the Foreign Office has begun to move and asks for information. There must be more information as to the restoration of the property to us. Unfortunately the two O'Neills some ten years ago agreed that we were only tenants of the place and held it from the *Fondations Anglaises*.

X

CORRESPONDENCE

I will be correspondent to command.

SHAKESPEARE

AS soon as Gasquet became a literary figure and the best-known authority on Monasteries and what is called 'Church junk,' he found himself much exposed to correspondents.

Out of considerable accumulations we have chosen specimens of letters which arrived from all sources. As far as possible, he attempted to deal with them and to give advice and information gratuitously to Catholic or Protestant. Antiquarians, clergymen, liturgists and every kind of historian plied and pestered him with their queries. A considerable part of his timetable was choked by letters he felt bound to read and when possible to answer. They certainly prevented him giving the further hours he needed for any great work. The public seem to have regarded him as one of those amiable and ambulant members of the British Museum's staff: to be stopped, consulted and tapped by all.

But Gasquet was not a public servant. He belonged to the Benedictine Order and his main business was prayer and monastic works. History was only a task set him in convalescence. What he gave to outsiders was of his liberality, and no doubt because he thought it was good for Protestant fellow-countrymen to correspond with a live Abbot once in a lifetime.

They make a quaint letter-bag: Anglican Bishops and Deans, Antiquarians and Heralds, Shakespeareans and Sacristans, Lawyers and Editors. No doubt there were letters on more intimate and personal subjects, but these were not of survival interest. The immense collections on Benedictine matters must be left aside. All that pertained to Benedictine struggles and anxieties was a family matter. When the Hierarchy consulted him, he felt he could act as an impartial umpire: for Dioceses as well as Abbeys

The truth was that this was the time of Edward VII's delicate mission to Paris and it was the object of the Foreign Office to deal with the Quai d'Orsay in velvet gloves. The monks and treasury of Douai were sacrificed to an *entente* with a rabidly anti-Catholic Government.

Curiously enough the French Government had paid compensation after the Revolution for Douai but the sum had been dishonestly applied to building the Marble Arch!

In all public stresses the Duke of Norfolk and his brother Lord Edmund Talbot (Lord FitzAlan) were employed like a Catholic Castor and Pollux. They were expected to enter battle whether to save a Benedictine Liqueur or Abbey: to protect a trade-mark or compensate flying monks. Without those noble brethren the Catholic interest was constantly endangered or lost. In later days the Cardinal thanked FitzAlan for his work on the Catholic Relief Bill and the ex-Viceroy wrote (December 24, 1926):

> The real work was done in the Commons and chiefly by Francis Blundell who has devoted three years of persevering effort to it.
>
> But it cannot be too widely known that we owe an enormous debt of gratitude to our non-Catholic countrymen in both Lords and Commons for their generous support, in many cases in spite of a certain amount of prejudice and suspicion that somehow or other we were getting more than we were entitled to. The Archbishop of Canterbury [Davidson] was really kind and went out of his way to help. He told me the day before, he wished to speak and support, though he added: 'I shall have to say one or two things you may not like.' Afterwards he said he hoped I had not minded. I said: No, it was most kind of him and I knew he would have to *hedge* a bit!

Gasquet was interested in Relics which claimed to have been in Abbey reliquaries. The famous Hand of St. James the Apostle had been listed in the treasures of Reading Abbey since it was brought by the Empress Maud. The Emperor Frederick had wished for its return, but Henry II had refused and it remained there till the Dissolution, when it may or may not have perished. At the close of the 18th century a workman preparing the site of Reading gaol found an embalmed Hand which passed through the possession of various owners until safely landed in Great Marlow Catholic Church. Gasquet collected the available testimony from the antiquarian Francis Weale: but he never alluded to its genuineness except with a wry smile and comment. It had been exhibited by the Philosophical Museum at Reading with its proper label 'Hand of St. James' amongst specimens of preserved fish, which did not even have the distinction of claiming Apostolic capture!

Welsh antiquarians wrote for help in identifying a chapel and skeleton, found under the sands at St. David's near St. Patrick's 'place of departure from Whitesand Bay and it is stated that he received his miraculous vision of Ireland through seas and mountains while he was residing in this district.'

With the turn of the century certain alleged relics of St. Edmund caused trouble amongst antiquarians. The body of a canonized English King could only be regarded as a wonderful prize and there was immense interest in England when it was announced that the Pope had arranged for the body of St. Edmund, the King, slain by the Danes and giving his name to St. Edmundsbury, to be restored to England! For centuries his body, pierced by arrows, had been the St. Sebastian of England. For centuries his shrine and relics had been venerated in Suffolk until they perished under Henry VIII with all the spiritual treasure of the land. St. Edmundsbury became a ruin and the shrine a dust-heap. And more centuries passed.

But lo! A rumour based on archaeology, as deceptive as that which once deceived the pious Mr. Pickwick, came from France. It was believed that St. Edmund's body had been providentially stolen during a French raid and deposited in the Basilica of St. Sernin at Toulouse, whence it was brought to Newhaven by the enthusiastic Merry del Val (July 25, 1901) on the way to the new Cathedral of Westminster, as a counterpart to St. Edward's body in the neighbouring Abbey.

No greater annoyance worried the mediaeval or Catholic mind than false relics. Rome has always been busy discriminating and sealing genuine survivals from 'pious frauds.' This unrecorded rape of St. Edmund's body was described as a '*dévot larcin*,' but a mistake had arisen when a label of '*St. Aymund confesseur du roy d'Angleterre*' had been carelessly read for centuries as '*Saint Edmond Roy d'Angleterre*' causing the body to be enshrined and venerated as such in Toulouse. The arrival of this astounding relic roused Suffolk antiquarians like Dr. Montagu James and Sir Ernest Clarke to frenzy. They delivered shafts in *The Times* as deadly as the arrows that ever pierced the martyr. They proved it could not be the real St. Edmund, for whom Merry del Val was wrestling with the Custom Officers. The belief was abandoned but the officials made no trouble over any 'false declarations' made to them.

Cardinal Vaughan was deeply grieved and appealed to Gasquet as the only possible champion. In the previous year he had already brought him into play (November 16, 1900).

> The Toulouse Commission has finished its investigation of the authenticity of the relics of St. Edmund and is ready to send it for examination and observation to the Commission I named, the whole matter to be treated with secrecy until the last result has been attained. I proposed for our Commission yourself, Mgr. Moyes, and your author of the *Life of St. Edmund*. Will you act as President?

The Cardinal wrote (August 26, 1901) during the controversy:

> I don't know whether anything more will be said in *The Times* about St. Edmund: probably a reply will be written to *The Tablet's* leader. It seems to me that, if the occasion occur, a letter from you, in your cold and impartial manner of placing facts, arguments and conclusions, would be more convincing for *The Times* readers, than such replies as others might be tempted to send.

Unfortunately the letters in *The Times* had proved devastating, and Gasquet could not reassure the Cardinal. With all the known facts of history at his disposal, he advised him how impossible it was to have moved St. Edmund to France under Louis VIII, when there was record that Henry VI had prostrated himself before the relics at St. Edmundsbury so many years later. Could the devout have continued pilgrimages to an empty box? Could two monks have been on guard day and night to prevent the pious burglary of an imaginary relic? As for the claimant from Toulouse: 'most people must admit that the body is found in very doubtful company.' The *doubtful* company included most of the Apostles and St. George himself, 'Knight and Martyr'! It should be added that the same fortunate church was endowed with the head of the chaste Susanna, her virgin body having been providentially withdrawn from prying eyes for ever.

There was worse to come. Ten years previously at St. Edmundsbury Gasquet had described a mediaeval procession in which an arm of St. Edmund was carried. It had been hoped that this was the arm missing from the body brought from Toulouse. Gasquet now corrected himself and the Cardinal almost cried aloud, writing (September 1, 1901):

Many thanks for your paper which came as a crushing surprise. I had relied much on your *arm* but it is St. Botolph's! I shall insert an episode, quite short and as illustrating something else, in my Newcastle address. I enclose it and would ask you to return it *at once* with any note or comment that may occur.

On the back of the Cardinal's letter Gasquet pencilled a note from Edmund Bishop: 'N.B. Father Hitchcock's recollection according to Weldon of the taking down of the Shrine of St. Edmund—the *body there* at that time and hidden.' There was an exciting chance that like St. William in York Minster and St. Cuthbert in Durham Cathedral, the body of St. Edmund had been concealed. But it was too slight to build on, even for pious antiquaries.

On September 9 the Cardinal withdrew belief in the relic, which reached the chapel at Arundel and went no further.

Mgr. Hugh Benson, who was opening his literary Apostolate, wrote in 1904: 'I am beginning to think about a book on the times of Henry VIII a sort of romance'; and asked for lists of books on the Cluniac Rule, the Tudor Court, Lewes Priory.

Pius X had ordered Benson to be ordained Priest in his first year of Roman studies much to Archbishop Bourne's indignation, but as the smiling Pope said on the occasion: 'Who is Bishop of Rome?' Benson was shelved if not suspended and took to writing novels. The Bishop of Southwark was kind enough to allow him to say Mass in his mother's house (widow of the Anglican Archbishop). That good lady kept two separate cupboards for vestments in her chapel. One was labelled belonging to the Archbishop of Canterbury and the other to the Bishop of Rome! Benson's novels bore the mark of Gasquet's historical advice, although the tone and psychology were more modern than Tudor.

Reformers of the Calendar besought Gasquet to restore the Gregorian Calendar by obliterating March 21 for March 20 and enabling the Bull *Inter gravissimas* to regulate Time for the civilized world. He was implored to bring Mussolini into co-operation with the Pope on this matter.

Hadrian Allcroft appealed to him to settle whether Archbishop Cuthbert of Canterbury was the first to introduce cemeteries within town limits, as asserted by Weever and Dugdale. Edward Pennock wrote to confirm his statement that St. Gregory had directed heathen temples to be used as churches, for he had found burial urns in Lincolnshire churchyards, and Freeman, the historian, had told him the same thing of the West.

Canon Augustus Jessopp, the Norfolk antiquarian, wrote (March 8, 1892) from his rectory:

Many thanks for the *Scriptorium*. It is capital. . . . We shall have to get up a Society for printing unpublished Monastic Documents when the Camden comes to an end! You are quite right about these second-rate people who rush in where Angels fear to tread. As Lowell says:

Bad work's like sin
It's always wanting to be done agin.

I am earnestly longing to bring out my theory of the relation of the Secular to the Regular Canons.

Hartwell Grissell, the great collector of relics, Papal Chamberlain, and an amusing character claiming that he could produce a relic of some Saint of the day at breakfast throughout the year, wrote (July 30, 1892) to say that the only Pallium in England ever worn by a Pope was in his possession at Oxford. It was the Pallium with which Pius IX was invested but as he was buried in another, it had been acquired as a possible relic. Grissell was chortling because Archbishop Benson had written admitting that the Pallium was an anachronism in his arms. Benson had been carved on the Truro Cathedral throne wearing the Pallium, but orders were now given for its removal.

And there was the doubt about what oath of homage Anglican Bishops took. W. Bliss wrote:

> There is at least one living Anglican Bishop who does not know *what* he swore! It has often been quoted by Allies etc., but what is needed is to verify Lord John Russell's quotation of it in *The Times*. Where did Lord John get it?

An Anglican curate wrote anxiously to know whether the Excommunication of Queen Elizabeth in April 1570 was the real parting of the ways for English Churchmen. When was the date of the formal cleavage?

Mr. Fitzherbert Brockholes was much exercised about old stone-stoups 'which may have been Holy Water stoups and which were being used as drinking troughs in Lancashire farms.'

The veteran Positivist Frederic Harrison wrote (June 25, 1907):

> May I say how heartily I second your appeal in *The Times* today as to Roger Bacon—far the grandest man on the roll of Oxford. I hope to see the Pageant and I trust this ribaldry may be dropped. I have been on the foundation of Wadham now exactly 59 years and I am to occupy rooms I first entered from school.

Gasquet, who had a particular devotion to Roger Bacon, had protested in *The Times* on his behalf.

A Vicar wrote to ask if there was truth in the legend that, when Montalembert saw the ruins of Fountains Abbey, he threw himself on his knees and vowed to write the *Monks of the West*.

The Anglican Bishop of Gibraltar asked (May 2, 1908) help

in finding portraits of some mediaeval Archbishops of Canterbury, Kilwardby, Courtenay, Sudbury, adding 'is it rash to say that I forecast the far more eminent address which will naturally be yours in Rome before long?'

From Sarum Close came a request to ask whether the entry DE CATI PETRI in a Calendar could be a contraction of *Dies Catenati Petri*—the day of St. Peter *in vinculis*—in chains?

A glass-painter wrote: 'I am directed by His Grace the Duke of Norfolk to apply to you for the favour of information and authority as to the occasional use of a *cope* by Abbesses. Could St. Etheldreda be properly dressed wearing one?'

An interesting letter from Dean Robinson of Westminster (February 5, 1907):

> I have no ground for thinking that any breath of scandal touches Westminster. Under Islip it must have been well and his successor was a mere stopgap from Peterborough: for by 1532 it was pretty plain that all would have to go. But even though things were breaking up, I know of no scandal. Mr. Rackham is *desolé* to find he mistook your title. He knew of you only in your capacity of historian—too eminent for titles or prefixes!

From Cambridge the Public Orator, Sir John Sandys, wrote in 1905 for information, 'having been privately informed by the Vice-Chancellor that it will be proposed to confer honorary degrees on Father Deniflé and on Father Ehrle of the Vatican Library . . . you would be much better able to tell me of the points that an English audience would like to hear about both these eminent scholars.' Deniflé was a Dominican, who had hammered the Lutheran legend. Ehrle, later Cardinal, was the Pope's book-keeper in the great sense. Their 'honorary doctoring' did Cambridge credit, and the undergraduates improved the occasion in the Senate House by chanting from the gallery 'Call me *early*, mother dear,' which the good ecclesiastic mistook for an Anglican hymn to the Blessed Virgin being sung in his honour!

From Corpus Christi College, Oxford, Dr. Plummer wrote (June 26, 1904) in gratitude for Gasquet's edition of the oldest life of 'our Father Gregory who sent us baptism' and referring to 'the common interests and studies which unite us in spite of many things which divide.'

At the time of Archbishop Bourne's enthronement, the *Surrey Herald* was writing anxiously (March 7, 1904):

. . . nor do I like the *fimbriation* [colour-border] of the *pall* but prefer the *pall proper* as borne by the earliest Archbishops and now by Decree of His Holiness Leo XIII *gules* (in honour of the English Martyrs) an Archbishop's Cross *or*, over all a *pall proper*. All this was definitely arranged and I made the required drawings and supposed that the grant would suffice for ages to come as had been the case from the days of St. Edmund till the Funeral of Reginald Cardinal Pole. To my astonishment I find on the ceremonial for the enthronement the double-barred cross at the back of the shield is ignorantly repeated thereon and is meaningless, null and void. You and I have formerly enjoyed old English Heraldry and will sadly see the *invincible ignorance* on the subject. . . .

Such are the tragedies of Heraldry!

'The arms of the See of Westminster are those of the ancient Archbishops of Canterbury—on a *red* field instead of azure.'

From Hornby a clergyman announced the precious find of a half-ton bell dedicated to St. Benedict, which he was anxious to rescue from 'dishonourable obscurity,' that is to say—it was suspended in a Protestant church tower.

It has always been a slight scandal with English Nonconformists that the Religious Orders should brew expensive liqueurs. Gasquet was interested in the trade-marks of the foreign Benedictines selling their brew. In the action taken to restrain thieving traders using their name it was successfully proven that the ancient recipe existed in the Order 'and that in most ancient Orders a laboratory for compounding liqueurs and medicines for the use of the poor and sick has existed without being recorded.'

When Gasquet was tackling the most famous Divorce of History—Henry VIII's, which depended on whether he was properly dispensed to marry his brother's wife, Nevill Geary wrote (July 26, 1899):

I rather drew the conclusion that if the case had been argued out before the Rota, there was as a matter of mere law a very good chance of nullity being decreed. The Dispensation did not remove the impediment *publicae honestatis* which coexisted with affinity. Also its validity was impugned as obtained *obreptione vel subreptione*. I don't think Froude even attempts the question of Law.

From the King's Armoury, Sir Guy Laking wrote (December 22, 1916) for information about the goldsmiths who worked for the Vatican in the second half of the 15th century, producing the famous ceremonial swords which:

1. Pope Pius II gave to the Duke of Brandenburg.
2. Pope Innocent VIII gave to William of Hesse.
3. Pope Alexander VI gave to the Duke of Pomerania.

'Can your Eminence substantiate this statement, as I am anxious of proving that these workmen existed and carried out the work they are stated to have done?'

The Diplomatic Bag was employed to forward an antique Cross from the Duke of Marlborough to be blessed by the Pope and duly returned, Mr. Harris having 'told him that I thought your Eminence would be able to get it done. The Duke is going to become a Catholic and is anxious to present it to Cardinal Bourne.'

James Bryce invited Gasquet to a *tête-à-tête* (May 8, 1904): 'We have so many historical interests in common that I should highly value an opportunity of having some talk on historical topics.' So the author of the *Holy Roman Empire* met a future Prince of the Holy Roman Church.

After a tussle over Shakespeare the actress Mary Anderson wrote:

You have thrown a new light on many things for me—a light that was needed in many dimly lighted corners. I find that there are five signatures of Shakespeare *authentic absolutely*. I was talking with a great Shakespearean yesterday and he feels that Shakespeare had much help from many poets but agrees with me that one master-hand had done the plays. I was wrong about his signature in the marriage register, but I am glad about the other things. I can never bear that Shakespeare should have anything taken from him. It is so hard to build up, so easy to pull down and I am always ready to fight for Shakespeare (as you saw) but in this case you knew so much more than I did.

When Father Thurston attacked the Rosary tradition sacred to the Dominicans, as an antiquarian, both he and his critics sought Gasquet's opinions. Thurston wrote:

I have expressed myself ill, if I have anywhere left the impression that I am laboriously trying to prove that the Rosary vision is not authentic. That would certainly be flogging a dead horse. My point is that before Alan de Rupe there is not a shadow of evidence to identify the Dominicans in any way with the Rosary. It all goes to pieces when you touch it. For all proof we are referred to documents that have disappeared and which cannot be examined or criticized—Bulls that Alan de Rupe says he saw. . . . Bollandists and Dominicans alike have assumed that a *Paternoster*, wherever mentioned, was to be interpreted as a pair of beads for saying the Rosary; when once that presumption is destroyed, the whole aspect of the evidence changes . . . I have not the slightest wish to pose as an iconoclast; all my instincts are conservative. When I first began to work seriously at this Rosary question, I had only a vague idea where it would land me! I hoped to come to something which one could recognize as a real immemorial tradition. Like yourself I should regard that as relatively speaking a bit of *terra firma*.

I cannot too often repeat that it would be much more to my taste to vindicate a papal tradition than to attack it. I should be delighted to unsay upon evidence given what I have hitherto said. But a tradition which can only be traced to such a personage as Alan de Rupe, 250 years after the event commemorated, I own does not satisfy me.

Thurston could be just as hard on Benedictine scholars, one of whom he reported to Gasquet: 'It has accidentally been my fortune to read a good deal of him. He seems to have very odd ideas about the correcting of proofs and the use or neglect of

inverted commas. I think that intellectually there must be a screw
loose somewhere.'

From Dublin Father Walsh wrote to ask him to persuade
Lord Coventry to permit search for a document covering the
examination of an Irish Dominican, Father McGeoghegan,
executed at Tyburn in 1633.

Cardinal Vaughan was asking:

> Did not St. Thomas of Canterbury kiss hand of the King?
> Is there any tradition as to what Bishops did in the way of
> homage to the King before the Reformation?
> Can you give instances of the term '*Roman* Catholic' being
> used among Catholics in England before the Reformation?
> Can you give me any rules governing the liturgical services
> and attendances in Cathedral Choirs by Secular Canons before
> the Reformation?
> I hasten to thank you for your valuable hints and for Mr.
> Bishop's pamphlet which I will keep a little longer. . . . I have
> said that the opening will depend upon the readiness of the
> Clergy and Choir. I am quite resolved not to open with the soul
> of the Cathedral inchoate and untrained. The structure is no
> more the Cathedral than flesh and bones are the man.

Anglican parsons were constantly in Gasquet's blotters. Father
H. M. Evans (who became a priest in Southwark) was writing
many years before his conversion asking an interview 'as I really
want to hear the Roman Catholic side of this dreadful controversy which separates us fairly stated.'

Father Evans was Rector of St. Michael's, Shoreditch, when
he came over with his curate and most of his congregation. He
was sent to Rome with Hugh Benson and shared in the speedy
ordination ordained by Pius X, as he said to show the English
Bishops he was Bishop of Rome!

From Pusey House came a letter from a future Abbot of
Downside to say he had resigned the office of Vice-Principal of
Wells Theological College—Henry Leander Ramsay. Requests
for interviews came from future Monsignori like Arthur Barnes,
and Somers Cocks, all Anglicans at the time.

From Bishop Moriarty of Shrewsbury: would he consider an

Archaeological Society's request to correct the Bishop's rendering of a mediaeval document? 'It is to be published in the *Transactions* and I think they are somewhat jealous of my name being mentioned.'

Though he corresponded with historians and antiquarians in the different Orders, his most familiar and informing letters were reserved for his own.

The Benedictine Abbey of Stanbrook was a favourite resort and source of family affection. During the years of his Presidentship (1900–14) he was a frequent visitor, bringing his work to be discussed and typed. The actual typing was done by a blind nun, whose work, so he gladly told, was specially admired by the printers. He gave forth his excellence in retreat or recreation, which an Abbess described as 'splendid, happy and very hilarious.' He was a Father amongst his children.

A considerable correspondence was filed by Dame Laurentia, with whom he exchanged information, dear to pious antiquarians and mediaevalists. He was genuinely pleased when elected to the Athenaeum Club. 'As I only knew one of the committee personally and had many most eminent competitors, we must take it as an honour done to St. Benedict' (February 7, 1903).

April 14, 1907: Your discovery about the Commentary of Odo of Asti is very interesting indeed. Mr. Cockerell's letter is very interesting. Poor fellow, he wasn't an 'infidel,' only one of a large type who 'don't know.' . . . As usual work is turning up. I wish I could turn myself into a 'limited liability' Company. Since Thursday I have had to undertake an *Introduction* to a new translation of Jocelyn of Brakeland and a volume to be illustrated by water-colours on *Great Abbeys of England*. The publishers are to spend £1,000 on the production.

August 1, 1907: I fear you will think I have been treating you rather badly: but the fault is your own. You and Mr. Cockerell together brought a perfect hurricane down upon me in the shape of Edmund Bishop. He is adding and 'swearing' all day long. He's been to the Museum daily and after all it has strengthened our former conclusions and he is now writing a second part to make it clear that we were right. The proofs must stand yet a little while and I think that the Calendar of Bosworth will have to be put in tabular form with the other Canterbury ones. Meantime enjoy your retreat and pray for me.

December 7, 1907. *S. Anselmo, Roma*: Here, as the light is really too bad to read at night, I am in bed at 9 and so get always the pig's allowance of 8 hours. I wonder whether I shall ever see straight through this job. It is like a terribly tangled mass of thread and where the end or ends are I don't know. The Pope has written me such a nice letter and to have got it within three weeks is a thing to be proud of. The poor *Bosworth Psalter* looks as if it would never appear. I should like to have copies sent here.

January 23, 1908. *Sant' Anselmo*: I have got my head in a bag and cannot find time for anything else whatever. The days fly by and the nights go as they haven't for 20 years, for I have for the most part delightful sleep. I have got two excellent aids, D. Donatien de Bruyne of Maredsous and D. Henri Quentin of Solesmes. They are quite the best people I could have got. They don't agree always; but it is delightful to get these foreigners by the ears and then 'bang their heads together.' They don't quite understand me yet. I am so different to their own Reverendissimes. At present we are just beginning to print a *text* for the purpose of collating. It is to have a twin column of text and the rest of the page blank, to collect the variants. The book will be a bibliographical curiosity I think, but I shudder to think what it is going to cost. However Stanbrook must have a copy. I am beginning to think the *Bosworth Psalter* is destined never to see the light!

This he signed '✠ (his mark)', as though he were illiterate or a Bishop!

July 6, 1908: I have had great trouble about the MS. with the Trustees of the Estate, who naturally want to get all they can in the interest of the Estate. Meantime the Museum authorities are pressing to know whether the MS. is to be offered to them or no. I don't think you need wait for my corrections when you have Bishop's, so push on. I have not got the MS. but handed it back to the owners at once. So we must get the Calendar through with the photos as you promised you would.

Yes, make up the verses indistinct in Bosworth from *Vitell. E. XVIII.* [MS. in British Museum].

November 30, 1908. Sant' Anselmo: I have treated myself to three days in the Archives of the Vatican away from the Bible. I went to try and find something more about *St. Albans* and Cardinal Morton. I have unearthed in my three days *three* unknown documents which all are confirmation of my article in *The Tablet* and I hope to find some more if I can manage to steal some more time.

Abbot Pothin is here next door. He looks feeble but is sanguine about his *Antiphonar*. Would that someone could stop him! I always detest the Hymn-tunes of the Solesmes. They destroy the Feasts for me with their unmusical phrases! I'll ask the old gentleman (I mean Abbot Pothin) where he got his Psalms but he is a difficult man to talk to as he seems as incapable of expressing himself in human language as he is ready to compose ancient melodies.

The manuscript of the *Bosworth Psalter* with another found at Turville Petre was sold to the British Museum for £3,000 by Gasquet. 'The officials are quite satisfied that, though a big price, it is a fair one and in confidence told me that I had exactly hit upon the figure which they had set as the maximum they would ask for.'

January 18, 1909: I am sending you a copy of our Gospels for you to make the collations. If you mark the capitals under the letters and correct the text it will then represent the text of your Gospels. I fancy that these must be of Anglo-Saxon origin. . . . Here the whole thought of everybody is still apparently in Messina and the possibility of an earthquake here. I am glad to hear about the *Hymnal*. It will be a great matter to have some of our old English folk-songs. Next door the 'holy old gentleman' is still occupied composing his 'ancient' Gregorians.

August 9, 1909: The four pages of the Gospels are very early 8th century, if not end of the 7th. They are not unlike the great Canterbury Gospel Book in the British Museum. The other two are very curious. I have never seen a hand quite like them but they are probably of the Ninth century. I am spending the mornings collating the Psalter of St. Augustine and it suits me well.

January 20, 1910: It is a pity about the diocesan *Imprimatur* but mistakes will happen in the best regulated convents. . . . Just now I have in hand a very interesting Psalter of the 8th century and am preparing for a meeting of all our Commission at Easter time. I told the Pope how the nuns at Stanbrook were at the collation of a Bible from photographs. I think he was much impressed by the learning of the ladies.

January 22, 1912: Though I don't think I waste my time, still the days race by and at the end of each I have to say another gone and so much left undone! Well so much the better, if one is only fit and with the help of *strict* diet I can work against anyone now. Today I began at 4 a.m.—had my Office and Meditation finished by 5—

5–6 work at the old MS. of Vercelli (such a terrible task).
6.15 Mass.
7 Breakfast.
7.15–8 MS. again.
8–11.30 work at bringing collations together with Dom Cottineau.
11.30–12 Little Hours etc.
12 Meal (and quite ready too).
2–3 Walk.
3–4 Office.
4–5.30 more work with Dom Cottineau.
5.30–6.30 letters (Four) and now 6.30 I am writing—see you have my day.

[After 1914 he humorously added a 12.30 dinner followed by a drive in the Cardinal's funeral coach!]

Abbot Pothin returned last week. Of course the new Psalter has upset his applecart and whether he will get it to go again remains to be seen. *Semper cantat* (next door) *Semper componit* (ancient melodies) *Tu autem Domine miserere nobis*!

October 13, 1912: Yesterday I had a most delightful chat, for that it was, with the Pope. You should have seen us winking at each other and almost nudging each other. At least he

13

nudged me and ruffled my hair with his blessing as I went away. I had gone with the intention of getting something settled about my present state as a carpet-bagger with no home to call my own, but he wouldn't listen to that at all and so here I am quite the same with all the larger issues of my life still uncertain and my age now 67.

Father Philip and I had a very pleasant visit to the Austrian Monasteries. The Lord Abbots live in rather more state than I try to do at Harpur Street: but I'd rather *not* try, I think. Marble halls, vassals and serfs in evidence and compelled to live as a great *panjandrum* isn't my style at all . . . I find the Primate really better but not what he was. The Pope had got it from the Beuron people that he was coming to resign his office. I don't think this was what he intended by any means. His idea I fancy would be to *be pressed to continue*; quite another pair of boots.

April 23, 1914: This is St. George's Day so I steal some time to write a letter to you. This place is getting into some order now and last night we had the electric light for the first time. This is a great advance and at night the huge corridors don't now look 'spooky' as they did. It will be ideal for our purposes and I hope a centre for Benedictine work long after the Vulgate is finished. The Pope talked of this as his ideal and hoped the Order would take up a monumental edition of the Fathers done on the same plan. The garden is a joy and in my workroom from early morning to sunset I have the sun when there is any to have.

The repairs and furnishing are running away with the money. But the Pope said—don't fear. I'll see that you do not want. See what a letter I've scribbled, for which you must be grateful to St. George and not expect another for ever so long.

Dame Laurentia noted:

This letter reached me on Monday April 27. On the same day, at 11.30 a.m. a telegram from Downside announced Gasquet Cardinal. Two days later came a postcard—'Will you please let me have a copy of my arms which you have at Stanbrook. In the present circumstances I should prefer "legs" but "arms" are required. Oh what a rush and what a lot to do.'

The Cardinal's Arms were very handsome. Upon his shield the insignia of an Abbot-President were empaled:

Sinister a double cross with PAX enwreathed in a crown of thorns. *Dexter* a *soleil d'or* on a sky *azure*. And on *vert* below a cock *argent* combed *gules*. The whole shield was surmounted by the *Rubra galera* or Red Hat with the fifteen tassels fluttering on either side.

Gasquet wrote scores and scores of letters to his correspondents of an antiquarian nature. Writing to F. J. Baigent, the Hampshire historian, about a Nun's Brass in Nether Wallop Church (December 13, 1888):

> One line. My instinct was right—a Rot. Pat. 8 HEN V m 14 is royal assent to the election of Mary Gore formerly sub-Prioress of Ambresbury to the office of Prioress vacant by the death of Sibilla de Montacute October 12, 1420. I feel great satisfaction in having unearthed this good lady.

To this letter (the only one of Gasquet preserved in the British Museum) Baigent noted: 'As the Gore family were settled at Wallop at the time of the Dissolution of the Monasteries, there is no doubt but that this brass was brought from the Abbey Church of Ambresbury.'

It is preserved in the *Baigent Papers* which Gasquet later presented in 36 volumes to the Museum.

Gasquet had been the only Catholic subscriber to the Anglican Canon Randolph's Exeter Registers, who wrote (Xmas Eve, 1888): 'I shall be very proud to number you amongst the subscribers . . . it is my most earnest desire to do justice to the great Prelates with whom I have been living in spirit for these three years past.' Baigent later wrote (May 20, 1889): 'How grateful such praise coming from a Catholic must be to his heart especially from a priest. There is a hidden power in it we little know, we who are in sunshine while others are in shadow and mist.'

To James Durham, F.S.A., he wrote (December 15, 1906):

> St. Michaels Mount in Cornwall was an alien Priory of men and annexed to *Mont St. Michel* in Normandy when at the

beginning of the 14th century the alien Priories were for political reasons suppressed, but *St. Michel* appears to have continued as an English House for another century. We learn from the Register of Bishop Stafford of Exeter (F 124) that the last Prior was appointed in 1410. His name was William Lambert and he was a monk of Tetbury—a Benedictine House in Staffordshire. I have not got Oliver's *Monasticon Exoniense*; but that should give an account of the House. But I think, without going into the question, I can say that the house of Mount St. Michael belonged to the Benedictine Order not to the Gilbertine, that it was a house of men and not women.

Two correspondences lasting over a great many years must be illustrated, for through them Gasquet kept in touch with Roman affairs before he had been made a Cardinal. Both correspondences dated from the strenuous Nineties, when they were all deeply involved in the Commission on Anglican Orders. Merry del Val (Cardinal after 1903) and Father David Fleming (Franciscan, Consultor of the Holy Office and Secretary of the Biblical Commission) wrote to him continually.

LETTERS OF CARDINAL MERRY DEL VAL

Gasquet and Merry del Val prided themselves on their English birth, but their extraction, French or Spanish, gave them the larger view of a Universal Church. What their united efforts on the Commission had done to bring the *Ecclesia Anglicana* in or out of the Communion of Rome can only be realized in time. The later Malines Conferences and every surreptitious approach between the two Churches was bound to break on the breakwater which Gasquet and Merry del Val had laboured to build. Merry del Val later as Secretary of State did not find Gallicanism so easy to crack as Anglicanism. The paths of the two Cardinals separated, but they kept in touch and Gasquet received letters such as:

August 26, 1897: I have not seen the Holy Father [Leo XIII] for some days but I will see to the matter you mention as soon as possible. It is a question which, if brought up at all forcibly, will probably be passed on to the Holy Office, where I fancy your view would be considered the most acceptable. . . . I should like to have a talk over this Canadian business. My mission was a painful one in many ways. I don't know how I got through it. Looking at things from the standpoint of the interests of the Church and of the salvation of souls (and I can take no other) I consider the situation out there most serious and critical. Since Cardinal Taschereau's illness there is no one at the helm in Lower Canada and the line of action followed of late is, to my mind, simply suicidal. Under wise and prudent guidance Canada might be the bulwark of the Church on the American Continent.

It was curious how the Dreyfus Case and the Boer War had combined to cut England off from Catholic sympathies abroad.

November 9, 1899: I am afraid that some recent events in England (*e.g.* the passionate and foolish outbursts in connection with the Dreyfus case) make people here wonder whether the tradition of common-sense of English people is not beginning to wane. At present correspondents of some English papers are sending malicious misrepresentations of what the Catholic papers say commenting on the War. I am surprised that the Cardinal [Vaughan] believes all these to be well-founded. There is certainly scant sympathy here for England in the War now going on in Africa but the feeling is general and not exclusively Catholic. As far as Catholics, it is due to a variety of circumstances which make it natural however unpleasant it may be for Englishmen and for those who love England. The disgraceful breach of faith on the part of Lord Salisbury's government with the Holy See in regard to the marriage question in Malta, the language question in that island, the Irish University add strength to the anti-English feeling among ordinary Catholics and which is traditional since the Italian Revolution.

During the troubles over Modernism (April 4, 1906):

I had already heard years ago that Newman had declared that he was not a theologian, but I had never learnt the source of the information. I must say I should not have styled him a theologian. What I do think is deplorable is to push one's worship for a great man to the pitch of claiming infallibility and all but inspiration for every word he ever said or wrote

during a long life. No Father of the Church could be defended
in that way. At present poor Newman is being made use of as
a pedestal for Wilfrid Ward. I hope the Duke and the House
of Lords approve.

Wilfrid Ward, as editor of the *Dublin Review*, was gallantly
defending Newman from the accusation of being the grandfather
of Modernism. Under Pius X and his Secretary of State the
pendulum of the Church seemed to have swung far in inhibiting
Liberal thought. Thinkers like Ward and von Hügel were compelled to use their literary talents to defend themselves from
Roman Inquisitors. It has been remarked that English theologians
never get into trouble at Rome until their writings are translated
into Italian. Possibly Ward and von Hügel became too involved
in their English styles to suffer translation. In any case they
survived the Modernist scare when angrier and clearer writers
like Loisy and Tyrrell went under. Cardinal Bourne courageously
refused to condemn Tyrrell as he considered he was suffering
from disease.

Gasquet kept a judicious but unjaundiced eye on the Modernist troubles. Very few Englishmen understood what was in the
Pope's mind. By his Encyclicals he was determined to pursue
and chloroform the will-o'-the-wisp called Modernism. Gasquet
talked to the Pope and wrote to the Duke of Norfolk that the
Pope 'has Italy always in his thought and he assured me that the
inroad of Modernist principles among the clergy was very
terrible.'

Wilfrid Ward and Baron von Hügel believed that Catholic
thought could be modernized without incurring the guilt of
heresy. Gasquet wrote to Ward from Rome to say: 'I believe
I induced the Pope to think that we in England are practically
free from Modernism.' At the same time he wrote twice to *The
Times* denying that the Pope had condemned Newman's theme
of Development in the Encyclical *Pascendi*. He bade Ward to
hold back nothing in his *Life of Newman* in the interests of
edification. 'Be very careful at first in your philosophical statements. There are heresy-hunters after you. *Verbum sap!*'

When Lord Hugh Cecil warned Ward that he feared Rome

would give a blow to his *Life of Newman*, Gasquet remarked that 'it was as unlikely that Rome would condemn the Biography as condemn an Encyclopaedia.'

As for the heresy-hunters: 'I quite agree with what you say about the danger of having men like —————— who don't understand modern thought or language but unfortunately we have got to suffer them.'

As it was increasingly difficult to say where the limits of Modernism could be drawn, it needed Gasquet's fine balance yet unimpeachable orthodoxy to assure the Pope on one side and to advise men of intellect on the other where they could safely stand.

The Pope of course was obeyed by the clergy, whether they understood what Modernism was or was not. Laymen like Ward and von Hügel side-stepped, awaiting the arrival of more Liberal days.

Gasquet's discretion, and especially his striking letters in *The Times*, increased his favour with the Pope, and Merry del Val was able to insert his name in the list of new Cardinals, no doubt on a hint from the Pope.

It was a great pleasure for one friend to acquaint the other of the approaching honour:

Confidential.   *April 25, 1914.*

My Lord Abbot,

It affords me very great pleasure to inform you that the Holy Father, wishing to reward your merits and the valuable services which you have rendered to the Apostolic See, has decided to raise you to the high dignity of a Cardinal of Holy Roman Church at the coming Consistory on May 25th.

Allow me to express the particular satisfaction which I derive personally from the announcement of this token of special esteem which His Holiness is about to bestow upon you and to congratulate you most heartily on your entering the Sacred College.

Returning to England with the *Galera rubra*, the crimson head-piece of the most eminent, Cardinal Gasquet settled down to duties, monastic, literary and social. So little murmur was there of approaching wars even at the sounding board of the Vatican that Merry could distress himself over a matter of etiquette as late as July 10, 1914:

> I have been astonished at a photo which reveals the fact that my enterprising brother [The Spanish Ambassador Merry del Val] actually *presided* at the *Salisbury* between two Cardinals. That was not in order. He ought to have sat opposite to the two Cardinals or on the right of the Senior Cardinal as his position does not allow of his taking precedence over Cardinals even though acting as Chairman. You will have noticed our reticence and reserve in regard to the conflict in Ireland and you may be sure that we shall continue to be very cautious.

Gasquet's Cardinalate was a matter of tremendous congratulation from Merry del Val, who prided himself on having pointed out the merits of the Abbot to Pius X. In the same batch was Cardinal della Chiesa, whose merits poor Merry had signally failed to point out to the Holy See on successive occasions. Even as late as May, 1914, Merry had excluded della Chiesa's name from the Cardinal's list but this time the Pope inserted it in his own script. However events were rushing with unseen force and unsuspected speed. Within a hundred days Pius was dead and della Chiesa Pope with Merry del Val dethroned from power in the Vatican for ever. It had been so with his predecessor Rampolla before him. The Papal pendulum moves slowly but it crosses the dial in the end. As Gasquet once said: 'The great thing to remember is that there is Providence to reckon with on these occasions.' Della Chiesa had the satisfaction of murmuring that the stone which the builders rejected had been made the headstone of the corner: and more practically asked Merry to vacate his rooms in the Vatican in the same terms which Merry had once served on him. 'We forgive but we cannot forget,' said Benedict XV. Only the President of the Accademia had stood by della Chiesa in 1903 and to him the new Pope gave his first audience. Only the American Cardinals visited the fallen Merry, who cried out to O'Connell: 'Here we have no abiding city!'

During the new Pontificate Merry del Val was no more consulted than Rampolla had been under Pius X. His future was
dedicated to the Basilica of St. Peter with one great flashing
promise of return at the Conclave of 1922, but even that died
down before the inscrutable voting of the Sacred College.

CORRESPONDENCE OF FATHER DAVID FLEMING AND GASQUET

Something must be said about the redoubtable David Fleming,
whose influence was thought to have been decisive with Leo XIII,
when the Commission was sitting over Anglican Orders. He was
a staunch supporter and lively correspondent of Gasquet. His
letters for many years supplied the gossip of Rome, the veerings
of the Papal compass, the criss-cross and excitements of the
ecclesiastical world. No doubt Gasquet found him a useful
informant. Father David was a well-known figure in Rome,
indiscreet in his letters but not without the humour lacking to
Manning's 'special correspondent' in the Holy City, the Mgr.
Talbot whose letters spiced ecclesiastical biography of that time.
Fleming did not stand so close to the Pope as Talbot, so that his
letters, as history, must be considered second-hand, but they
helped and entertained Gasquet immensely.

On the guidance of the Franciscan Order, Modernism,
Biblical questions, Americanism and every question of the *Curia*
he retailed the latest anecdote. He was always fighting 'Frenchers'
and foreigners. He seemed to think he was a chosen instrument
to steer the Church. When there was a vacant Bishopric in
England, Fleming had his candidate but, including Gasquet, they
were seldom successful. Irish of blood, with the style of an English
schoolboy, he amused Leo XIII, while Gasquet found him worthy
of affectionate trust. He took himself very seriously, but his
roughness will be forgiven for his gaiety, which was that of Our
Lady's Troubadour.

Father David was a candidate for Generalship of the Franciscans, when word came that the Pope wished to reserve his
services to himself. Shortly afterwards he was appointed Secretary
to the Biblical Commission, whereby his influence was felt
throughout the Church. He was often mentioned for a Hat,

though he had once proclaimed his personal opinion that a Cardinal could be an ass!

Gasquet's letters to Fleming are equally full of sallies and wit and shrewd little asides. They have been preserved by the Franciscans at Forest Gate. Gasquet wrote:

November 3, 1896: Here we are experiencing the temper of our Anglican friends. Moyes, one paper says, may be excused because of his ignorance; but Gasquet must have known better! Moyes is itching for the fray. *Pour moi* I have buried deep in Bacon. He is worth all the Anglican Orders put together. I am beginning to doubt very much the way the Franciscans are said to have attempted to prevent Bacon doing anything. We must have a proper edition. Only Catholics can do that. I am thinking of having the rest of that MS. in the Vatican photographed. If you can make your way to Dr. Ehrle. . . . I have had 12 years work by order of the Pope and have been out twice about this greatest of modern questions Anglican Orders at considerable expense to myself and loss of time. Don't be too heretical or revolutionary in your course of sermons.

November 24, 1896: I suppose that if you become Consultor of the Holy Office you will *have* to remain. What is wanted really is to have Consultors who are in touch with real life in these parts. The De Augustinis and the rest of the Professors are living in a perfect fool's Paradise. What I should like is that they should face the problems of the day, not pretend that they don't exist.

December 6, 1896: . . . The Roman authorities ought to have had a lesson in the danger of trying to work off a serious question without asking the people concerned. Anglican Orders should have taught them this much . . . you might put in a word for some settlement and warn them not to trust to any foreign advice. I have no faith in the *Primas* of S. Anselms. The Beuron military system is both un-Benedictine and perfectly unsuited for the English. What you said about the East is confirmed by Père Badrom, a very capable Persian of the Latin rite. He told me that the late change of policy has done harm beyond description to the chances of Catholicism in the East.

December 10, 1896: Since I wrote to you I have heard that the *powers that be* have *funked* sending me out to Rome as *Procurator in Curia.* I presume this means fresh delays and stagnation. However such is life! and my point is that there is now an end of my coming out at present. . . . The Bacon idea interests me very much and I am getting together the necessary literature. The proofs of the Italian translation of my *Introduction to Montalembert* were sent off yesterday. I shall be glad if you will spread it about among our friends: Cardinals Mazzella, Parocchi, S. Vannutelli, etc. I am anxious to give the Roman authorities the *tip* about what I hold to be sound principles for the Benedictine Order.

December 16, 1896: *Entre nous* I hear that —— is in bad odour. I don't wonder at it and cannot say I am sorry. He was too decidedly made in Germany. The Cambridge authorities are projecting a large work under Lord Acton. They have asked me to write the Chapter on Catholic England on the Eve of the Reformation.

Fleming's letters preserve the froth of the ecclesiastical currents. Especially he interested himself in Gasquet's work in editing and glorifying the greatest of all the Friars, Roger Bacon. Nor was he content with his work in Rome. At one time he was carrying out Visitations in Croatia where no less than 105 Houses required his attention.

After the Bull on Anglican Orders, came the great Bull on the Benedictines. All this is religious history. Rome in the latter days of Leo XIII swarmed with gossamer gossip, pious excitements, struggles between Religious Orders or rival Nationalities. Gasquet's correspondence livens when David Fleming is at the other end of the line. He was useful, intensely loyal and always fighting behind the scenes. In those halcyonic days, when the world was not traversed by general wars nor the Church pierced by persecutions, different countries fought spiritual warfare in Rome: Irish against English, Americans against Germans and Father Fleming against all. Above the Orders and the Nations the Holy See stayed secure: occasionally issuing a Bull and there was peace for the time. This is illustrated by one of Fleming's scraps which reads: 'Volpini wrote the Bull. Things are going on splendidly. All opposition ceased at once. The Holy Father is very pleased.' *Secura judicat Ecclesia!*

Gasquet wrote (January 1, 1897):

> I do not fancy there will be any counterblast from Canterbury and York about the Bull. Our meeting about *Development* was very interesting. Even Moyes has the fear of progression in this. Rivington was most amusing. He didn't think much of Petavius and thought development of doctrine most mischievous. Father Butler and I were the only two to take what Rivington regarded as the heterodox view. The discussion seemed to elicit the fact that people don't draw the proper distinction between *truth*, which of course can't develop, and the *tracking* of it or doctrine.

Newman's *Development* was simply evolution applied to Dogma and was later used as a stalking-horse by Modernists.

Father David replied (January 30, 1897):

> I'll send you a few views on the Development question. You are right as to *Revelation* and the *teaching* of the various points of it. A momentous distinction is to be drawn between the *dogmatic* teaching and the merely *theological* development by drawing conclusions. St. Paul could certainly not have written the *Summa* of St. Thomas especially with the blunders in it! . . . The fixing the meaning of terms adopted to express Christian ideas took time and trouble but it is erroneously put down to development. . . . The *row* in America will blow over. They are passing through a crisis similar to that of England in the Sixties: minimising *versus* maximising. They will find their level in due course. . . . An Irish Augustinian has been appointed Consultor and a German Franciscan at the Index. The foreigners are coming with a vengeance.

Gasquet wrote (July 15, 1897):

> I was interested in what you said about the Bible translation. The S.J. would spoil everything. There is no doubt that the Anglican *revision* was undertaken too soon and the first measure is a critical edition of the Vulgate—so said Bacon in the year 1260. What a disgrace that it has never been done.

Then there was the question of a new translation of the Bible into English. Fleming believed 'we could not have a good English translation until we had the Vulgate revised, which I did not think the Pope would undertake.'

This was a pointer towards the great unfinished work of Gasquet's life, the revised Vulgate, though Mgr. Knox has managed to English the Latin before the Vulgate revision was complete, half a century later. Slowly germinate the Church's ideas.

Gasquet wrote (October 12, 1897):

> I have been working away at Bacon since I saw you and I want you to find out for me whether the Annalist at S. Antonio knows anything of a Chapter at Paris of the Order in 1278 at which Bacon is supposed to have been condemned to imprisonment by the General, Jerome of Ascoli. The only authority apparently is the Chronicle of St. Antoninus 150 years after the event, which I don't believe. Till I can clear up this point I am waiting to do Bacon's life. Meantime I am doing for the next *Dublin* an article on Roger Bacon and the Bible or English Biblical criticism in the 13th century. . . . By the bye in the last number of the *Revue Bénédictine* the Rector Janssens of S. Anselmo has an attack upon the memory of Cardinals Manning and Newman. I have called attention of *The Tablet* to the libel but I know not whether they will do anything. The impertinence of these foreigners! If you should see it, pound into it in Rome.

The Church has also her Bacon problems (but not Shakespearean). Gasquet was engrossed in Friar Bacon and his manuscripts. Fleming wrote (October 16, 1897):

> You are quite right about the Chapter of 1278—no Chapter at all. S. Antoninus is *most* untrustworthy in many of his assertions and Wadding [the great Irish Franciscan] equally so. Wadding was a most laborious *compiler* but no *critic*. . . . Your life of Bacon will be a most opportune contribution to the history of Theology and Science in the 13th Century and the part played by British intellect. The idea that it is wanted again is rapidly gaining ground here. We want a few bold and yet

cautious spirits to upset the southern *Manualists*! *That* riled many but did good even here. The narrow *Thomism* is *dead*. . . .

There was much hunting for Bacon manuscripts. There was one in Trinity, Dublin, and 'the last part of the *Opus Majus* must be found somewhere in England. It may be found at Oxford unless it has got into some private collection. Would it be at Lambeth?'

Gasquet wrote (October 31, 1897):

I sent off a copy of Bacon's *Opus Majus* to you as the book has, I believe, now been withdrawn by the Clarendon Press. I believe that the Preface is really what Bacon in the *Opus Tertium* calls the *Opus Secundum*. If you have Brewer, you will find the exact description of this Preface under the title of *Opus Secundum*. . . . I am very glad to hear you have been put at the head of the higher studies and I hope you will smash into the *Manualists*. How delightful Bacon's position is in regard to the Manualists of his day. Have you ever made out who the great teacher is that he attacks with Alexander of Hales? I can hardly fit *Albertus Magnus* into the description and St. Thomas hadn't the position.

Father David wrote later on the German trouble, which the Church experienced before the rest of the world in both Continents (December 23, 1897):

The Americans have succeeded in ousting Schröder the German Professor from Washington. You have seen about the row in Fribourg. All the Germans have resigned. Things are coming to a head. It is now the psychological moment to write to Cardinal Vannutelli about your affairs in England. Write a nice letter in French or Italian. . . . The Vatican is becoming more and more alive to the necessity of keeping the Germans in order.

In America their educational scheme called after Cahensly was routed by Archbishops Gibbons and Ireland.

February 8, 1895: It is necessary to be on our guard as I heard that many people are beginning to take an interest in Bacon. Your last article in the *Dublin* has given the matter a new

impulse. . . . I have read Wiseman's *Life*. I quite agree with
you that it is too long and too late. I don't like some of Ward's
sayings, too much *ex cathedra*. [One chapter was withdrawn.]

July 13, 1898: It is said here and there that under a new Pope
Roger Bacon will take the place of St. Thomas. I agree with
you that the Americans have brought odium on themselves
by their aggressiveness without learning to back them up.
They made an active propaganda of their doctrine in France
and here. . . . They want people to believe that they are
amazed and shocked at the Americanism propounded by the
French! There is quite as much dodging going on as there was
in our Commission. I don't think the Pope will publish the
letter to Canterbury and York. What a nice pickle our Ritualist
friends are in? . . . Poor Spain. I am sorry the Americans did
not get a good licking at least once. They were sure to win in
the long run. Our Hungarian people [Franciscans] may keep
their top boots and coarse broad cloth if they will only fall into
line on other matters. I had a long interview with His Holiness
last week. He looks well but tired. Rome has a sort of *Ante-
Conclave* aspect just now [when a Pope is dying].

In spite of his advanced or Liberal views Father David was
made a Consultor of the Holy Office. Mgr. Moyes wrote
(January 1, 1897):

So they have caught Fr. David! *Et angariaverunt eum*! I was
afraid he could not long escape the tentacula of the Inquisition.
The Semi-evolutionists will have a friend and spokesman in
the Holy Office and if Dr. Hinsley cannot get Fr. Zahm reduced
to ashes, he will know the reason why. It is the irony of fate
that Fr. David whom Duchesne supposed to be in danger of the
cells should have been called to the counsels of the Holy Office
while the savant has been left out.

St. George Mivart was the most brilliant Biologist on the
Catholic side. His criticisms of Darwin were said to keep that
great Naturalist awake at night. Lord Acton recorded that in
consequence the Darwinians blackballed Mivart for the
Athenaeum. He held chairs at Louvain and at Manning's futile
University in Kensington. Unfortunately his mind became

distracted by illness and he wrote such oddly unorthodox views as "Happiness in Hell" ! Though he was condemned from Westminster, his friends Gasquet and Father Fleming never lost touch or friendship. Mivart died suddenly on the very evening the Darwinians were expecting to entertain him. 'There is a Providence to reckon with'! Though he was buried out of the Church, Cardinal Bourne felt misgivings and arranged on his own terms to give him consecrated ground on the special pleading of his Liberal Catholic friends. So all can be well that ends well.

Gasquet wrote (January 16, 1900):

Poor Mivart has distinguished himself in his usual way as you will have seen. Nothing can defend what he has written but I think Moyes in *The Tablet* was wrong. It would add to the terrors of Catholic life, if there was to be excommunication by *leading article*. I always thought a person was not to be considered outside the Church until he was a formal heretic, by refusing to retract opinions plainly heretical. Mivart has been very ill since Xmas and the doctor thought that he might die at any moment, so I went and got him to see a priest and receive Extreme Unction. . . . I wish something could be done to condemn the practice of the Nine First Fridays, as I am sure harm will come from what is rapidly becoming a superstition. I have a letter from a mother whose son died of a long illness and who refused to see a priest or do anything on the ground that he had made the Nine Fridays— that Our Lord had promised that anyone who did so should be saved and that he expected Him to keep His promise.

March 25, 1901: I wrote to the Cardinal to say very plainly what I thought about his French Benedictine scheme. It is very sad how completely out of all touch he appears to be with everyone. Altogether the general outlook in England is very depressing and one has to say one's prayers and mind one's own business as best one may. Certainly the position of Catholics made by Cardinal Manning has been very much lowered.

April 21, 1901: I have tried to find out something about the visit of Consalvi to England; but beyond the fact nothing is apparently known. It is said that he was received quite *privately* by the Royal Family and this may account for the difficulty of finding any account. I spent a morning in trying to get some clue but without success. . . . Curiously enough within a week of Father Taunton's book on the Jesuits in England coming out Major Hume has published a volume called *Plots and Treasons* which also deals with the unpleasant subject of the Jesuit designs in England in the reign of Elizabeth. I wish the S.J. people would only throw Father Parsons over; but they can't do that I fear. These books and Father Thurston's attack upon the Dominicans and the Rosary will cause a great flutter.

November 29, 1903: I quite agree with you about poor Loisy and am more than sorry. Would it not be possible to condemn him for the reasons of *inexpediency* without going into the merits? If this were stated it would obviate great harm to many, for it must be obvious to all that his books are certainly inexpedient at present. Try what can be done. It is very curious that you say what I have also felt that Merry del Val cannot be relied on as a friend. Now he has *arrived*, his peculiar *twist* will be accentuated. I am very pleased indeed to hear that the Archbishop has been defeated *re* Amigo. It would have been the cause of great trouble and soreness. As to myself. Of course, if it comes, I should not refuse as I have always made it a point in life to be guided by what turns up. I believe that one could do good among the Bishops if one was there.

December 31, 1904: I do not know what use I should be in Rome or whether I want to go; but the Pope so clearly said that he intended me to come there, that if it is to be, it had better be soon. After 60 it is hard to transplant anyone. The only thing that would make me desire it is that the Roman authorities should do something in the way of showing that they understand I have served them well. I certainly think I have in the Anglican Orders Commission and in settling our Benedictine business. The only return for work and money expended for them was the *snub* over the Westminster business. Such is life!

January 16, 1905: I do not know what to say about your saying a word to the Pope as to my coming out and think you

14

had better leave it to chance. If the opportunity comes, you might use it. I wrote to Merry del Val strongly about the danger of leaving the English-speaking world without proper representation or without some of the officials knowing something about the nations they were governing.

With Modernism and the Pope's Encyclical of condemnation liberal-minded clerics were worried more about their friends than themselves.

> *October 26, 1907*: What the Modernists are saying now is something like this . . . an indirect censure not only on many of Newman's writings but on the whole scheme of thought. . . . Send me a line to say what is the best answer briefly to make to this. The parson who puts the question is disturbed and is worth making an effort to satisfy.

> *November 28, 1907*: I have been here just a fortnight now and have surveyed the situation. At present I am *sitting tight* till I know where the *needful* is coming from. I told the Pope plainly that it would be better to say plainly that the work could not be started for lack of funds than to start and find we had not counted the cost. I am at present working at the Vatican Library to get a rough survey of the MSS. of the Vulgate in Europe. My interview with the Pope was delightful and he was really charming. He had on his table the two letters I wrote to *The Times* which had been translated. He said with a real wink: 'They say I am a poor peasant and can't understand what I write!'

> *June 29, 1911*: Lepicier has apparently not given any decision on the case between Westminster and Southwark. He is apparently most interested in the question of dividing up England into three Archbishoprics and several Vicariates. . . . Bourne's point is to destroy Southwark and St. George's and to get all London and twelve miles round added to Westminster. This would in my opinion be fatal to religious interests. Had South London been under Westminster from the start, it would have been as neglected as East London is still. Westminster puts its energies in the *western* parts too much. If there were a Bishop for East London something might be

made of it and Heaven prevent South London being put in the
same case. St. George's at any rate is a centre of energy. This
mad scheme must be put an end to. At any rate I hope the Pope
will not consent to such drastic changes without full inquiry.
At present Bourne hasn't even suggested the matter to the
Bishops. Even the Bishop of Southwark has not an idea of what
is going on.

November 4, 1911: Well wonders will never cease! The
surprise Consistory came as a bomb to all. The Archbishop
himself had not heard anything of it till Saturday night late.
The division of England into three Provinces was certain, but
I did not think it would have come till the Bishops had been
consulted. It is evident that they had not been told anything
about it. The most astonishing news however to my mind
is the Franciscan *coup d'état*. How an Order of the antiquity
and size of the Minors can be treated by a *Proprio motu* is
past comprehension. As far as I can make out all your
work under Pope Leo is swept away. . . . Keep the flag
flying.

—which certainly Father Fleming did till he died.

Mgr. William Barry was a learned correspondent and very
much on the Liberal side, writing (February 7, 1902):

I want more information about Colet. I can't be sure
whether Colet was, like Wessel, a Protestant in germ, or only
a dissatisfied reforming Catholic. Green is, I hope, extravagant
in his view. What is yours? I remark that you don't discuss the
point. Do you think he wished to get rid of confession, celibacy
and the rest? Bishop is a loss to you. How seldom can one say
that of Bishops? Would not half an ounce of Erastianism be
worth trying if it can put Gore at Birmingham? There is a
sort of good in things not so good. The charge against Gore
was put thus to me that he is a Rationalist who believes nothing
and a Papist who believes too much.

Gore became Bishop of Oxford but contrarily it was
Cambridge that put him in a glass window.

Barry hoped that the condemnation of Loisy's book could be averted (February 16, 1903):

> I write as hoping you have access to the Bible Commission and would be listened to. If Father David is as strong as some think, he might get them to accept a *via media*. I put it in one word, Correction not suppression. The time is short.

Of Gasquet's threepenny sketch of Church History, Barry wrote (March 12, 1903):

> I have had your sketch and I find it clear, interesting, impartial. . . . I don't think anyone has told the story of Henry VIII—Elizabeth in so small a compass with such distinct setting out of the necessary points to be considered. On the British Church, the Celtic monks, Theodore, I believe you express the sum of the truth. On Dunstan and *à propos* to celibacy, perhaps more should be hinted with regard to the secular clergy, who, as far as I can see, had made up their minds that the law was obsolete. It was certainly not observed. You imply severe judgment of the Roman Curia *temp.* Henry III but are very gentle in speech hereon. I am struck with your limitation in regard of the term *spiritual*. Had the Curia recognized this fact, how much less odium would attach to *spiritual* Courts. In the Middle Ages *spiritual* meant the claim of ecclesiastical persons to the money of layfolk, five times at least out of ten. Your page is luminous though not a fiery flame on this question.

It is amusing to note tracks of the pseudo-historian Frederick Rolfe (Baron Corvo). Abbot Sir David Hunter-Blair wrote (March 2, 1901):

> I mentioned to Mr. F. W. Rolfe that you would be willing to see him if he consulted me as to his projected work on the Borgias. However, apparently he does not wish to see, or to consult, *anyone* and writes that he wishes his communication to me on the subject to be considered *strictly private*. How under the circumstances he expected me to help him in any way, I cannot imagine; nor does it much matter. I can only do as he seems to desire, viz. ask you kindly to refrain from mentioning him and his alleged literary discoveries.

Corvo's *Chronicles of the Borgias* is a patch of glittering white-wash.

On a point of Sabbatarian discipline Alfred Pollard wrote:

> *Do* tell me, when people began to fast from midnight to midnight instead of from sunset to sunset. It is not a merely antiquarian question. I honestly believe that if the people, who want to be religious, could be got back to the old way it would do more for the religious life of the country than almost any other change of the kind I can think of. Didn't St. Hugh die after sunset and isn't that the reason why his feast is kept the day after he died? What I am chiefly interested in—keeping Sunday. I get infuriated with the Protestant idiocy which doesn't care a cent what is done on a Saturday night as long as no-one plays cricket on Sunday afternoon. But if midnight to midnight holds the field for fasting, and always has held it, I'm afraid history is agin me.

The learned convert Johannes Joergensen wrote in some distress from Assisi on the credibility of the Holy House of Loreto, which of course is not a matter of faith (February 8, 1922):

> When I turned Catholic 26 years ago, I did not accept the Translation by Angels of the Holy House of Loreto. It was a difficulty that there existed a Mass for the Feast. But I passed by this difficulty. I went twice to Loreto and prayed there saying to myself: I will pray here, as if it was really the House of Mary at Nazareth.
>
> This spring I was at Nazareth and spoke with a Franciscan Father who said that he himself never accepted the miraculous translation, that Rome had abolished the Mass and the Office of that Feast. . . . I read the letter with which the Pontiff is delegating His Eminence Gasparri for accompanying the new statue of the Virgin to Loreto and I read this phrase *prescelto della Divina Provvidenza ad estrarre La Santa Casa di Nazareth.* I wondered very much at this expression. If the Pope, in a solemn occasion, calls the Chapel in the Loreto Basilica 'the House of Nazareth,' he must believe in its *miraculous* translation and is going, so far as I may understand, against historical truth. The proclamation of the Virgin of Loreto as patroness of

airmen is pointing in the same direction. All this is very hard food for me. I know perfectly well that the Infallibility, *stricto sensu*, is not in question. But it seems to me that the ordinary teaching of the Church is tending to corroborate a legendary tradition as historical. And that troubles me. Your Eminence might wonder why I address myself to you. But I know nobody else who would appreciate perfectly my difficulty and from whom I might expect a solution.

The venerable Dr. Murray, second only to Dr. Johnson as a lexicographer, consulted Gasquet on several points (November 8, 1905):

> Can you kindly give us a little help in behalf of the Oxford English Dictionary with the names Pied Friars, Freres of the Pie and Pied Monks. The former are mentioned in Piers Plowman. We should like to know something about them, whether they were a distinct Order, etc.

On the subject of 'Holy Pokers' (March 18, 1906):

> Can you give us any help as to the *pillars* said to have been borne before Cardinals as signs or emblems of their office or dignity? There are several references to these in the case of Cardinal Wolsey and some in the case of Cardinal Pole.

The good Doctor had found them in the ornamentation of Christ Church as used by Wolsey and wondered whether they symbolized 'pillars of the Church'?

Lawyers consulted Gasquet as to the State election of Anglican Bishops and the rights of opposers to make known their views. Were Catholic Bishops thus confirmed of old? 'The Attorney General insists that its origin must be known. Speaking confidentially, the Crown is very anxious to stop these opposers and the origin of the form might clear up one of their difficulties. The Statute of Henry VIII says the Archbishop is to *confirm* the person elected. Where did the Archbishop get the form from?' Anglicans are free to protest against new Bishops suspected of Romanism or Rationalism.

Dame Laurentia of Stanbrook Abbey asked advice as to an

'Ingoldsbian' story in her MS. of St. Egwin, which had startled Mr. Bishop, who had scribbled: 'this is rather strong! But if Father President has passed, *good*. And perhaps the crabbed and cross-grained Protestant, peevish, perverse and opposite may be left to snarl.'

Of this St. Egwin, Gasquet wrote to Dame Laurentia (October 29, 1903):

> I have received from Abbot Snow his opinion about St. Egwin. He does not approve of the old mediaeval stories and I think that we have to guard against scoffers in these days. I think also that some word about these legends really being regarded as indications of the honour and reverence in which the Saint was held rather than as facts. *E.g.* the startling miracle on p. 7. I do not suppose that anyone really credits the fact that St. Egwin really walked to Rome with chains or at any rate that the key which locked them was thrown into the Severn or Avon. See how you can guard against misconception and then the book may be printed. I think that as I have to give the *imprimatur* it would not do to mention me in the preface, especially as I really have done nothing to help you.

The aged Editor of *Punch*, Sir Francis Burnand, had a Biblical difficulty (May 8, 1904):

> This is to request you to give me a reference to some *satisfactory* explanation of the story of the bears eating the children who called out to the prophet 'go up, thou Baldhead.' I cannot find the subject in the answer of 'certain Jews to M. Voltaire' where I thought I might find it. The facts of the case seem so strangely out of proportion. A good all round birching would as it seems to me have been a sufficient deterrent.

Longueville the historian was writing asking for an Introduction to his book (May 15, 1904):

> Did James II become a Catholic mainly from conviction; or because he thought that the Church was the strongest pillar of the Monarchical principle?
> How was it that a convert was so zealous as to be ready to sacrifice his worldly prospects and if necessary his chance of a Crown for his Faith and yet persisted in adultery?

Was James really aware of the cruelties of Jeffreys during the campaign in the West?

I would like to ask whether you think Petre was a knave or a fool; but it would not do to tread upon the corns of our friends the Jesuits.

There was the Jesuit John Gerard hard on the scent of the Gunpowder Plot and the signatures of Thos. Winter or 'Wintour,' finding that the plot more resembled a Protestant trap than an orthodox hope of blowing Parliament to Limbo.

August 18, 1897: The case looks strong. Can this be the reason that the original was withdrawn from public view to Cecil's private Archives? It is curious that the copy made by Salisbury's secretary—from which the printed version was evidently taken—leaves out the signatory's name altogether and instead of finishing off 'I remain your L L penitent prisoner Thomas Winter' ends simply 'I remain etc.' I will send copies of all for your perusal and Mr. Bishop's.

When the project for canonizing the English Martyrs was on foot, Father Pollen wrote for advice on how to present the processes (Pres. B.V.M. 1921):

How can we introduce our documents to Rome? A small series of *nota* signed by Catholic *periti*. . . . Also the political troubles, the Armada, Oath of Allegiance—so that no one should say we were stifling inquiry. In the case of Ven. Thomas Tichburne 1602 there is I regret to say an accusation of unchaste life, against which there is little which we can oppose. But this is the only case. The case of Ven. Edward Coleman in Oates plot will never quite commend itself to Protestants and I fear will fail over the *tuto*. But we have such a great number 253 that the loss of a few won't matter.

Archbishop Walsh of Dublin consulted him (April 11, 1906) on the names of Legates, when writing about Canon Law in England, 'and I do not know which form of the names of the two Legates to take—Otto, Otho, Ottoboni, Ottobuoni, Othoboni, Othobuoni, Ottobon. I am sure you have considered the matter and made up your mind on it, long before this.'

November 19, 1904: I only want to know a few salient facts, as to the object of their coming. All I have is as follows: (1) Otto; what Rohrbachen tells and this is practically sufficient.

(2) Ottobon; *nil* beyond the fact that he held a Council in 1266.

P.S. Are you acquainted with Mr. Maitland? I should like to write to him about one or two points.

Sir Frederick Kenyon from the British Museum (November 30, 1921) reported the ex-King of Portugal was making research into his country's history and anxious to seek in the Vatican.

You have done so much to make those archives accessible to historians that you, if anyone, can say whether the thing is possible. He does not appear to know anyone in Rome whom he could ask to make the search except a Portuguese Bishop, whose scholarship may not be equal to his piety. I shall be very grateful if you can help me in this matter. I had a very grateful letter from Mercati about the Catalogue of our Library.

Later King Manuel wrote (February 25, 1923):

Monsieur Quintella de Sampayo, my private Secretary, is going to Rome to settle some private affairs. Taking advantage of your Eminence's great kindness I take the liberty of introducing to you Monsieur de Sampayo who is a very devoted and dear friend of mine. . . . Very affectionately, MANUEL R.

Later the British Museum and the Vatican found themselves contending at auction for Cardinal Pole's letters which 'plainly have an interest for the national collection, as well as for the Vatican.' As the patriarch of the house, Kenyon recalled old friends and assistants like Thompson and Warner and forwarded 'respectful homage to His Holiness'—who was the Pope of all Librarians (Pius XI).

One question occupied a large corner of the correspondence: the trouble between Southwark and Westminster and the proposed changes in the boundaries of the two Dioceses. This question was waged between Cardinal Bourne and Bishop Amigo as long as they lived to the perplexity of the laity. It must be allowed that Gasquet's sympathies were entirely with Southwark as appears in the pile of letters from Amigo.

When coldly received at Rome, Bourne asked Gasquet what he had done and was frankly told that his relations with Southwark were a scandal.

The Popes maintained impartiality while the quarrel reached serious stages. At one time the Pope ordered them to shake hands (the kiss of peace perhaps would have been too much) in the presence of laity. In vain the Holy See demanded peace, but both Diocesans were roused and remained hostile until death united them, convinced that each had the better case for what was best for London Catholics.

Pope Benedict looked upon Gasquet as an umpire in English Church matters so puzzling to the Italian mind, and amongst the autograph letters which he wrote to him one was written asking him to allay the fears of Amigo of Southwark that his Diocese would be diminished without consultation and underlining certain words in the Latin: 'nullatenus esse faciendum, *nisi auditis Episcopis interesse habentibus* et salvis integrisque cuiusque mensae episcopalis reditibus.' (April 16, 1917). It was signed '*suo affmo Benedictus PP XV*' and it really settled the matter.

The Pope's letter was exquisitely diplomatic as between the two appellants. His Holiness continued that unless the Bishop concerned gave his consent, nothing would be done. The Pope justly reproved the version of His Holiness' Letter to Cardinal Bourne as given in *The Tablet.* In the matter of their Dioceses the Bishops were free to increase them, but it was not expected that they would. Southwark need not doubt, for the Holy See could not contradict herself. The Holy See remained judge of the situation.

Secura judicat mater ecclesiarum! It was clear that the Holy See waited for one Bishop to bury the other.

This immense and unending case between Westminster and Southwark might be described as a Tichborne Trial amongst Dioceses. War or peace might descend on Europe but the Bishops stayed unreconciled. With his grandiose idea of uniting all London under one majestic See, Cardinal Bourne could not brook the refusal of Bishop Amigo to allow his claims. It is difficult to say whether Gasquet was interpreting the Pope's wishes or whether the Pope had accepted Gasquet's views of the case. Certainly matters in Rome remained as they were during the Pontificate of Benedict XV. And subsequent Popes have not made any advance or change upon this *grandis Epistola*, which reads so worthily of the patience and prudence which the Holy See ever pours upon the troubled waves of Episcopacy tiding around the Rock.

XI

THE GREAT WAR

Non Angelus sed Anglus

IN May 1914, Gasquet became John Bull's other Cardinal. England had secured two representatives in the Sacred College. From the moment the Cardinalate was announced, Gasquet's life belonged to Rome. He proceeded thither after warm send-offs from his English and Benedictine friends. Created a Cardinal-Deacon, he received the Red Hat in the last Consistory held by Pius X. He was nominated to the Deaconry of Saint George *in Velabro*, a title which had been given to Cardinal Newman, but like Newman he never took possession. There was some difficulty raised by the Italian Government. Before the end of the year 1915 he was enthroned in the Church of St. Mary *in Campitelli*, which had once been held by the Cardinal Duke of York, last of the Royal Stuarts.

The Revision of the Vulgate he continued as his final life-work. The Commission had moved from St. Anselm's College on the Aventine to the Palace of San Calisto in the Trastevere and here the Cardinal prepared to settle down in peace. Unfortunately the Great War broke out and scattered the band of scholars he had collected to his assistance.

On May 25, 1914, he received the *Biglietto* or announcement of his Cardinalate with the modest surprise which tradition expects from Eminence elect. He spoke of the three English Benedictines who had been raised to the Sacred Purple in the past. One was a nephew of the English Pope Hadrian IV and a monk of St. Albans, of which Gasquet held the titular Abbacy. Another was Archbishop Langham and a third was a Norwich monk, Adam Easton.

Meantime the First World War. His principal work in Rome became the elucidation of the Allied Cause and the reception of the rare British visitors who penetrated through the veils of war. He comforted his soul by writing his spiritual treatise on the Religious life which had so strangely brought him to this position.

In 1917 he became Librarian of the Vatican, and in 1920 the Pope made him Archivist of the Holy Church. He served on Congregations touching Propaganda, Rites, the Religious and the Oriental Church. He became Protector of the English College and the Beda as well as of numerous devout Communities.

During the war he kept tenacious grip of passing affairs and earned without receiving the gratitude of his country whom he defended in an undefended pass.

The Diaries which he kept during the war years abundantly prove and illustrate his action during the greatest difficulties and depressions. He kept his soul high and cheered up the few Allied sympathizers around him in St. Calixtus.

Here he kept vigil, here he kept court, here he kept the flag flying. No English ecclesiastic ever played so lonely or interesting a part as Gasquet. The diplomatic chessboard is always spread in Rome. The last refinements of the great game played in the eighteenth century are surviving. Since the fall of Rome from temporal Theocracy to the temporary Kingdom of Savoy, a double diplomacy had emerged—white and black, which under the pressure of the war was merged under the colours of the many nations striving to influence the ancient capital of the world.

The intense ecclesiastical world of Vatican politics, Congregations, Propaganda, sacred intrigues, Modernist scares and strife between Bishops had continued under the dispassionate and deciding supremacy of the Pope, but after 1914 there was but one controversy. The foreign powers, Catholic or Protestant, ranged at the Quirinal, always added to the strident notes if not to the melody of the European concert. They now divided into pro-German or pro-Ally, dragging as many neutrals with them as their resources allowed.

The outbreak of war threw the two worlds of Rome into intense excitement and some confusion. Cardinal Gasquet found himself faced by one and engaged in buoying up the other.

The confusion was embarrassing, for the Pope was neutral while Italy joined the Allies. As the French Ambassador Cambon said, she was bound to go to the rescue of the conquerors. But 'conquering Kings' were still far from appearing on Belgian, British or Italian horizons. There ensued four years of swaying agony.

The Pope's neutrality was balanced between a Catholic Austria and the religious enmities of France and Russia.

It was the reverse in the Second War, when Italy rushed to join a triumphant Germany, while a later Pope found himself invisibly at war with a German New Order involving the destruction of the Old Religion. In a generation the trends of History and Diplomacy may turn full circle.

It was Gasquet's duty to play a part in the front trenches of intrigue and battle for the honour of the Allies, where they were feebly represented. As a Foreign Office veteran wrote: 'Gasquet fought a brave battle with few supporters and not much ammunition in face of highly organized offensive.' At his desperate suggestion the Foreign Office though divided against itself despatched a British Mission to the Holy See, where the Central Powers were strongly entrenched. It is true Belgium was already represented, but neither France (like Prussia) nor England nor the United States. Sir Henry Howard with a handpicked staff including 'Bogey' Harris, Duncan Gregory and Gaisford arrived in Rome ostensibly to inform the Pope of the innocent and Christian intentions of the Allies. It had hardly struck the Foreign Office (save the sagacious mind of Sir William Tyrrell) that the Vatican in return could inform the Foreign Office of European opinions and pulsings in their most secret and delicate bearings.

No doubt all the Embassies and Legations to the Holy See in those days sought to persuade the Pope through his Secretary of State of the predominance and propriety of their own governments: but the Holy See possesses a susceptible machinery of her own for judging such.

On arrival in Rome for the conclave which elected Benedict XV, recorded Abbot Butler in the *Dictionary of National Biography*:

The English cardinals found strong pro-German influences at work. On Cardinal Gasquet, as the resident English cardinal, fell the task of countering the anti-English and anti-Allies propaganda of the Central Powers. . . . He took a leading part in negotiating the appointment of a British minister to the Vatican in December 1914.

The work on the Vulgate was suspended while the workers retired to their several countries to become chaplains.

During the war years Gasquet took a villa at Leghorn where he insisted on sea-bathing in spite of the marine etiquette for Cardinals. The local nuns, recalls Henry Harris, used also to bathe, looking like wet seals in their black draperies. They all scattered at Father Philip's approach while the Cardinal's bathe was watched by anxious attendants all wearing the black gloves of a Cardinalitial suite.

He was very English in spite of his Gallic blood. Sometimes the Romans must have murmured to themselves—'*Non Angelus sed Anglus.*' But he kept his flag flying amid all the international complications at Rome during the war of 1914–18, when the Central Powers seemed not only invincible but the self-appointed claimants for Catholic interest and influence. British isolation made it difficult for Italian priests to realize that England politically had returned to Christendom. An English Cardinal *in Curia* was as strange a phenomenon as a Patagonian Eminence in the Roman corridors. No decoration that the Foreign Office could give could possibly have covered his services. No Ambassador was ever in a position to achieve more. His Embassy could be compared diplomatically to Stratford Canning's lonely watch at the Golden Horn. The curious hypocrisy of British Governments facing the Papacy has always aimed at securing all possible benefits while giving no signs of gratitude, at least no external favours to those who have brought them about. Not that Cardinal Gasquet wanted a Grand Cross any more than Cardinal Bourne. They had the distinction of being undecorated and the Government ignored any representation at their funerals.

It was a different Rome to the Rome of scholars and friends that Gasquet had known of old. In his guarded position he was no longer a freelance. His old friends were dead and whom could he now trust? He was suspected, feared and disliked on account of his unofficial position. He was the eye and voice of England.

As Abbot Butler commented with amusing understatement: 'The Vatican had not yet settled down into the attitude of firm neutrality maintained by the Pope.'

For the benefit of Lord Grey the Cardinal wrote (November 20, 1914):

> Really with all the Catholic interests in the Empire, it seems absurd that there should be no official means of communication between the British Government and the Pope. The matter has been very evident in this great crisis. The Pope and his Secretary are quite correct in their attitude, but the mentality of the clergy generally is astounding. . . . Germany and Austria and Bavaria have been at work for the past two years and more and when the War started they had the ground well-prepared. Prussia doesn't leave things to chance and had a good deal of the wisdom of the serpent. Muhlberg the Prussian Minister to the Vatican is a very clever and charming man. We English here have had by no means a pleasant time, but we have not kept quiet and the Italian translation of the *White Book* has done a great deal. We shall welcome Sir Henry Howard with all our souls and do all we can.

Old friendships with Germans were broken off—amiable relations with many of the Sacred College suspended. Merry del Val alone dined with Gasquet.

The Pope seemed uncertain. Henry Howard wrote (December 1, 1915):

> As to the Pope and peace, I feel sure that the Germans, through Cardinal Hartmann and others, are bringing great pressure on His Holiness to propose some sort of intervention. . . . He has recently told two of my friends that it was not the moment. All the same one can never tell what His Holiness may not do or say.

Pro-allied prelates were rare. A letter from Archbishop Ireland (December 10, 1915) was treasured:

May the New Year be for you one of joyousness, one of
fears allayed, of hopes fulfilled. You see, I join with good wishes
for yourself personally good wishes for the causes of the
Quadruple Entente. You have a very weighty mission incum-
bent upon you—that of spreading through Rome, even into
the very citadel, truth and light with regard to the great War.
. . . How sorry I am that 'Father David' is gone from us. A
picturesque and most interesting figure has disappeared from
the battlefield. There is a vacuum in Rome which nothing will
fill.

As a matter of fact Gasquet's friendship with Father David
had been severed by the war. The Irish Franciscans for three
centuries have furnished the Resistance movement against the
English at home and abroad.

The British Legation were left by the Foreign Office to fight
their battles blindfolded. They were not informed of the secret
clause by which the Allies, in their anxiety to bring Italy into the
war, had excluded the Holy See from the Peace. Three months
later Cardinal Gasparri, Secretary of State, had found out and
asked the British Legation frankly. They looked very foolish but
they had not played the knave. This was only one manner in
which the Foreign Office misused the Papal confidence.

Gasquet soon found that the most effective personage in the
Legation sent by the Foreign Office was Henry Harris. A collector
of Italian art, he would have been at home in the circle of Lorenzo
de' Medici. A freelance in his political views and disinterested in a
career, the only Catholic layman whose opinions were accepted
by the British Government, he played a large but unrecorded
part behind the scenes. When something important had to be
settled (and needless to say the more important it was, the less
decision or answer was returned from the Foreign Office) 'Bogey'
Harris was speeded to London to pay an effective visit to Lloyd
George's secretary Miss Stevenson. In Harris' opinion de Salis
was the ablest of the Ministers of the Holy See. As a compromise
with Protestant feelings, Curzon, after a visit to the League of
Nations at Geneva, was later induced to send Sir Theo Russell to
establish the precedent of a Protestant Minister. It was Harris

15

who in his own phrase later prevented so great an institution as
the Vatican going 'under Woodrow Wilson's umbrella.' The
Holy See took Harris' advice and Cardinal Ceretti would travel
all the way to London to obtain it on some delicate point in later
days.

It was typical of Gasquet that he never took pains to learn
Italian well, though it fell to him to speak almost like a father to
the Pope on questions of the war. He left all business requiring
the vernacular to Father Philip Langdon who knew Italian and
Italian ways better than the Italians. When Irish affairs grew
troubled, 'Bogey' Harris was sent to talk to the Irish College as
he had the gift of patiently hearing Ireland's woes. But relations
between the Irish College and San Calisto were severed. The
Irish students did not salute Cardinal Gasquet in the streets and
his invitation in later days to meet the Prince of Wales received
no answer. At least the Irish were always genuine and outspoken,
but the 'Black' aristocracy of Rome veered according to the
defeat or victory of the Allies. The British diplomatists found
themselves cut at parties when the Germans were winning and
tolerated when the fortunes of war had changed. But the entourage of the Vatican and the entire Catholic Society during the
First War remained stiffly pro-German. It was Gasquet's great
achievement to have penetrated the aura of neutrality around
the Pope and to have warned him what the *Curia* were doing to
antagonize the possible victors.

Benedict found his very neutrality compromised by the
Sacred College and, to keep the balance, showed especial attention by conversation and pen to Gasquet and Mercier. To the
Belgian Primate he wrote 'your cause is my cause': and to
Gasquet he wrote a series of personal autograph letters no doubt
intended to assure the Allied Governments where he stood. Such
a correspondence between a Pope and a Cardinal *in Curia* must
be unique.

Rome, the original mother of Propaganda, was subject to a
flood of influences from every warring direction. Not unexpectedly
a cloud of Germanic informations hung visibly over the paths
of the Vatican. If the Allies had a case, they were careless of

promoting it in Rome and even less after they had obtained the assistance of Italy.

But neither the diplomatists at the Quirinal nor those at the Vatican are of absolute and ultimate importance in Rome. The ear of the Pope has since remote ages afforded a sounding-board to Europe and his judgment alone counts. The direct approach to the Pope has been rare and difficult. Few Englishmen have enjoyed it. The effusive and well-meaning Monsignor Talbot had a personal influence with Pius IX. Cardinal Manning made direct approach to Pius IX and Leo XIII, but only as a visitor. Subsequently no Englishmen played any part in Rome, though Lord Halifax and the Duke of Norfolk by their prestige as devout Milords drew the Pope's attention to matters which most interested these noblemen.

But it was unique for an Englishman to find himself living in Rome, a Cardinal *in Curia* with direct access to the Pope. Gasquet's appearance proved providential for the Allies. To the German influences in Rome he seemed a formidable opponent. Perhaps they attached too much weight to his power of intrigue. Certainly they regarded him less as an innocent fly on the wheel of diplomacy than as a spider in their mess of spikenard. They nicknamed him *il punto di nero*—the black spot! and in the scarlet of the Sacred College his dark robe gave symbolism to the jibe.

Gasquet's supreme duty was to uphold the Allied Cause against great odds as truthfully and agreeably as possible. It was not only a duty to his country but to his Pope. The process has been formulated in the past as the skilful changing of a Pope *male informatus* to a Pope *bene informatus*: from a Pope deceived to a Pope in a better state of mind, the Infallibility not being available in matters political and diplomatic.

The unfortunate but courageous Benedict was compelled to gather political truth from tainted sources of information. His moral view of the war, his opinion on the invasion of Belgium, he kept to himself. He required no help on matters touching the higher planes of International Law. But the evidences, the propaganda, the exaggerations on both sides ceased not to assail him from the salaried diplomatists surrounding his Court.

The Allies continued to be represented by Sir Henry Howard, who was succeeded by Count de Salis, and their excellent staffs. They were a gentlemanly team. If it had not been for Cardinal Gasquet they would not have been there at all.

Having reached the Vatican they were overwhelmed by the assertions of the Central Powers. The Pope retained a model neutrality, but there were pro-German streaks in his entourage and spies amid the machinery of the Vatican. It is vital to distinguish between being neutral in the First World War and pro-German in the Second. Historians realize the wide differences in the causes and propaganda and hopes in the two wars.

In the First War the United States took a much longer time to dispossess themselves of neutrality. The German, the Irish and the German-Jewish communities (with isolated exceptions) were strongly pro-German; that is in welcoming the arrival of Germany to the mastery of Europe. The defeats of Russia and England were not unwelcome aspirations to Jewish and Irish sections. America did not distinguish the moral gulf between the Allies and Teutons, certainly not officially, until nearly three years had elapsed.

In the First War the Irish at home and abroad felt a conscientious pro-Germanism if a German victory could compel Irish Freedom. The Irish in Rome showed themselves as Irish as Gasquet showed himself British.

In the First War the Vatican herself could contemplate a victory of the Central Powers with equanimity. In Austria the Holy Roman Empire would survive. Catholic Germany would remain a religious and flourishing block in the German Empire. France had for a generation bitterly and officially attacked Catholicism. Russia was an immense rival ecclesiastically and her Communist potentiality had not been revealed. Instinctively the Pope opposed Russia, orthodox and autocratic. Benedict was entitled 'Patriarch of the West.' In every way Russia entailed the East. And East and West mingle as difficultly in religion as in politics, as Kipling's verse has told.

It was not to be wondered if the Vatican should have appeared pro-German subconsciously. Against the German claims to merit

Orthodox Russia, although represented by a Minister at the Vatican, could hardly be counted as a friend to the Catholic Church. Consequently the British Colleges and Clergy in Rome were alone in upholding the British case for the war, and Cardinal Gasquet was their obvious mouthpiece. It was fortunate for us that we at least had a resident Cardinal in Rome, and a universally popular one. But of course he was not the official representative of His Majesty's Government with all that entails.

But the despatch of the British Mission was not quite as easy as it might have been. No sooner had the French Government heard of our intention than they took considerable umbrage and in fact formally protested. It is a little difficult at this date to understand why they objected so strongly, but it may be presumed that it was a dog-in-the-manger policy. Aggressively anti-clerical as they were—it was not long before that the Prime Minister Viviani had talked in the French Chamber about 'extinguishing the lights of Heaven never to be re-lit'—they probably reckoned that we, being the first to recognize the Holy See as by no means extinguished, should be playing into the hands of their Catholic opponents in France. . . . Who knows? At all events His Majesty's Government decided to pay no attention to their protest and to *passer outre*. But it somewhat delayed the departure of the Mission.

Its arrival in Rome was certainly a relief to Cardinal Gasquet, and he at once set to work to sponsor it and to promote its activities in every direction. Luckily the work of the Biblical Commission for the Revision of the Vulgate, the execution of which Pius X had placed in his hands, had brought him a spacious residence, the Palazzo San Calisto, where he could back his personal qualities with suitable pomp and circumstance. The first reception which he gave in honour of the British Mission, to which all British residents in Rome were invited, was an impressive display with illuminated state-rooms, uniformed and liveried retainers and all the rest. It gave the Mission a good send-off.

In 1915 the British Mission, backed by the Cardinal and its Allied friends, had two distinct functions to perform. Officially it had to supply the Vatican authorities with information relevant to the British case in the war, and unofficially to counter enemy propaganda in Catholic circles throughout Italy. As regards the former, the Mission was fortunate to have two such sympathetic and intelligent prelates in charge of ecclesiastical foreign affairs as Cardinal Gasparri, the Secretary of State, and Monsignor Pacelli [the present Pope Pius XII] in the capacity of what we should call Permanent Under Secretary of State. All dealings with Gasparri and Pacelli—they involved weekly visits at least— were conducted in the most friendly atmosphere, although controversy necessarily played a big part. The Mission arrived in the thick of the German occupation of Belgium accompanied with allegations of German atrocities, which were exciting great indignation at home and the hope that the Vatican would be willing to make a pronouncement condemning the German Government. In cold retrospect it is clear not only how unwise, but how impossible such a condemnation would have been. Apart from parallel information at the Vatican that our Russian Allies were behaving in similar manner in Galicia and would merit an equal condemnation (which obviously would not have suited us), if there were to be any condemnation at all, an external authority could hardly be expected to pronounce judgment on any but its own judicial investigation on the spot, and this was not practical policy. Yet passions run high in war time, and there were occasional and sometimes excitable debates in the *coulisses*, especially in regard to the violation of Belgian neutrality, apart from any question of atrocities, debates which may or may not have been justified in themselves, but which at least prevented enemy representatives and agents from having it all their own way. It was also the time of the sinking of the *Lusitania* and other war incidents which gave the members of the Mission an opportunity of dealing a blow at the pro-Germans. But it never was a question of pro-Germanism on what are now called the 'highest levels' and contacts with the Pope himself, the Cardinal Secretary of State and Monsignor Pacelli, while they made it clear that they would never depart—and time has proved them amply right—from their 'neutrality,' there was never any doubt at all where their personal sympathies lay. There was for instance a specific indication of Papal feeling when the Pope signed a photograph for Cardinal Mercier with the inscription 'Your cause is my cause,' though of course he may have meant it in a strictly limited sense. In every case all these matters were discussed as a matter of course at San Calisto, with Cardinal Gasquet taking part and giving the benefit of his experience with the *Curia*.

The other, if perhaps secondary, aim of the Mission, namely to influence Italian Catholics generally, was also in certain ways facilitated by the intimacy with the San Calisto community, particularly where the Catholic press was concerned. It was there that duels took place with the editor of the leading Catholic paper *Corriere d'Italia*, Monsignor Pucci, in which the dynamic Father Philip Langdon, the Cardinal's secretary, could give full vent to his linguistic volubility and become in fact as vocal as his peaceful Eminence could tolerate, despite the spaciousness of the state-rooms.

Although the headquarters of the Mission was at the Palazzo Borghese, where official business was transacted and formal entertainments given, San Calisto became the informal centre for local activities, press interviews and meetings of Allied friends jointly engaged in promoting the Allied case among wavering Italians. A particular group, which in time became almost a permanent unofficial committee, was of an exceptionally international composition. It consisted of Monsignor Deploige, the successor of Cardinal Mercier at the Philosophical Institute at Louvain, who had been driven out by the Germans: of Admiral Yamamoto, at that time Naval Attaché at the Japanese Embassy to the Quirinal: of Prince Wladimir Ghika (afterwards a priest and prelate): of Monsieur Louis Canet, subsequently head of the Ecclesiastical Department at the Quai d'Orsay: one or two other young Frenchmen and Belgians: and members of the British Mission. To all these Cardinal Gasquet extended perpetual hospitality, and indeed without his sponsorship it would have entailed carrying on the work under far less easy circumstances. Resident at San Calisto were the high lights of the Biblical Commission, distinguished scholars like the erudite Abbot Amelli, Dom Quentin, and the versatile and gifted Dom John Chapman (subsequently Abbot of Downside), all O.S.B., the Cardinal presiding over the work. The administration was in the hands of Father Philip Langdon (subsequently titular Abbot of Abingdon), popularly known in Rome as *Don Filippo*, whose energy and resourcefulness in the affairs of the Mission largely contributed to its success. In January 1915 there occurred a catastrophic earthquake in the Abruzzi, which shook all Rome without doing any material damage. Within an hour or so of the shock Father Langdon had hired a car, filled it with clothes, food and relief necessities generally, and was off to the scene of the disaster with members of the Mission.

Parenthetically, the cosmopolitan and somewhat romantic team just described did not confine itself to the purely political. Its spiritual ambitions were equally unbounded, to the extent that in company with the monastic inmates of San Calisto, under the superb musical direction of Dom John Chapman, the Cardinal presiding, they sang in entirety the Holy Week offices in the chapel of the Palazzo, the British, Roumanian and Belgian members taking it in turn to sing the Lamentations at Tenebrae—undoubtedly a unique experience in the annals of diplomacy, which deserves to be recorded. It also obviously strengthened the bond which held the little group together and so powerfully contributed to its political co-operation.

It is therefore not too much to say that without the help of the Cardinal the Mission would have had very uphill work to get going at all, and, even when the initial difficulties were overcome and the first phase of the Mission over, the Cardinal continued to advise the Foreign Office and make recommendations which were of great use. When it was time for the first Head of the Mission, Sir Henry Howard, to retire, it was largely owing to the Cardinal's intervention that a particularly able successor was appointed in the person of Count de Salis. It was during his term of office and greatly owing to his popularity that the Mission gradually took firmer root, helped to overcome prejudice at home and so became transformed into a permanent Legation to the Holy See. Thus from first to last Cardinal Gasquet continued to preside over the destinies of the Mission and his name should always be associated with its inception.

To return to 1915, it was the crucial moment in the war when the intervention of Italy on our side hung in the balance. Giolitti was agitating for compromise with the Germans and Austrians, and against him D'Annunzio, emerging from his Paris exile, was touring triumphantly through Italy inflaming, with picturesque speeches, the Italians to join us. The Palazzo Farnese, housing both the French Embassy to the Quirinal and the pundits of French erudition under the famous Monsignor Duchesne, was the focus of Allied propaganda, and here again one of its most effective younger members was also one of the little Allied group at San Calisto. So it was there on the whole that co-operation could be most practically pursued. Whether, or how far, any of this contributed substantially to Italian popular backing for the Anglo-Italian Agreement of April 1915, it is impossible to say. But it acted as counter-propaganda to the Germans, who had made a big effort by sending down to Rome Prince Bülow, equipped with several millions of lire, to say nothing of violent threats, should the Italians depart from their neutrality—while incidentally it may be said, the British had no funds to corrupt the press, whose correspondents stood on the doorstep, waiting to be corrupted. Our propaganda was peculiarly straightforward and truthful, but in those days propaganda was in its infancy. It was considered quite sufficient to proclaim the justice of the British cause. Strange innocence!

It is here worth recording that in 1915 it so happened that the British Mission had an action to perform which was totally independent of war propaganda or of any of the objects for which it had been despatched to Rome. Diplomatic relations with the Holy See were not an entirely new thing, though they had been spasmodic and always *ad hoc*. Since the days of Cardinal Pole there had been no British Diplomatic Representative resident regularly—Odo Russell, who was for some time resident, was not officially accredited—and there had been no official Mission until that of Sir Lintorn Simmons and later of the Duke of Norfolk, who had come respectively for a specific purpose. The only question between His Majesty's Government and the Holy See which had required a species of concordat—and a concordat it was—concerned the appointment to the Archbishopric of Malta, and it bound the two Powers to agree between themselves on the appointment. It so happened that the See was vacant at the time of the arrival of the British Mission in 1914, and consequently it fell to the latter to implement the Agreement. The candidate proposed was Monsignor Caruana, O.S.B., and, as he was commendable to both parties, the presentation and confirmation were carried through without any discussion. Monsignor Caruana was consecrated in the Church of Santa Maria Trastevere, the church that adjoins the palace of San Calisto, and so it was appropriate that it and the subsequent reception should take place under the aegis of the Benedictine Cardinal.

That the existence of the British Mission, afterwards Legation, has been justified, should by this time be patent to all. It was perhaps necessary, in order to stress its political, and not its religious, character, to appoint subsequent Ministers who were Protestants. When this was put up to Cardinal Gasparri, he saw the point and agreed without hesitation. Since the precedent of 1914 most nations, and not only the European, have established diplomatic relations with the Holy See, and there are now among others both Moslem and Hindu Ministers representing their countries, to the immense advantage of peace policies and of co-operation between the principal creeds of the world.

Moreover, apart from questions of high policy, there are many routine matters which require consultation between His Majesty's Government and the Vatican Authorities. For instance, in the shortage of British priests, the Vatican has frequently been obliged to appoint foreigners to Sees in India and our colonies, and unless there were a good understanding with the Vatican, appointments displeasing to His Majesty's Government, though not known to be displeasing, might easily be made in the absence of any regular channels of consultation. In this way alone the utility of the diplomatic relations has been proved. Finally it is universally acknowledged that the presence during the last war in the Vatican City of a British Minister—in the person of Sir

Francis D'Arcy Osborne—was of the first importance, and it may therefore be hoped that the continuance of the post will never be seriously questioned again.

With the death of Cardinal Gasquet, the removal elsewhere of the Biblical Commission and the appropriation to other uses of the Palace of San Calisto, the memories of the early days of the British Mission will fade, but its association should be a tradition in the annals of the Legation and the Cardinal remembered as one of its founders.

The diplomatic and private papers of the time show without doubt that the Vatican was pro-German and only hoped to retain enough influence to modify what seemed certain in 1914–15, a peace in Germany's favour.

But amidst the hostile tangle which the friends of the Allies found arrayed against them they found encouragement from two historical characters—Pope Benedict and the future Pope Pius XII, who from Gregory's letters showed themselves in favour of the Allies in private.

Pope Benedict made himself accessible to the bitter reproaches of the Allies, and realized that bad-intentioned advisers were responsible for what were called his *gaffes*. For instance, he sent for Gregory spontaneously (January 17, 1915) and during three-quarters of an hour asked questions about the exchange of prisoners and 'asked earnestly that England should do all in our power to make Russia play the game.' Gregory took the chance to let the misinformed Pope know that the English were sincere and determined in the war. He quoted Lloyd George's Christmas message in the *Methodist Times*. When Gregory referred to the cruelties practised in Belgium—

> the Pope nodded approval and said they were indeed abomin-able! But he then observed that with regard to the neutrality of Belgium, of course the Germans had asserted to him over and over again that they had not violated it. I then proceeded to tell him what a deplorable effect the silence of the Holy See was producing even in the large world which did not recognize

16

his spiritual authority. What, I asked him, would his predecessors like Gregory VII or Innocent III have done in a similar case? I added that the world would have preferred their violence to the present silence. . . . The Pope then said he certainly sympathized with what I had said but that he must remember that if he did what I asked him he would unsettle and perhaps alienate all the millions of Catholics who were fighting against us and make their position intolerable.

Gregory pleaded for a Papal condemnation of the philosophy that might is right, since 'the Vatican was very fond of condemning errors.' Gregory proposed that the Pope, to save his neutrality, should add a few British names (presumably Kipling and Admiral Fisher) when he condemned Treitschke and Bernhardi. Gregory apologized for speaking so frankly and fiercely, but the Pope's

warmth and affability with which he dismissed me showed he had not thought it cheek on my part. He is exceedingly quick and at the same time enormously sympathetic and very much a gentleman, in soul as well as by birth, and it seems the greatest pity that he has been fed on German lies. He might have done so much for us, but perhaps he still will.

There were signs of the Pope's feelings. Gregory wrote (February 23, 1915):

The *Mulo* has been at it again, but we came down like a sledgehammer the day (the caricature) reappeared, and the Vatican are going for it hotly once more. We must give them their due, for it cost them 3,500 francs to stop the appearance of the number that was about to come out.

Later, a bright and friendly figure appeared (May 23, 1915):

I had a very straight talk to Pacelli last Wednesday. He is the best of the gang and I have seen him twice since. For the first time, he really unbent as to the inner workings, and confirmed my worst suspicions. But I think I have captured him at last, and he certainly realizes the gravity of the situation for the Vatican. He is accordingly bent on trying to get some Papal pronouncement in the good sense, and even went so far as to ask me to draft something in my *perfectly private* capacity.

A quarter of a century later Pacelli became Pope Pius XII.

XII

ROMAN DIARY (1914–16)

ON May 12, 1914, the Cardinal began recording events in Rome from the time of his return till the death of Pius X, filling a large book in his fine British Museum script.

August 19, 1914, found him in Scotland staying with Sir Stuart Coats. The following day he telephoned to Cardinal Bourne on reading rumours of the Pope's illness and death and 'learnt in reply that a telegram had been received saying that the Pope had died that morning at 1.30 a.m. Later a wire from London by Father Birt conveyed the official notice from Cardinal Merry del Val and urged an immediate return to Rome.'

He needed no urging. A Conclave gave the Historian his first chance to dabble in making history.

On August 22 the Cardinal left Charing Cross with Father Langdon and Mgr. Jackman, picking up Cardinal Bourne at Folkestone. 'In France, just near Amiens we passed a train of the Irish Guards going to the Front and wished them God speed. . . . Throughout our journey both in France and Italy we received the greatest kindness and attention and in Rome we found the royal waiting room prepared for our reception.'

During a *Sede vacante* every Cardinal is *papabilis*, and the Vatican for the time is really a vacuum.

August 27 (Rome): For the next days all the Cardinals attended the *plenaria* held in the Vatican to arrange business from the time of the Pope's death till the Conclave and also the Requiems for the late Holy Father. On August 31 we had one last meeting and the final drawing for rooms in the Vatican for the Conclave. All the Cardinals had arrived except the two Americans, Gibbons and O'Connell. Cardinal Farley was in Europe and so was present.

As the last of the Cardinal Deacons it fell to my lot to act in the Conclave as general manager and Master of Ceremonies, to act as door-keeper and to see that everything was ready that was required. This kept me moving about and busy during the whole time and brought me into relation with all their Eminences and I was very glad to have had the office. I merely note that in spite of the terrible War which was going on, there was no sign during the whole time of the slightest difference between us. My next neighbour was Cardinal Piffle of Vienna, in the Conclave.

From the first there was evidence that the assembled Cardinals did not understand the position of Belgium, or the attitude of England in coming to its support. Cardinal Mercier was told plainly enough that many, if not all, considered that Belgium had brought its misfortunes upon itself by refusing to allow Germany to pass through the country in order to attack France. . . . With the exception of the English-speaking Cardinals and the French this was almost the universal opinion. Possibly I should not include Cardinals Maffi, Ferrari. On August 29 when the news of the sack of Louvain reached Rome, Cardinal Mercier suffered terribly from the lack of sympathy. The general opinion was to deplore the acts but to regard them as a necessary incident of a war. . . .

On August 31 at 5 p.m. the Cardinals took up their places in the Vatican and a couple of hours later the Conclave began by the closing of the doors. The next day the Mass *de Spiritu Sancto* was said and the Cardinals all received Holy Communion. By the new Constitution of Pius X there were two scrutinies in the morning and two in the afternoon. On September 5 Benedict XV was chosen at the second scrutiny and by five o'clock on the same day the doors were unlocked and we were able to return to our homes.

At San Calisto it soon became evident to me that the whole sentiment of ecclesiastical Rome was distinctly pro-German. There was hardly any attempt to conceal this, although the Holy See was by declaration, and so far as the Pope was concerned, certainly *neutral*. The so-called Catholic Press hardly took the trouble to disguise its partisanship. The reason appeared to me obvious. The German side had been represented at the Vatican constantly by the Ministers of Prussia, Austria and Bavaria whilst the Allies only had the Minister of Belgium, who had been in Rome a very long time and had become timid and retiring. Russia was uncertain and much distrusted owing to its failure to keep promises in the past. France not only had no representative but the present Government represented the anti-Catholic spirit. England of course had no one to represent its side in the quarrel of nations. . . . Some of the Cardinals regarded Germany as the nation of Law and Order. One Cardinal argued with me that the War was entirely made by English and French Freemasonry, which was striving to drag Italy into a War which would overwhelm the Church. This and the vision of Russia, which was always present to the ecclesiastical mind in Rome, as *the peril* to be dreaded made it expedient to lean on the side of Austria and Germany. . . .

At the time of the Conclave the position of France as a nation was discussed. The account of the wonderful revival of religion in the country, of which Cardinal Amette of Paris and Cardinal Sévin of Lyons gave testimony, was hardly believed. Cardinal Sévin pointed out to the Hungarian Cardinal what the Church of France had really achieved since the breaking of the Concordat. He asked what the position of Catholics in Austria-Hungary would have been, had the State not only cut itself off from the Church but had confiscated all the Church possessions and imposed an irreligious system of education. The Hungarian prelate replied that it would have been fatal to religion and quite hopeless to have expected the people to have come to the support of the ministers of religion.

Cardinal Sévin then related how his diocese had recovered its full Catholic life and the many reasons there were for considering France still a Catholic country in spite of her governing classes.

I had long talks with many Cardinals and Roman ecclesiastics, but nothing prevailed in disabusing them of the idea that it was English and French Freemasonry that was responsible for this European conflagration.

After the Conclave I saw a good deal of Cardinal Maffi of Pisa and we formed a warm friendship, which I trust will last for our lives. I never came across anyone who was more *sympathetic* to me.

A fortnight after the election of the new Pope I had an audience and freely discussed with him the situation as I saw it. I had been thrown with him a great deal during the days of the

Conclave and found that he was a man to whom it was as easy to talk as to the late Pontiff. He possessed a great heart, was most quick in seizing an idea, but he was above everything a trained diplomatist. I endeavoured in this first audience to try and insist that in these early days of the War, it would be to the interest of the Church for the Pope to make some general pronouncement upon the Catholic principles which should guide all Christian combatants in the conduct of the struggle. . . . The Holy Father, whilst hearing me with sympathy and patience, considered that his only attitude was one of strict *neutrality*. Any condemnation of practices would, he thought, be construed into a condemnation of Germany. I saw plainly in this interview that the pressure exerted by the Austrian, Bavarian and Prussian ministers at the Vatican was so constant and insistent that there was little hope of any declaration being made at this time.

During a holiday at Leghorn the Cardinal soon conceived the idea of a British Mission to the Holy See, 'if we could induce the Pope to accept and the British Government to send a Mission, even during the time of the war.' A fortunate chance brought him into correspondence with Rennell Rodd, the British Ambassador. The Archbishop of Malta had providentially died and there was an agreement that the Holy See should consult the Foreign Office concerning his successor. This gave the Cardinal the opportunity to broach the question of a Mission to both sides. He found the Ambassador and the Pope consenting parties. 'The Pope immediately expressed his agreement and I asked him in the event of my being able to work the matter, if he would wish me to try. He gave me all authority to do so.' The inevitable Duke of Norfolk was induced to write a letter.

Before success was obtained, the whole position was nearly wrecked. The idea leaked into the spiteful spying of the Press and raised Protestant feelings in England. The Foreign Office was frightened and toned down the idea of a Mission to a visit by Sir Henry Howard, to congratulate the Pope on his accession without any thought of remaining. 'Cardinal Gasparri drafted a telegram of a very curt nature and had written a letter to the effect that the proposition was altogether different to what had

been suggested in the letter to the Duke of Norfolk.' Cardinal
Gasquet wisely kept Gasparri's letter back until Rennell Rodd
could communicate with Sir Edward Grey: 'Unfortunately it
was a Saturday and the telegram to Sir Edward Grey remained
in London unopened as the latter was away for the weekend!
Thus no reply was received on Monday. Cardinal Gasparri came
on Monday to San Calisto to express his and the Pope's anxiety
for some reply.' The curt telegram would have been sent but in
the nick of time arrived word that Sir Henry Howard would
come with full powers as Minister Extraordinary. 'Father
Langdon immediately went off to the Vatican with this message
and took back the telegram and letter, which I had held over,
bringing back another telegram accepting cordially the proposal
of the British Government. This was on Wednesday, December 9,
and the same night the letter went by the Embassy bag.'

This concluded a neat piece of work which at one stroke
brought England into the Vatican.

Later Cardinal Gasquet took up the Pope's proposal to make a
Christmas truce in the trenches, which fell through owing to
France and Russia. The German Press announced that the
Prussian Minister had convinced the Pope there was nothing in
the reported destruction of Rheims Cathedral. This Cardinal
Gasquet countered by a letter from Cardinal Luçon which he
took to the Pope who promised to write to Luçon direct.

Sir Henry Howard arrived and held his official receptions at
San Calisto. Some fourteen Cardinals and 150 Prelates attended,
'all the British Colleges attended in force with the exception of
the Irish College. The reception was boycotted with some un-
necessary rudeness by the Vice Rector and students. Father David
Fleming, a very old friend, went so far as to return his card of
invitation. It may be well to note that I believe this boycotting
was more to show the dislike of the Irish for the Mission than
their objection to having an English Cardinal *in Curia*.'

Gasquet was bewildered by Irish politics and by the attitude
of Mgr. O'Riordan and Dr. O'Hagan who presided the Irish
College (who he thought were good friends). Unfortunately

they had mistaken him as an enemy to Home Rule, though Gasquet insisted: 'I had never in my life said a single word about Home Rule to the Pope and further I had never received a single letter from the Duke of Norfolk nor from any Irish Bishop on the subject of Home Rule.'

The intense feelings in Rome tended to bring out Nationalism and under their Catholicism the Irish were more Irish than their leader John Redmond, who had privately aided the sending of the British Mission. By all accounts the French and German ecclesiastics were even more French and German than their representatives. And the old type of English Catholic like Sir Henry Howard was always more royal than the King. We cannot blame the actions of the Irish College, which had always regarded the Vatican as an Irish preserve, when they found in these vital days not only an English Cardinal but a full-fledged Mission descending upon them!

Cardinal Gasquet had several severe skirmishes with the Catholic Press in Italy of which he complained bitterly to Gasparri. The climax came when the *Mulo* of Bologna

had a most vile picture of Blessed Joan of Arc between two English soldiers. This was sent broadcast to the priests and even to religious women of Rome! Mgr. Herzog and the Rector of the Canadian College came with copies and begged me to protest against such an outrage. I wrote a very strong letter to the Holy Father on the subject and enclosed him a copy of the incriminated paper. To this the Holy Father replied in the letter I here insert:

The Pope's letter translated from the Italian

Eminence,

I do not delay for a moment in replying to the letter which Your Eminence has written to me this morning because the same deals with a subject so important as to require immediate attention. The Cardinal Secretary of State had already informed me of the just complaints against the *Mulo* of Bologna and similar newspapers. Although it is well known that the said journals do not depend on the Holy See—which does not in any way deal with them—Cardinal Gasparri told me last hoped that a better reply would have been in the statement made by the *Osservatore Romano* on Thursday. In effect I know that the Belgian Minister has declared himself fully satisfied, and that he has said the incident is closed. But now I learn that the English Colony does not show similar satisfaction. I am surprised at this, and all the more because England was not directly interested in the matter. I pray Your Eminence to use your influence to calm people's minds, inviting them to reflect that though the incident was certainly regrettable, none the less it was given an importance greater in fact than it deserved. I have renewed my advice and orders that greater attention be given to not wounding the reasonable susceptibilities of anyone; and thus I hope that incidents of this kind shall not be repeated, though I would wish that should they unhappily arise, there shall be no further doubt as to the good faith and loyalty of the Holy See.

I am, with special esteem,

Yours very affectionately,
BENEDICTUS PP. XV

March 13, 1915.

A very lame excuse for the offence of the *Osservatore* was inserted in the next number.

With the month of May the situation in Rome became very critical in political matters. The idea that Italy had become very restive as regards relations with Austria was prevalent. It was known that von Bülow had moved heaven and earth to secure continued neutrality at any cost.

On Friday May 8 came the news of the sinking of the *Lusitania*. I felt impelled to try and obtain from the Holy Father some expression of condemnation. The *Osservatore* appeared to associate the Allies in these barbarous methods of modern warfare. The Holy Father's reply was the following:

The Pope's letter translated from the Italian

Eminence,

My desire to help, whenever it may be possible for me to do so, the requirements of Your Eminence, has made me give

special attention to what is contained in your letter of the day
before yesterday. But I have not considered it possible to depart
from the usual practice of the Holy See which as Your Eminence
knows, is accustomed to submit each case on its own merits to
competent persons when any unusual measure is to be taken.
The question here is of making a protest against the sinking of
the *Lusitania*.

I hasten to say that the wise reflections of the Consultor do
not encourage an immediate protest from the Holy See, but
instead I intend to accelerate the date for the holding of a Consistory already announced so that I may have occasion to
renew the condemnation of all *methods of barbarism* which, alas,
we see have been introduced into this war and which among
other sad conditions have caused the deaths of so many victims,
such as the barbarous sinking of the *Lusitania*.

With especial esteem I rejoice to reaffirm myself yours most
affectionately,

BENEDICTUS PP. XV

May 12, 1915.

It is worth noting that there is no manner of doubt that the
Vatican authorities were entirely ignorant of the fact that the
furnishing of munitions was allowed by all International Law.
The Pope thought that it was against the Law of Nations and
intended this, though he did not expressly say as much, in his
celebrated *interview* for the American *World*.

Previously to the incident of the *Lusitania* I asked and
obtained an audience to explain my views about the *interview*,
which caused so widespread a feeling of indignation in France
and as it seemed to suggest to America that it was wrong to
furnish munitions of war to England. The Holy Father had not
expressed this exactly . . . but he admitted with regret that
he had himself corrected an Italian version of what he had said.
He was much disturbed when I told him the character of the
World and how it was not looked upon as a respectable paper
in the States. He clearly admitted that the whole thing was a
mistake and it should never happen again. The whole was
evidently a German plot engineered by Mgr. Gerlach and I
think by the Bavarian Minister.

These are only passages from the Diary written in the first

1925

April 22: A letter from the Queen [Mary].

April 25: Princess Helena Victoria came to tea.

May 17: Canonization of Little Flower. Began at 8.30 and finished a little after two.

May 24: Cardinal Mercier has arrived, his conversations with Anglicans finished. It is said that they are agreed that nothing practical can be done. No compromise on doctrine being possible!

May 25: Paul Claudel, Ambassador of France to Japan, called. His great desire is to see the *Vie Monastique* established at Tokio. He thinks that this is the best way to convert the Japs. Great numbers are ripe for conversion and the Government is well disposed.

Cardinal Mercier found English ecclesiasts as chilly over his Anglican venture as he had found Roman Cardinals during the war.

October 24: I had an audience of the Holy Father. We discussed the question of the Malines Conference but though I spoke very plainly he still approved of the fact that conversations in private could do no harm. I replied that unfortunately they were regarded as semi-official. He did not put any value on the alleged falling-off of conversions. Even if people were wanting it, it showed that they were not prepared to take the step etc. One thing he said which was important, that of course there could be no compromise about the Eucharistic beliefs and Ordinations.

So Gasquet found himself back again with the questions of Reunion and Anglican Orders after thirty years. It was strange to find Mercier in Rampolla's place trying to find a way of squaring the ecclesiastical circle and making valid the invalid.

The Cardinal was famous for his humorous little asides. English visitors carried away morsels.

Mr. Harold Anderson repeats a story from Mrs. Arthur Strong of a lecture given in the Hypogeum, where one of the frescoes represents a woman who appeared to be weaving figures including a naked youth. The Cardinal was heard to observe, when Mrs. Strong suggested the scene was possibly emblematic of Charity: 'It looks as if it will be a long time before that poor young man will receive his clothes!'

He had no use for modernism applied to Church subjects in art or wood-print or painting or even in literary form. His heavy John Bullism did not allow him to appreciate Father Martindale's style of prose or Eric Gill's sacred statuary. It was an irony of fate that his features in death were graven in the style of Gill upon his Downside tomb.

Yet he was no Philistine. He loved the mediaeval beauty of the Lord's House and exulted in the giant proportions of Gothic. At the same time he wrote an exquisite mediaeval script.

The Irish Banshee is heard from time to time and in a sanguine moment the Cardinal sings *Te Deum* over the prospects of Irish Peace.

He settles questions from the ends of Christendom for nuns and religious. He resettles the Beda and English Colleges. He delves into the secret Archives of the Church. As Librarian to the Vatican he has access to the lost and secret history of the past. The revised Vulgate slowly issues until Genesis is in print. There are holidays in England: visits to Downside, Ramsgate and Brighton. There are speeches and papers to be compiled and read. There is a visit to Cambridge to preside over the Catholic Biblical Congress. A meeting in the schools is rudely interrupted by Dr. Coulton in person. Father Philippo stands between the twain and frustrates Coulton of his hope of engaging in a public wrangle. Slowly he winds his way downhill to the terminus. Walks with Mgr. Pisani and talks with the Pope become rarer. New Cardinals take their place. He attends the Consistory raising Lucidi and Galli to the Cardinalate, little dreaming that they will accompany his *terna* of death when he comes to die. For Roman legend insists that Cardinals die in threes. And Gasquet will be no exception.

He became more proudly and pronouncedly English in exile. When he led English visitors into his study, he used to stop to point out the carpet and say: 'You see it is quite like an English room.' He never took to Italian ways or even to the Italian language.

Mrs. Arthur Strong, when in charge of the English School of Archaeology, 'insisted that one should always kiss the ring of Cardinal Merry del Val but never that of Cardinal Gasquet, for he was *too English* and preferred to shake hands.' After Mrs. Strong became a Catholic, the Cardinal's car 'was frequently to be seen outside the school. Occasionally she would arrange an excursion for one or two of the archaeologists to the English College or to San Calisto.' It all shows how the Cardinal drew all English folk and English interests in Art or Society under his mantle.

Was it his island spirit or his naval descent that led him to say that he preferred to come from England by sea and proudly mentioned his powers to remain well even in stormy weather.

The old round of Congregations and Canonizations continued. Like the other Cardinals he found the stubborn Pope had no use for his advice. They all found themselves loosely harnessed to the Papal dray without sharing in its direction.

Little requests were always granted. Gasquet notes that he recommended Hinsley, the future English Cardinal, for promotion. It was a brilliant suggestion.

1926

April 30: Audience with Holy Father. Discussed many things. Strongly recommended Father Philip to Holy Father for a post in future. Also asked him to honour Mgr. Hinsley, Rector of English College, by making him a Bishop.

To Mussolini, the risen portent, there was but one allusion in the Diary: the attempt which the well-intentioned Miss Violet Gibson made on his life. But History refused to be diverted and she only snipped his nose. Her brother was the convert Lord Ashbourne.

A great triumph came his way which brought him the honour of being photographed with the Pope:

June 6: Presented the Holy Father with the first volume of the corrected Vulgate and was taken with him surrounded by the Fathers of San Calisto.

The revision of the Vulgate proved an immense and unending work. Gasquet might have quoted words from the Prologue to the Wycliffite Bible, to his own effect making an astonishing parallel:

A simple creature had much travail with divers fellows and helpers to gather many old Bibles and to make one Latin Bible some deal true and then to study it off the next text.

He had never spared himself. When he had taken his first Report to Pius X, the Pope noticed that the work was completely in Gasquet's handwriting and said: 'I do not expect the President of a Commission to do all the work himself.'

Gasquet had made no reply but glanced meaningly at a pile of papers on the table covering all the accounts of money received by the Holy See to help the victims of the Messina earthquake. They happened to be written entirely in the Pope's handwriting!

Once when showing the stacks of photographed texts to an English visitor he exclaimed in utter weariness:

'I sometimes wish I had never seen it!'

He was a worker working himself to a standstill.

1927

January 5: I received from the Holy Father a silver medal of the Vulgate presentation.

January 7: The Pope wants to know how many medals should be set aside for chief benefactors. I have made a list of seventeen.

The *Action Française* is now put on the Index and so I must stop its reception here.

This was a sore subject amongst Gasquet's French assistants: perhaps as piercing as Modernism has been amongst his English friends. The *Action Française* of Charles Maurras represented Fascism, Caesarism and Paganism under a Catholic cloak. But it was spiritualized by many devout followers. French Catholics were acutely divided and even the French monks working at the Vulgate. Gasquet found it necessary in the end to forbid the mention of the *Action Française* at all. Moved by his French followers, he ventured to speak to the Pope on its behalf but received a cold reply. The Pope would ask his opinion when he needed it. Cardinal Billot went further and found it necessary to resign his Red Hat.

Entries become fewer. A new friendship came into his circle typical of the many English clients he received.

April 12: Evan Morgan to tea. He says that the impression in England is that we shall have an Election about July. Also that Baldwin is tired and that the next Prime Minister will be Winston.

Evan Morgan (Lord Tredegar) had come into the Cardinal's perspective in 1924 and had afforded him much entertainment and some anxiety. A convert from High Society to the Church, he had had the courage to stand as a Tory for Parliament against Mr. Attlee in Limehouse. He then entered the Beda College (with his suite!) to pursue his studies for the Papal Diplomacy. Like Baron Corvo and Ronald Firbank, he was one of the eccentric offerings which the age had added to Our Lady's Dowry. The Pope himself took interest in his case, advising him to marry, while the Cardinal recognized him as a charming character returned from the Renaissance.

Halcyonic days followed the First War in the Holy City, where all that was agreeable and amusing from the shattered Societies of Christendom could still meet under the shadow of the Papal prestige. Exiled royalty, disenchanted statesmen, wandering ecclesiasts passed from salon to salon if not from Basilica to Basilica. The fragments of Europe coalesced in Rome. The Cardinal built up an English centre such as Rome had

never known before or since. The English flourished as never
before. Eugenie Strong was lecturing at the English School to
student and expert alike. English Monsignori like Mann or
Barnes were informing unlistening Romans about the history of
their Popes or the location of St. Peter's bones. The English
College and the Beda were full of war veterans or 'invalid'
parsons. And, as Lord Berners wrote from Rome at the time,
'occasionally Evan Morgan is seen carrying a sheaf of lilies to
some distant shrine and all is serene and beautiful.'

For the Cardinal, sought and honoured, by pilgrim or
professor, by Catholic or Protestant fellow-countrymen from
England, the War's aftermath was continuously happy.

None were closer to him than Mary Anderson, most beautiful
of Catholic actresses, and her family. When Lewis Waller was
rehearsing the *Garden of Allah* with her, he could not understand
why the hero returned to the monastery. Mary and Gasquet tried
to explain the Catholic belief in a *vow*. To Gasquet's great
amusement the matinée idol answered: 'I would go to Hell for
the woman I loved. Wouldn't you, Abbot?'

XIV

LAST DAYS

His body to that pleasant country's earth
And his pure soul unto his Captain Christ
Under whose colours he had fought so long.

SHAKESPEARE

DURING the winter of 1926 Gasquet was sorely stricken by illness and was able to visit England only in an enfeebled condition. During that summer he paid his final visit to Downside and chose his last resting place between the columns of St. Benedict's Chapel on the Epistle side of the High Altar. Returning to Rome, he refused to quit his work at the Vulgate, which was carried on by relays of Benedictines. As a Cardinal he was still attending monthly audiences with the Pope or presiding at long and elaborate functions in churches. On these occasions he used to return much exhausted and comfort himself by saying: 'One feels that one is not entirely on the shelf.'

He was not destined to live into the 'thirties, so full of tragedies for Christendom. Although he had kept his old diabetic enemy at bay, he was suffering from disease of the heart. He could not walk easily. When his legs failed him, he would murmur humorously: 'I have kept my reason but I have lost my *understanding*.'

His last production was the *Obit Book* of the Venerable English College which he compiled and printed in 1929. Therein, day by day through the year, he compiled the names and memories of the College patrons, ecclesiasts, students, Martyrs from the old books. It was the sort of industrious work he did so well.

The Cardinal's last days in Rome were amongst the happiest of his long and energetic life. He could look back at many achievements and even more initiations. His ambitions for the Benedictine Order in England had been met and reached. He had found them diminished and scattered. He had restored them to something like their old national position.

Sitting in the warm sunlight of Italy, in the perennial light which played upon the Palace of San Calisto, he had time to meditate, not only the meditations of the monk, but of an old man who looks back on a wonderful and unexpected career.

What were his crowding memories?

From the early days in Bayswater he had always lived amongst Ecclesiasts and men devoted to religious life. The serving of Cardinal Manning's Mass at Bayswater rose in distant memory. There were the Oblates of St. Charles, eager converts gathered about their determined leader. They were all dead many years. He had known those followers of the old Archdeacon before he became Cardinal, men like Cyril Forster, who became the first Chaplain of the Irish Guards, and Francis Burnand, who became editor of *Punch*. They had all called him 'Frank': little Frank Gasquet, the doctor's son—far back in the 'fifties.

Followed the memories of old Downside. There was the historic moment when he had come over the Somerset hillside driven in an old-fashioned carriage, and his eyes had fallen for the first time on lowly buildings nestling amongst ancient trees. There were secluded old-fashioned days at the school, with the quaint old monks chanting and the boys playing traditional games. The Benedictine ideal shadowed and sheltered that forgotten corner of the English West. The splendid figure of old Ullathorne, the last of the Vicars Apostolic, crossed his life. He remembered the dauntless old monk, who had served his chaplaincy in Botany Bay and by his determination swept the horrors of convict life out of Australia.

The monks had passed easily and friendliwise into his existence. He had never wished to leave them and he passed into Noviceship that he might stand with them in the House of God. He was learning to pray and chant at Belmont. Then he was back at Downside working in the school amongst knife-scarred desks and boys and inkpots. He could remember what the school was and the old monks who wanted no change, and the quiet coming and going of dark-robed figures to the missions and parishes. And he had begun to dream—dreams of a bigger school, bigger monastery, bigger community and at last of a towering minster like the great English Abbeys of old.

From his haven in Rome he could see the great tower of Saint Gregory the Great, from which rolled the thunder of bells across the pastures and meadows of the West. It was more than the ghost of Glastonbury. It was one of the great Abbeys re-arisen from the pages of his first Book as though Glastonbury were restored, rebuilt for England.

He could remember the long laborious days, hundreds and hundreds of days, scribbling in the British Museum and the Record Office. He must have crossed tracks with hundreds of unknown students and with the whole school of English historians. But he had wrested his history of the English Monasteries out of those faded manuscripts and he knew that his work was good enough until better took its place.

He remembered Edmund Bishop ever at his side, never at a loss for a book or a date or some rare trait of Liturgy. And he remembered the monks who worked with him, like Stephen Rawlinson and Norbert Birt in the Museum, and at Downside, Edmund Ford and Leander Ramsay, who had come to their Abbotship and been entombed in the mighty choir which he had built.

He recalled the Popes for whom he had worked personally— Leo XIII with his bright puzzled eyes questioning the validity of Anglican Orders, the bewildered Benedict XV, whom he had seen coming out of Conclave, and the bibliophile Pius XI, for whom he had voted among the Cardinals of the world. Above all he remembered Pius X, who had created him Cardinal and thereby placed an English monk in the Sacred College; Pius X, who had called him to Rome and laid the revision of the Vulgate Bible on his shoulders.

And the difficult years of the First War in Rome when the flag and honour of England seemed entrusted to his vigilance: and he was slighted as the 'punto nero,' the black blot on the Sacred College.

18

He recalled bringing the British Legation to the Vatican and the unending struggles and protests and Papal Audiences pleading his cause. And the happier days of Peace, when the Pope had given him the Keys of the Vatican Library, the Archives of Holy Church. Those were days when he could hunt for manuscripts and *incunabula* and first editions and lost letters to his heart's content with no one to hurry or harry him. He had ruled supreme in the Vatican Library.

Thenceforward he had lived in Rome, sometimes revisiting old haunts in England, Monasteries and the Universities as in a dream. About him lived and worked the Benedictines, while the slow work of comparing and collating Vulgate manuscripts never ceased. The great Order, to which he had dedicated his life, would finish his life's work for him when he was gone.

He could sit back at last and rest and dream awhile. There were still Audiences with the Holy Father to be attended and ceremonies to be slowly and solemnly presided in the magnificence of his black robe crowned with the Cardinal's scarlet biretta on his old head. And there were constant funerals of other Cardinals. It was after attending one that he himself had sickened and found himself weakening but in serenity and peace. He was glad to receive the Last Sacraments given by monks of his own Order. He was passing away from Rome and from England—sinking into the arms of Saint Benedict. He belonged to his Order now and for ever. The dark-robed monks moved about him as though about to take him from the busy world of Rome unto themselves.

He looked round for the most faithful and strenuous of them, Father Philip Langdon. But in vain. It was the last little sacrifice he was required to make. What Ambrose St. John had been to Newman, Don Filippo had been to him. . . . It was Dom Urban Butler who cared for him in his last hours. And the *Dream of Gerontius* was upon him: the Litany of the dying and soon the prayers of Requiem with all the restrained passion of the Church for the dying and the dead.

He would be going home very soon to Downside. It had been his last request of the Pope, and leave had been granted. .

The end came soon after he had risen from a bed of sickness

to attend the funeral of Cardinal Galli. He caught a chill which
led to pneumonia which rapidly proved fatal. He passed some
uncomfortable hours between bed and armchair, but feeling the
end was near he summoned his brethren and gave them his last
blessing. In his last words he uttered his monastic ideal '*ora et
labora.*' On April 5, 1929, at four in the evening he passed away
with 'an eye full of gentle salutations and soft responses—
whispering soft like the last low accents of an expiring saint,' as
it is written in *Tristram Shandy.*

Mary Anderson wrote of the death to the Benedictine Nuns
in Stanbrook Abbey (April 5, 1929):

I have just wired the sad news.—Cardinal died 4.30 this
afternoon—Soon after lunch today Tony was rung up to say
the Cardinal was dying and at once went to Palazzo San
Calisto. His Eminence was sitting in a chair and looked like
dead. Father Butler said, here is Mr. de Navarro! He opened
his eyes, smiled and said: Oh, Tony—and held his two hands
and then said: 'How is Mamie? (me).' Then he closed his eyes
again and in an hour and a half was dead. We are ever so upset
as we were seeing a lot of him. A week ago tomorrow he was
here lunching with us in wonderful form, amusing and looking
really splendidly well. He came at one and remained to four
and Father Butler said he enjoyed coming here so much. He
was full of the Abbot of Downside's death and so pleased with
the letters about him in *The Times*, but he was very annoyed
about a letter in the same paper, bringing up the old Boccaccio
story about the books at Monte Cassino and told us (this was
a few days before the lunch last Saturday) that he was going to
answer the letter. He did and said he had simply stated facts and
that if the writer of the ugly letter said anything further, he
had everything ready to answer him but he said: 'He won't
say another word. My letter will shut him up.' Day before
yesterday he did far too much and when Tony saw him
yesterday, he found him *very* tired out, also he told me he had
taken a hot bath and couldn't get his breath after, but he had
been very bright and well and said to Tony: '83 and not out!'
Tony stayed by him till he died at 4.30 and has gone out with
wires now so as to get prayers for him. Father Philip can't get

here till seven too late and Father Butler got us to wire
Downside.

P.S. Father Philip has been with his sister in Florence some
days. I may tell you the Cardinal was difficult with his diet.
He came here to lunch in January and Father Butler said he had
great trouble to get him to wear his overcoat. He said 'I won't
go there looking like a trussed fowl!' Well he died quickly and
peacefully and had the Last Sacraments. The Holy Father will
feel his going, as they were such friends and he saw a great deal
of the Pope. Cardinal Bisletti came in while he was dying.

Father Wilmart, O.S.B., added details (April 7, 1929):

On Easter Day the dear Cardinal showed me your letter
and spoke with me about the Life of St. Wulstan. He proposed
to go again to the Library in order to appreciate the chances of
recovering the lost text. On Wednesday he came back a little
tired from the funeral of Cardinal Galli after which he took
lunch with some friends (The Navarros). It was too much for
his strength but even all the following day we kept confident.
On Friday morning the Cardinal received the Last Sacraments
but only because it was insisted on. Even then he did not think
the end was approaching quickly. At 2 o'clock he inquired from
a visitor if Sir Frederick Kenyon had been well received at the
Vatican on the preceding day. At 4 he was obliged to leave and
the doctors supposed he would be able to continue the fight
several hours. The main thing seemed to be the feebleness of
the heart and he understood everything up till the end.

It was a domestic tragedy that the faithful Don Filippo was
not present, being absent through illness at Florence, but Dom
Urban had remained continually by his side and brought his body
back to Downside by land and sea.

Don Filippo was able to attend the lying-in-state which was
carried out with all the Roman ritual. For two days and nights
the Cardinal lay on a bed of purple clothed in his Benedictine
robe. On the third day he was vested in his pontificals and the
customary eulogy was read over his embalmed body.

Sealed in his casket, surmounted by his Red Hat, he was
carried to Santa Maria in Trastevere and placed beneath a blazing

catafalque. In Rome Cardinals are laid upon the floors of their Titular Churches. Dying in the Holy City, they are expected to be buried where they fall, but in Gasquet's case the Pope had permitted translation to Somerset.

The Requiem was sung in Rome by the Abbot of Monte Cassino and the Absolutions were given by the Dean of the Sacred College, Cardinal Vincenzo Vannutelli, old 'Indestructible,' as Gasquet used to call him. His body was taken to the railway station and it was noticed that he passed St. Gregory's on the Coelian Hill on the journey to St. Gregory's in the Mendips. The saying in Rome is that Cardinals always die in threes. Cardinal Gasquet's companions in sepulchral trilogy were Galli and Lucidi.

Dom Urban hastily seized the Cardinal's Red Hat which by appealing to privilege he refused to disclose to Custom officers. Was a Cardinal not reckoned in rank with a Prince of the Blood? Yes, he was!

Don Filippo was left to convalescence and executorship of the Will permitted by the Pope. The hard and fast rule of Poverty had been relaxed and Cardinal Gasquet's poor possessions and trinkets were accounted property which could be divided amongst friends.

His body reached Downside on April 12 where Abbot and Monks were waiting at the West Door. The Solemn Dirge was sung on April 14 and on the following morning Cardinal Bourne sang the Solemn Requiem.

At noon the *Libera* was chanted and Francis Aidan Gasquet was laid in the haven where he had wished to be and whose breakwaters he had built.

Over the grave a striking though somewhat oriental effigy has been erected of the Cardinal lying in full length in prayerful repose. The likeness scarcely recognizable in the smoothed grey marble seems symbolic rather than natural. An angel is represented clasping his pillow, while a minute almost gnomelike St. Benedict upholds his feet. It is all very moving and mediaeval and especially the richly painted *testa* of carven wood surmounting the tomb, betraying the exquisite hand of Sir Gilbert Scott. In the space towards the soaring roof hangs the scarlet-tasselled Hat, the sublime reward upon earth for so many works and struggles, so many dreams and achievements, so many hours of study, so many vigils of prayer: the fantastic reward which comes to so few; the Hat which the Church in her sublime humour allows her most Eminent to dream they can carry with them into the next world but leaves dangling over their graves between Heaven and Earth!

'*Flos Nigrorum Monachorum*,' Matthew Paris wrote of a great Benedictine Bishop in his day. Thou, also, Francis Aidan Gasquet, wert Flower of the Black Monks in thy day!

The tomb is inscribed:

AIAE. IMPLORA PACEM. FRANCISCO AIDANO GASQVET. S. MARIAE IN PORTICV S.R.E. PBRO. CARDINALI. S. GREGORII MONACHO. OLIM S. ALBANI ABBATI TITVLARI. QVI A.D. NON. OCTOBR. MDCCCXLVI NATVS. OBIIT NON. APRIL. MCMXXIX. AMICI POSVERVNT.

which may be rendered:

Pray for the peace of soul of Francis Aidan Gasquet, Cardinal Priest of St. Mary *in Porticu*, monk of St. Gregory, formerly titular Abbot of St. Alban, who was born 5 October, 1846, died 5 April, 1929. Placed by friends.

POSTSCRIPT

Out of the volume of Press notices few carried biographical value except *The Times*. Later Abbot Cuthbert Butler summarized him in the *Dictionary of National Biography* as 'A man of slight build, but overflowing with energy, he threw himself into every phase of the school life, including games and music, and was a successful teacher of history and mathematics.' Ordination did not impair his 'good-humoured enthusiasm.' His Priorship of seven years was 'the turning-point in the history of Downside.' He was the ideal monastic head, 'not a strong ruler, but he ruled well by the power of his personal charm and understanding sympathy.'

Whatever he required of others he failed not of himself. Seven years of reading into the night and working all day had undermined his health. He was the last to quench the lamp at night and the first to appear in the Choir at dawn.

As a monk his Benedictine climax was achieved with the opening of the new century. Abbot Cuthbert Butler summarized his position during the next fourteen years:

In 1899 Pope Leo XIII put into his hands the execution of the Bull whereby the old English Benedictine Congregation was released from the conditions imposed since penal times, and reorganized on more traditional Benedictine lines, the monasteries being raised to the rank of abbeys. The Pope named Gasquet chairman of the papal commission appointed to carry through this reform and to draw up revised constitutions. In 1900 the general chapter of the Congregation elected him abbot president, to give effect to the new order of things; and to this office he was re-elected up till 1914.

This was the year of his Cardinalate and the beginning of his historic residence in Rome.

In his Obituary of April 6, 1929, *The Times* said:

It was Gasquet's merit that more than all others since Cardinal Erskine he used his high position to serve his country's interests. At the outbreak of the War neither France nor England was officially represented at the Vatican. On the other hand, the Central Powers had their Embassies, which were active *foyers* of German thought and influence. Besides the Embassies, there lived in Rome many German clergy, heads of colleges and of religious houses, men justly held in esteem for their learning and integrity. Their views on the War, freely expressed, were naturally pro-German, and frequently diplomatic falsehoods coined in Germany were accepted and circulated by them. From the first, Cardinal Gasquet set himself to combat vigorously this campaign of misrepresentation. The appointment of a British Envoy to the Vatican strengthened his hands, and with both Sir Henry Howard and the Count de Salis he worked in cordial co-operation. At the same time, his influence steadily went to convey to the highest quarters a fuller knowledge of facts and a clearer appreciation of the Allied Governments' aims.

This was true enough although it put the achievement very mildly. The Cardinal had performed a difficult and patriotic task with a success which could never be sufficiently estimated or requited by his fellow-countrymen. Pope Benedict purged the Vatican of German spies and discouraged German supporters. Succeeding Popes never allowed the political German influence within the *limina Apostolorum* again. In prestige and influence the British Legation stood and remained highest. This was Gasquet's work and it is marvellous in the eyes of those who remembered the old days.

The Cardinal's legacy was threefold.

1. The British Legation at the Holy See.
2. The School and Abbey at Downside.
3. The turn of the tide in the national estimate of the Religious Orders in English History.

In his practical mind he would probably have considered the third and last achievement as the least. He had no literary ambitions nor desire to use his historical sense and industry to his power and glory.

He was surprised himself at the success of his first books.

Whatever furious criticisms and hysteria were aroused by less popular and over-biassed historians, nothing could take away his claim to have laid the first whitewash where all had been tar.

Certainly during Gasquet's lifetime the Religious Orders, great and small, returned to England, not without a general tolerance and appreciation of their ideals and of a life far at variance with the national tradition. To this change of view in England Gasquet's contribution was probably second only to that of Cardinal Newman.

Then, Soul, live thou upon thy servant's loss
And let that pine to aggravate thy store;
Buy terms divine in selling hours of dross;
Within be fed, without be rich no more.

SHAKESPEARE

INDEX